DREAMBEASTS

A Magical and Divinatory Directory of Animals

WENDY TREVENNOR

GREEN MAGIC

GREEN MAGIC
Seed Factory
Aller
Langport
Somerset
TA10 0QN
England
www.greenmagicpublishing.com

Designed and typeset by Carrigboy, Wells, UK.
www.carrigboy.co.uk

ISBN 978-1-915580-05-4

GREEN MAGIC

This book is lovingly dedicated to my wonderful Coven and outer circle, for their inspiration, their support and encouragement in all aspects of my life.

My thanks to my good friend Karen Thomas, for her care and patience in proofreading and checking my work.

Contents

Introduction

The high street of any town is a barren place for wildlife, isn't it? Lots of concrete and plate glass but very little in the way of jungle or veldt, let alone beasts and birds. Or so you might think. But a second glance will show you a lion on the pub sign above you, a black horse galloping across the front of the bank, a man dressed as a chicken giving out leaflets, dinosaurs pictured along a frieze, and even a dragon. Pandas, wolves, stags, buffalo and kangaroos romp around you. Not real live beasts, of course, but testament even so to the close relationship, even obsession, man has always had with creatures lower down the evolutionary scale. Some of these creatures provide food and clothing, others domestic companionship and still others have a working relationship with farmers, with shepherds, with enforcement officers, with sportsmen and hunters, with disabled persons.

Animals have crept, swum, flown, leaped and cantered into the recesses of the human mind in a way the plant kingdom and non-living objects have not – and into the heart as well. Most people, if asked, will describe themselves as animal lovers, and those who reply in the negative tend to be in receipt of wondering or even judgmental looks from their fellow man. For almost everyone loves animals. They are fascinating, often magnificent, frightening or stunningly beautiful "other" beings who often exhibit strangely human traits or seem to understand us better than we do ourselves. Close relationships are maintained with them – without the possibility of exchanging speech. Many people say they prefer animals to other humans; they are "nicer" than people. Stories abound of their wisdom, compassion and love: dogs pulling toddlers from water and dolphins saving swimmers from sharks, horses refusing to proceed in the dark onto a bridge that has fallen, cats waking their sleeping owners to alert them of fire.

Their individual qualities of beauty, strength, affection, loyalty, ferocity, flight and speed have made them symbols – animals make up a huge proportion of heraldic charges and, in more recent times, commercial logos; they are found in jewellery, religious symbolism, on greetings cards, in advertisements, cartoons, literature, film and games, on shoes and clothing, ornaments and gifts, tattooed onto people's skin. Their importance to us is demonstrated everywhere.

Often, animals appear in our dreams. One of the delights of being a witch is that people will often open a conversation with you with the words: "Can you explain this weird dream I had?" Almost always, their dream will centre on an animal, perhaps a deceased pet or something exotic, like a tiger, or even a mythical beast.

Animals mean so much more to us than the value of their meat or their skins or their companionship ... they are embedded in our subconscious, side by side with Jung's archetypes. We share so much more with them than the occupation of the planet or a large proportion of our DNA.

The idea for this book came from one of my magical children, the sort of intelligent student who asks constant questions instead of just absorbing what they are told. On one occasion, she shared her dream of seven mice and a teapot, which just caught my imagination.

For all readers who have dreamed of seven mice, or tigers riding bicycles or bears arriving to stay with a suitcase or a goldfish working as a postman, I hope this book will enlighten, entertain and inform. But it has a more serious purpose as well; to enable practitioners of magic and divination to use animal symbolism and imagery in their Craft, to provide, if you like, a set of Correspondences for animals.

WENDY TREVENNOR

CHAPTER ONE

Man and Beast

Animals: cuddly, cute, adorable? Perhaps more like us than we realise? While people today may often think of animals in these terms, this is not an attitude our forebears would have shared. Their relationship with animals was much more complicated. Ancient man may have seen them as near-divinities which could withhold sustenance by refusing to be hunted and killed, or as the embodiment or gift of deities who could grant food by sending game towards the humans and withhold it if they were displeased. The vital importance of animals to hunter-gatherers seems to have produced a religious feeling, as demonstrated by the artworks found in caves (such as those at Lascaux, France) which have been seen as a type of shamanic or magical working intended to encourage the game to be plentiful and easy to catch. One major feeling that one derives from these artefacts is that of respect: it is easy to see that early man respected and honoured the beasts he sought to slay, perhaps even carried out rituals of gratitude to them.

The relationship modern man has with animals is rather different and a great deal more diverse. It can't really be called love or even respect, can it? Or else we would not have industries devoted to killing and butchering so many of them, or taking away their young in order to steal their milk, or their eggs. In the past, some have attempted to prove their so-called manhood by slaughtering magnificent larger animals "for sport" – and even today this goes on, along with the callous treatment of animals used in non-lethal sports, such as horse racing. Unbelievably, bullfighting continues to this day in Spain, France, Portugal and Latin America. Many cruel sports go on underground in countries where they are illegal: fox hunting, badger-baiting, hare coursing and lamping, dog- and cock-fighting and ratting for bets. Fishermen catch beautiful water creatures "for sport" then tear the hooks from their living jaws and put them back, still suffering, not even using the excuse of eating what they have caught. The film industry has been responsible for many acts of cruelty against animals, well into the current century, despite the efforts of American Humane. Circuses, animal theme parks and other animal shows have long been criticised for their treatment of their "stars". Dogs are deliberately bred to produce features that their owners consider desirable, and yet which may impact dreadfully on the creature's health. Animals are often ill-treated in various food industries (veal and pâté de foie gras being two salient examples). They are put through hellish and painful ordeals in the name of medical research or even (more shameful still) in the testing of cosmetics. Yet even these examples pale into insignificance against the behaviour of our less enlightened ancestors towards animals: cats burned alive in baskets while mediaeval crowds applauded and laughed, pigs tortured and hanged for "crimes", dogs dissected while still conscious by "scientists".

It was not until the early nineteenth century that the tide of human opinion began to turn, slowly, slowly, set afloat by philosophers like Jeremy Bentham: a man well ahead of his time who is best known popularly today for the preservation of his mummified head and body to demonstrate his lack of belief in an afterlife. The RSPCA has its roots in an early society formed in 1824, and Darwin's revelations about our close relationship to the great apes also played a major part in this sea change. Is it too big a leap to also suggest that at this time the stranglehold of Christianity, which has always insisted that animals are just objects without spiritual bodies, was beginning to loosen?

By Victorian times, the change was well under way, with Victorian sentimentality doing a lot to discourage public animal cruelty, as well as to enshrine the place of pets in society – pet cemeteries were even beginning to be created by the end of the era. However, for "working" animals and livestock, things were hardly improved. Anyone who has read that great novel, *Black Beauty*, will have an insight into the realities of animal welfare during this age, though at least gratuitous cruelty towards animals was now frowned upon.

Pets are now a well-entrenched part of our civilisation, primarily in the West, where their importance transcends any human-animal relationships of the past. Pets are "part of the family," "fur babies" – chihuahuas and other small dogs travel everywhere with their owners in a handbag or a custom pushchair, dogs attend funerals and appear at weddings dressed as bridesmaids. Veterinary surgeons, pet groomers, animal psychologists, animal behaviour experts and trainers, animal whisperers and animal astrologers have all bloomed in this era of pet-mania, alongside a growing industry producing not only collars but clothes, coats, shoes and even skis for our four-footed friends. Accessories for pets generally, including cages, beds, bowls, feed, treats and toys, make up a multi-million-pound industry in the UK alone.

Rather more exploitative is the breeding business, with pedigree animals being shown and changing hands for huge sums of money. Sadly, this ego- and money-led business has resulted in genetic modifications that can cause real harm to the animals, partly due to the issue of in-breeding, which results from too small a gene pool of animals considered to have the desirable points, partly from deliberate selective breeding to exaggerate features that are fashionable or seen as cute. French bulldogs with squashed-in muzzles who have breathing difficulties, inbred Alsatians with a genetic propensity for bad hips, short-legged and hairless cats which could not survive outside the home, Labradors (ironically, for a breed that has been the favoured choice for guide dogs) so inbred that they have chronic eye-problems and blindness – and don't get me started on docking and cropping.

Common pets are not enough for some people, who instead want snakes, lizards, spiders, monkeys and exotic birds, which has sadly led to a damaging trade in rare creatures captured from their natural habitats and transported, often under poor conditions, to be sold abroad. One can only hope that their high purchase price was enough to make their owners value and care for them properly.

Animal toys for children are surely another catalyst in the turning tide of opinion towards animal cruelty. Whilst, historically, toys were generally confined to the children of the rich (who were not obliged to work for a living), animal images have long been used for play. These would have been clumsy wooden or clay images, and it is difficult to know at this distance of time how they were played with. It is possible that many ancient items believed to have been children's toys were in fact ritual objects. Generally, playthings were designed to encourage or teach children how to act when they became adults: boys were given toy swords and girls dolls. As human life became easier, childhood became easier too, with children no longer expected to work for their families' livelihoods, and thus given greater freedom to play. Toys began to become more widespread. During the Victorian era, better-off families might have a rocking horse in the nursery, or poorer children might play with hobbyhorses.

The twentieth century ushered in the age of the soft toy, and since the early years of the last century, teddy bears have been the traditional primary toy and companion of babies, toddlers and older children. They derive their origin from an incident in 1902 when the then US President, Theodore "Teddy" Roosevelt, refused to shoot a bear that had been clubbed and tied to a tree for him [*sic*], considering this "unsporting". Toy manufacturers were quick to jump on this lucrative bandwagon and began turning out soft cuddly bears named after the President, later even adding a mechanism that allowed the bear to "growl". Practically all children in the developed world and many in developing countries have a stuffed bear, with modern teddies designed to look "cuter" and more human than the original pioneering bears, which had longer muzzles; like the real animal they represented. The importance and influence of this toy can hardly be overstated: it lived with the child day and night until the child reached an age to go out and play with balls, skipping ropes and other children. Even then, the bear would remain an important toy, kept in the bed or nearby, and later tucked away safely out of sight. Many adults still have their childhood teddy bear preserved in a cupboard.

To the cuddly ranks of stuffed toys were also added much loved children's books, in which anthropomorphised animals (or even toy animals) talk, wear clothes and have adventures. While animals have always been an intrinsic part of storytelling, the publication of hugely successful books, specifically for children, featuring talking animals began a new era with *Alice's Adventures in Wonderland* (1865) and *Alice Through the Looking Glass* (1871), the publication of the Beatrix Potter stories from 1901 and Kenneth Graham's *Wind in the Willows* (1908) and later AA Milne and Alison Uttley, although they were preceded by the rather darker tale of *Black Beauty* (1877). Cue Walt Disney and Mickey Mouse, and the great panoply of animal characters that were to emerge from his studios – and suddenly the world changed.

Further into the twentieth century, animal books took a new turn, entering the world of wild creatures and exploring their lives in a way that earlier children's books had not. *Tarka the Otter, The Call of the Wild, White Fang, Ring of Bright Water* and *Kpo the Leopard* all took the reader into the water, the forest and the jungle to experience a fictional but realistic version of an animal's life. Then children's animal fiction took a further step away from the cute and cuddlies with the appearance of anthropomorphised but serious stories like *Watership Down, The Plague Dogs* and *Animal Farm* – books which cannot really be said to have been written specifically for children.

Vegetarianism, which had disappeared from the Roman Empire with the onset of Christianity, is once again growing in popularity in the Western world. In the UK, a Vegetarian Society was founded in 1847, with other European countries soon following suit. Vegetarian restaurants were appearing in the UK from the latter end of the nineteenth century, and today most restaurants offer vegetarian and vegan choices, including non-dairy alternatives to milk in their beverages. Outrage at cruel farming methods sees online posts and more practical action growing every year. In fact, vegetarianism has been one of the biggest success stories of the 21st century with over 8% – more than one in 12 – of people in the UK, where it is not part of widespread religious practice, now identifying as vegetarian or vegan. Increasing amounts of corporate money go into the research and development of non-animal "meats", to which whole supermarket shelves are now commonly devoted. Whilst, historically, people were more likely to convert to vegetarianism for health reasons, the more common reasons now given are animal welfare and fears for the environment. The growth of paganism has contributed in no small way to this change. Whilst most pagan streams do not have set dietary rules, many adherents voluntarily avoid foods which rely on the slaughter or exploitation of animals because they regard all living creatures as being sacred to or part of deity, as being our "brother and sister creatures" on the planet.

Whilst in the West the tide of human opinion towards the treatment of animals is turning, it is hindered in developing countries mainly by poverty and by superstitious beliefs surrounding the therapeutic and magical uses of animal tissues which has encouraged the appalling things done to bears and other creatures in the name of Asian folk medicine and the ongoing poaching of endangered animals, such as tigers and rhinoceroses. Yet Western influence can be felt there as well: many animal lovers support animal charities active in developing countries or those torn by war (pets and animals were rescued from the Ukraine and one airlift took 150 dogs and cats from Kabul to sanctuary and the possibility of adoption in the

West). International laws protect endangered species and investigate the trade in their skins and other parts.

Finally, the very strangest and perhaps the most extreme aspect of humans' relationship with animals takes the form of animal wannabes…people who wish to look like or be animals and will often go to extremes in an attempt to achieve this goal. There is certainly a mental illness known as lycanthropy, in which those affected believe they can turn themselves into animals but in these days of plastic surgery, prostheses and tattoos, the transformation may no longer be just in the mind. While the subculture known as *furry fandom* involves the cult of animal characters in films, comics, books and games and even in pornography, with a small percentage of adherents admitting they are sexually drawn to real animals and even stuffed toys, some just want to be furry friends themselves and have gone some way towards achieving this. In 21st century UK schools it is now commonly accepted for pupils to "identify" as animals, for example cats, and to wear fake ears and a tail towards this end, and to expect allowances to be made for them in the same way members of non-indigenous religions would.

Dennis Avner (1958–2012) was a former American naval technician who spent a record $200,000 on fourteen surgical operations and procedures to make himself look like a tiger, achieving the world record for "most permanent transformations to look like an animal." These included tattooing stripes across his entire body, re-shaping his face and installing metal sockets for whiskers, re-shaping his ears and teeth to make them pointed, and wearing slit-eyed contact lenses and a robotic tail. Avner took his own life at the age of 54.

In contrast, professional circus freak, Eric Sprague (born 1972), known as the Lizardman, has made a successful career out of his own body modifications, which include head-to-toe tattooing of green scales, a forked tongue and implants to change the shape of his face and body.

In future chapters we will meet real, flesh-and-blood animals, of which there are some two million identified species (not including human imitations!) on the Earth – a number which is dwindling as we approach what may be a mass extinction event. These range from the well-known animals of farm, zoo and TV, such as goats, elephants and monkeys to extremely rare or obscure creatures, such as the tenrec, the caecilian and the bilby.

But right from the earliest origins of the human race, animals have shown a tendency to move from their own plot of grass, of mud, of water, of trees, of sun-warmed stone into the human imagination, where they join forces with creatures stranger than have ever walked the planet to embody ideas and cultures, populate myths and enable magic.

In the next chapter we will meet some of these magical beasts and what they have meant to people throughout history.

CHAPTER TWO

Here be Dragons

Our wealth of myth and story would be threadbare indeed, were it not for animals. From the snake in the Garden of Eden to Anansi the Spider and his close cousin, Brer Rabbit, they dominate ancient legends, fairy tales and traditional stories, print literature, cinema and games – but these are real animals, or based on real species, at any rate. Delving deeper into the realm of myth and magic will bring you face-to-face with animals that have never walked the Earth (as far as we know!): fire-breathing dragons, talking foxes, witches' cats, werewolves, water monsters, hellhounds and flying horses – all are part of our rich and inventive imaginary bestiary. Some of these ideas are very ancient; others, like the Chupacabra, the ABCs (Alien Big Cats), Mothman and the mokele-mbembe of twentieth century lore are recent arrivals.

Mythological beasts tend to fall into one of three categories: types of legendary creatures, such as dragons, unicorns, mermen and manticores; individual and unique creatures from distinct stories, such as the Sphinx, the Kraken, the Phoenix and the Minotaur; and finally, a more modern branch of the family: cryptids and urban myths, like the Beast of Bodmin, the Loch Ness Monster, Mothman, Ogopogo, Bigfoot and the Jersey Devil. This last category can include real animals which have gone extinct, such as the Tasmanian tiger (or thylacine), the Australian Megalania and the various kinds of dinosaurs still regularly glimpsed across the globe.

To begin with the more traditional monsters, such as dragons, hippogriffs, unicorns and griffins, what could be the origins of these creatures? Could they have existed in the distant past and then become extinct? Our fossil record does not include them, but absence of proof does not equal proof of absence. Moreover, some mythical creatures, for example the dragon and the sea serpent, are common to mythologies and art across the world. Ancient cave paintings show mythical creatures which are part-human, part-animal. So, clearly the belief in them goes back to the very dawn of human existence. The best known therianthropes (human-animal hybrids) of earliest times are surely the animal-headed gods and goddesses of Ancient Egypt, such as Anubis (jackal), Bast (cat), Sekhmet (lioness), Thoth (ibis) and Hat-Hor (cow). Archaeologists believe these may have begun as animal fetishes or totems, whose qualities and attributes were later added to human-form deities. They are typically portrayed as either an animal-headed human or as wholly animal. The Egyptian Sphinx (as opposed to the Greek mythical character) is the other way round: a man's (pharaoh's) head tacked onto a lion's body to represent his strength and courage. The Egyptians included numerous chimeras (creatures made up from parts of two or more real animals, for example the griffin and the manticore) in their picturesque belief system, including the Goddess Ammit (Eater of the Dead) – a mix of hippopotamus, crocodile and lion or leopard, who swallowed the souls who were so unfortunate as to fail the Weighing of the Heart test as they entered the other realm. The identity of the animal form of the God Set (a mysterious creature with a long, drooping snout and square-ended ears) has not been identified, and it may also be one of these chimeras.

It is easy to see how chimeras may have arisen. Humans are fond of trying to improve on nature, and it only took imagination to turn a splendid horse into a magnificent and magical winged horse or a centaur. Perhaps the qualities of two animals were required for a magical purpose or a story, so two animals were combined to create a single, magical creature. Still other creatures may have arisen from a glimpse of a strange animal, misinterpreted or misremembered by the seer, and from garbled descriptions given by travellers of beasts seen in other parts of the world: the unicorn may be an example of this, stemming perhaps from a traveller's attempt to describe a rhinoceros. Brief glimpses of manatees and dugongs nursing their young on the surface of the ocean may have given rise to the legends of mermaids; the sea is a particularly fertile area for sightings of strange monsters as it is not usually possible to see the complete form of any creature (unless you are a diver) or to see it close up and, of course, it may only appear fleetingly before vanishing into the depths. It has been suggested that stories of larger mythical beasts, such as dragons may have arisen from the discovery of fossilised bones from the periods when huge animals, such as diplodocus, megatherium and mastodon were alive.

The mind seems disposed to create monsters; our powers of imagination are one of the things that make us human and, as the poet TS Eliot once remarked, "Humans cannot bear too much reality." From bogeymen under our beds when we are small to UFOs and living dinosaurs, we see strangeness wherever we look.

As a witch, I see other explanations for some of these phenomena. Some may have been deliberately created by magic as guardians for a sacred place (my coven has done this kind of work on a site which had been disrespected). The Michigan and Bray Road dogmen in the US, which have been seen in several locations throughout the twentieth and into the twenty-first century, have been sighted increasingly as towns spread out towards sites regarded as sacred by the original First Nations peoples, who buried their dead and worshipped their gods there. Could the fearsome dogman be a simple thoughtform conjured to turn away outsiders who might desecrate the sacred land or the graves of the ancestors? The Loch Ness Monster appears to have no reality, despite the continuing sightings and photographs into this century. The loch has been declared too biologically poor to sustain a large creature, let alone a family of them, and scientific studies have produced little more than a few unconvincing sonar images which could be logs or boulders lying on the lake bottom. However, the topography of the loch has led some researchers to believe it could hold echoes of another time and that the monster is in fact a creature that swam in the loch in an earlier era and that modern people are seeing echoes of that, ghosts or time-distortions. Such an explanation might also work for the other dinosaur cryptids across the globe.

Dragons are everywhere: they twine along church architecture, strut across heraldic charges, fly across movie screens (courtesy of CGI technology) and dance through the streets of cities with Chinese populations on the heads and shoulders of costumed men celebrating a festival. While in Chinese belief dragons are spirits or deities, in the West they tend to have a more physical context: water monsters, "worms" that attack regions, beasts that terrorise until a knightly hero takes them on and cuts off their heads. The most famous are the Lambton Worm (Tyne and Wear) and the Worm of Linton (Scottish Borders), the former having grown from a strange fish or eel disposed of down a well. In both cases, a local hero takes on the monster and kills it using inventive methods. The dragon's close cousins, the wyvern and the cockatrice, also feature in many traditional tales.

Race memories of wolves might have inspired the many sightings of black "hellhounds" seen in remote places, such as East Anglia's Black Shuck (sometimes "Old Shuck" or "Shock") and Yorkshire's Padfoot and Barghest. These devil dogs are known for their great size, their black colour and their huge glowing or fiery eyes (sometimes only one, cyclops-style), and often as well for their ill omen: anyone seeing them is liable to die or at least encounter dreadful bad luck. Black Shuck is even said to have burst into a church and killed members of the congregation gathered there for a service in the sixteenth century. In the twentieth century, their place was largely usurped by the ABCs (alien big cats), which at least had their origins in real creatures. While some of these cats may have been escapees from animal collections or circuses, some may have been privately owned. Before the Dangerous Wild Animals Act (1976) it was possible, for those who had the money if not the sense, to own a tiger or a black panther and keep it around the house as a pet. The act demanded that such animals be kept in specially approved secure accommodation, and when it came into force it is believed some owners simply freed their beasts into the countryside, rather than go to the trouble of arranging this. If these animals survived and were able to breed, this could explain the thousands of sightings of large cats across the UK: the Surrey Puma, the Beast of Bodmin and the Black Beast of Exmoor, amongst others.

Phantom creatures are common across the world and often bring their own omens with them. In the UK and Scandinavia, the Church Grim is a guardian of the burial ground, usually in the form of a black dog, and sometimes said to have been a real dog killed and buried at the churchyard boundary for this purpose (such foundation sacrifices were common: some owners of old cottages have been horrified to discover a mummified cat in the walls of their home while making alterations or repairs). In the UK, the demonic black dogs are joined by many other creatures, often seemingly harmless, which nevertheless draw bad luck or even death to the seer. A new take on the Shuck dog, in Suffolk, is Rendlesham Forest's "shug monkey" – a hybrid of the more traditional black hellhound with a monkey, which has been seen as recently as the 1990s. Sometimes, they are just plain ghosts: the Tower of London has a ghost bear and London Zoo a ghost lioness. In Cornwall the appearance of a white hare (scarcely likely, now the hare has almost vanished from the Duchy) speaks of a young girl betrayed by her lover and dying of grief, in childbirth or by her own hand: such animals have traditionally been reported following the seducer and driving him to despair. The Baum Rabbit of Rochdale, a plump, white bunny which haunts the local churchyard, has been used as a bogey to frighten children into good behaviour, though it is said to be harmless. Norfolk has its own version: the Thetford Warren Lodge White Rabbit, and this animal does bring ill luck to anyone who sees it, it is said. The Merrivale Pigs of Dartmoor, a sow and her piglets, are even said to speak, complaining of hunger. A white owl is said to be seen at Windsor Castle before the death of anyone connected with the castle; this kind of family death harbinger is quite common, including the white birds seen around the Vatican before the death of a pope, the Closeburn Castle Swan in Dumfriesshire and, of course, the legend that Great Britain will fall if the ravens at the Tower of London fly away (not likely, as their wings are clipped to prevent this!). Owls, corvids and many white birds are often associated with death. It is not recorded whether the Windsor Owl appeared before the death of Her Majesty Queen Elizabeth II.

In the US, a phantom cat even haunts the White House, appearing as a tiny kitten but growing larger and more terrifyingly demonic as it is approached. The cat is said to be a sign of bad luck, and has appeared before the murder of John F. Kennedy and before that as a harbinger of the Great Depression. Nearby, the Capitol Building has a huge demon cat the size of a panther which roams the corridors at night and frightens any security personnel so unfortunate as to meet it. This creature seems to be a little more substantial, as it supposedly left half a dozen huge pawprints in wet concrete used to mend a section of flooring at the end of the nineteenth century!

In human belief, these mythical creatures can be as important as real animals, and certainly carry elements of power that can be utilised by those who know how. In the next chapter, we will look at the ways in which practitioners have connected with animals, both real and mythical, for their spiritual practices, healing and magic.

CHAPTER THREE

Animal Magic

Once we have satisfied the hunger impulse, clothed ourselves in skins and completed our travels, what man wants from animals becomes more intangible, more abstract. The animal under consideration now comes to represent something other, something more to do with ego and the power of identity. It has moved from the dinner plate or the coat hanger or the harness to the heraldic device. Totems represent man's earliest emotions surrounding the animals that he preyed upon or which might prey upon him: fear, desire, reverence and admiration. What modern child has not watched a horse galloping across a field (if only on TV), its mane flying in the wind, the sun gleaming on its polished, muscular flanks, and not wished to be that horse, if just for a minute? In early civilisations, animal names would be given to children, in the hope that those qualities of speed, strength, courage, fierceness and beauty for which the animal was admired might pass to the child in some degree. These animal-inspired names are still with us, for those who understand enough Latin and Greek: Leo, Philip, Agnes and Ursula. In some cultures, the name-bearer might be given a body part (such as a tooth, claw or small bone) or a carving of the name animal as a personal amulet, to continue this magical idea.

In the ancient past, leaders may have assumed as a name or even a hereditary title the name of an animal admired for its ability to inspire fear: bear (Arthur), dragon, wolf, lion, and bull. He may have worn the animal's skin, perhaps its skull, horns or teeth – especially into battle. Soon his men started adopting this image, marking their shields and breastplates with the same totem animal to show who they followed. Heraldry was born – it has always used far more animals (including mythical beasts), birds and fishes than any other kind of image and it is far from dead today, having also moved into the area of corporate and commercial logos. Brand names and advertising campaigns often use animals: cars, aeroplanes, lawn mowers, online services, kitchen appliances, alcoholic drinks, confectionery, fashion items, sportswear, breakfast cereal … the list goes on.

People's desire to identify with animals shows itself in many ways: they may have a tattoo of it on their bodies or a pendant around their necks; there has even been a brief fashion for men to topiarise their beards to resemble a curled animal clinging to their chins. They may adopt a nickname like "Cat" or "Tiger", have images of the animal around their home and, in modern times they may have the animal's name in their email address or as an avatar on their social media accounts. Modern pagans often adopt one or more magical names, which are used within the pagan community and often on social media sites and may incorporate the name of the animal to which they are drawn. As we have seen, people have sought to change their physical appearance with surgery to look more like animals. Some animals are seen as sexy: bulls and stallions are seen as virile, big cats are powerful and have elegant body shapes, small cats are slender and graceful (in an age when so many of us are overweight or obese), dogs and horses are fit, in the original sense of the word. So many people wish to become like this themselves, and work hard to achieve it, while in extreme cases the mental illness called clinical lycanthropy causes the patient to believe they have become or can transform into a wolf or other animal.

Practitioners of magic have used animals, their names, their images and materials from their bodies since time immemorial, and have gone themselves into the animals' habitats and into worlds where animal spirits live, to learn from them and gain power. Let us look at a few ways in which people have utilised animals in spiritual and magical practices.

TOTEM, POWER AND SPIRIT ANIMALS

Most people are aware of the Native American belief in spirit guides, which take the form of an animal. This is not necessarily an individual animal, but represents the spirit of its species. Once you have found your totem animal, or it has found you, they believe it stays with you for life as a guide and protector. It is a part of your identity: what makes you you and it lends you its own innate power on your journey through life. Individuals or groups, including whole tribes, may have a totem animal; in the latter case this may be depicted on the iconic "totem pole" erected in the centre of the tribal space like a European heraldic symbol with attitude! This is a snapshot of a revered animal making its way from fetish-hood towards becoming a deity (as must have happened in the ancient past), and individual totemic animals may be involved in ancestor worship as well.

Totems, power animals and spirit animals overlap to some extent but, as a rule of thumb, a totem is a sacred representation of identity, of individual, family, tribe, ethnicity – similar to the way that New Zealanders, for example, refer to themselves as "Kiwis". It can be thought to have some of the attributes of a deity, including bringing strength and protection to the person associated with it (in UK terms, this might be the heraldic British Lion which appears on so much of our national symbolism from flags to eggshells, or in the US the bald eagle). Power animals and spirit guides might better be described as friends along the way, who will help, empower and guide. These animals might be encountered in dreams or pathworkings, when they might deliver a message, warning or advice. While a puppy is for life, a spirit guide may change as you develop and gain knowledge and your needs change as well.

Animal deities may also form an important part of magical practice, with an animal god or goddess being invoked or their image being used in spellcasting. For example, the Egyptian Lioness Goddess Sekhmet might be invoked to give courage and daring, or the Hindu Elephant God Ganesh might be petitioned for help within His particular area of expertise (He is known as the Remover of Obstacles). Simply having the image of these gods or of their sacred animals on the altar as a focus might be considered an effective way of utilising their power.

Shamanism, an ancient practice which has gained popularity among neopagans, may involve the shaman calling up spirit animals for guidance, protection, help and healing; or entering their realms through trance, sometimes with the help of psychoactive plant substances.

FAMILIARS AND THOUGHTFORMS

The witch's familiar has a long history going back at least to mediaeval times and is showcased in the infamous seventeenth century woodcut created as a frontispiece for the 1647 book, *The Discovery of Witches*, by Matthew Hopkins. It shows a strangely relaxed Hopkins, self-styled Witchfinder General, standing in the background watching two witches from Manningtree with their collection of assorted familiars, all of which have cutesy names, most famously "Pyewackett". The illustration describes them as "imps", which is how the Church saw them, as devils or demons gifted to the witch after she had sold her soul to the Devil, and sent to help her with her evil work of cursing her Christian neighbours.

Neopagans have taken to this appealing idea, and it is common to see posters on social media pages sharing a picture of their real cat or dog and innocently describing the animal as their "familiar".

Actually, the authentic familiar – often called a "familiar spirit" – is not a live animal at all, but an advanced thoughtform created by an act of magic and will, a continuation of the totem animal concept. Not to give away too many secrets, the familiar is created firstly as an image, given a secret name, then an object is created in which to house it and it is then called into being with a series of rituals, the practitioner protecting him- or herself magically throughout the process in order to avoid calling up something not so desirable. If the familiar is maintained with proper "feeding" and attention, it will survive and may, over the course of time, gain some reality, even to the point where others can see or sense it. Its name must not be shared with others; the witch may even have a secondary or pet name to use when mentioning her familiar to her sisters of the Craft.

While the black cat is undoubtedly the most iconic form for a familiar, practitioners may use their totem animal's form or a range of traditional "creepy" animal forms such as snakes, toads, bats and spiders, and one witch I know has a blue-eyed white dragon. Modern witches and covens may use the familiar in a variety of ways, from being a spirit guide in pathworkings and shamanic journeys to sending it on ahead to keep a parking space!

Animal thoughtforms generally may play a large part in the practice of magic. They may be used to find lost or desired items or gain wealth, to help in healing oneself or others, even to assist with dieting! Probably the most common use of a thoughtform is protection. As we have seen, some animal cryptids may be the result of the deliberate creation of a guardian for a sacred site by magicians. Many practitioners create thoughtforms to safeguard their homes: a giant astral hound lying on your drive really can deter burglars! Others may use them more aggressively as "sendings" – magic intended to harm or frighten an enemy or someone they wish to influence to act in a different way. The occult writer, Dion Fortune, describes a variety of psychic attacks of this kind in her book *Psychic Self-Defence* (1930), including the appearance of a gigantic tabby cat "twice the size of a tiger" and a wolf-form created involuntarily by harbouring vengeful thoughts. In these cases, a witch or magician will choose the form of the sending based on their needs: a large frightening animal will be sent to threaten or intimidate, or perhaps a snake if the subject is known to have a phobia about snakes, for example.

Such temporary creations do not have the staying power of a familiar, yet should still be broken down properly when the need for them has passed. The occultist and explorer, Alexandra David-Néel, created, as an experiment, the thoughtform of a little Buddhist monk and allowed it to stay in existence for a while. After some time, the being gained sufficient reality for it to be seen by others, leering around corners in a sinister way; so she was obliged to break it down.

SHAPESHIFTING

The most famous example of shapeshifting is that of the werewolf – a myth which is found in many cultures across the world and in many guises. Remember Little Red Riding Hood? This seemingly innocent children's story has clearly arisen from a belief in werewolves, with the smart, loquacious wolf trying to trick Red Riding Hood and finally swallowing her grandmother in order to catch and eat the little girl (or is it the grandmother who is the werewolf?). The werewolf arrived in Hollywood in 1913 and has stayed there ever since, developing a mythology all its own as time has gone on, including its association with the full moon, its aversion to silver and its ability to generate new werewolves by biting people. Its origins are lost in the mists of time, but possible inspirations could include serial killers and rapists or ancient rituals involving ecstatic behaviour such as the Roman Lupercalia.

Witches are also said to be capable of shapeshifting (usually to escape from their enemies) and old stories abound of an animal being injured and the witch showing up the next morning with a wound in the same place as the animal. Witches are especially associated with shapeshifting into hares, which were once common in the UK and have behaviours that were considered more "eldritch" than those of rabbits.

Clearly it is not possible for a human being to actually change their body into that of an animal, but other kinds of metamorphoses are possible for those who have the knowledge and the willpower to effect the change. The spirit or energy of an animal may be called down into the practitioner, to utilise for certain kinds of work and the energy of an animal god or goddess may similarly be invoked. I personally have had the experience of being taken over in this way by an animal Goddess (Sekhmet) while clearing a house which had an unpleasant energy, possibly of demonic type. By the time I had finished the ritual, I was almost roaring like a lion, and I felt that if any Amityville-style phenomenon had shown its face, I would have eaten it! Since then, a similar change has come over me at other haunted properties, particularly where the inmates were very frightened and upset and I have felt protective sympathy for them. Where I feel the presence in me of Sekhmet, I have been told by colleagues that my appearance does actually change to some extent as I channel this lioness Goddess.

In some beliefs, shapeshifters may not be humans shapeshifting into animals, but the other way around; as for example the selkie: a seal being which may come ashore and shed its furry skin, becoming temporarily human. In Celtic belief, it was possible to keep the selkie in human form by hiding its skin.

PHYSICAL ANIMAL PARTS IN MAGIC

While many neopagans respect and love animals to the point where they would never eat meat or wear leather, others do use animal materials in their spiritual and magical practice. Many strands of Voodoo notoriously use animal parts in magic, and even the sacrifice of living animals (particularly goats, dogs and chickens) in ritual. In the ancient past, animal sacrifice (if not human sacrifice) was universal, from white bulls and horses sacrificed to Poseidon in Ancient Greece to the millions of cat mummies found in Ancient Egyptian temples, which may have started as an attempt to please the Cat Goddess Bast by paying for the funeral rites of a cat, but proceeded to abuse involving the breeding and killing of cats to sell to pilgrims and worshippers for this purpose. One thing we have to thank Christianity for is the ending of animal sacrifice, and modern pagans are more likely to honour animals sacred to their patron deities, perhaps making a regular donation to an animal charity in their name.

There are traditions of ancient British and Irish kings marrying a mare as a symbol of their connection with the land and the goddess to whom the animal was sacred. Whether the marriage was consummated, or the mare simply died on a sacrificial altar, is shrouded in the mists of time.

Wicca and many other streams of pagan belief place no restrictions on the consumption of meat or the use of bone, fur or leather – leaving individuals to make their own choices. The use of natural materials is much preferred by most neopagans, who see plastic, and to a lesser extent resin, as anathema, and certainly our ancestors would have made their own tools and ritual equipment from what was available in their environment – no magic shop in the high street for them. Drums, vital for much shamanic work, are often made from skin and some athames (the primary witch's tool, the black-handled knife) have handles made from deer antler or bone. Some pagans have actual deer antlers (sometimes still attached to the vault of the skull) on their altar to represent the Horned God. Feathers and snakeskin are commonly used in ritual, though of course the collection of these does not imply the death of the animal. Freshly spilled blood is known to be an enhancer of magical power and is still used today by Voodoo bocors (sorcerers), while most neopagans would prefer to use their own blood, if blood is called for.

In divination, some practitioners use animal materials, including bone dice and runestones, bone pieces for bone-casting (osteomancy) and scapulimancy (divination using shoulder blade bones). Divination which involved the killing of animals was common throughout history. For example, in Roman haruspicy, priests would inspect the organs of sacrificed animals for their divinatory messages, based on the colour, form and texture of the entrails, whether they twitched after death, whether they appeared normal and healthy, or were deformed or diseased; the latter being a bad omen.

Generally, most UK pagans today, even if they do use animal parts in their ritual practice, would ensure that no animal had been ill-treated or killed just for that part: roadkill is the magical practitioner's best resource! In cases where the use of animal materials is employed, it should be done respectfully and with gratitude expressed to the creature that has given up its tissues.

DIVINATION AND SCRYING

Whole divination systems have been based on the appearance and movements of birds, fish and animals; including the ancient Celtic Con-Ogham – a variation on the tree alphabet Ogham but utilising the appearance and behaviour of dogs. The Druids also used Bo-Ogham: "cattle Ogham", and En-Ogham: "bird Ogham". For those using other systems, such as runes, the appearance of the world around them, including shapes made by groups of birds or animals, can also be studied for meaning. It is common for migrating birds or water birds on a body of water to form letters or rune-shapes as they move, or even pictures which speak to the unconscious mind.

As we have seen, in classical civilisation animals might be killed for divinatory purposes, but live animals were also used. Sacred chickens and other fowl were kept and watched for their actions. If they were fed, and ate greedily, with food dropping from their beaks, this was a good omen. However, if they turned away from the food, this was taken as a bad sign. The shamans and diviners who watched the movements of prey animals soon developed the eye for seeing omens and messages not solely connected with hunting in the creatures' migrations. The migrations of birds, the rising of fish, the running of deer and the movements of sheep and other ungulates all had messages for those with the knowledge to see them.

However, it is better to use animals seen in scrying and animals in dreams and visions for divination, rather than the real live creature that might cross the road in front of your car. The reason is that the mind itself shapes the messages, from information it already has from the Universe. An oddly shaped cloud might appear to you as a cat or a dragon or a seal; your inner mind will make the distinction. A cat or a seal seen in the real world can only be a cat or a seal (if you see a dragon, let the nearest witch know ASAP!).

Scrying media, from tea leaves to coloured water to flames and smoke, will often form animal and bird shapes, and clouds do this better than almost anything else: try glancing at the sky and see if you don't spot a dragon or a humpback whale or a teddy-bear. Modern pagans now have systems available to them in the form of beautiful oracle cards featuring animals and birds, in which the animal symbols take their meaning from a universally accepted association of this creature. For example, a dog may mean loyalty; an owl may mean wisdom and a bee or ant industry. The classic tarot also uses animal images, like those created by Pamela Coleman-Smith among the complex illustrations on the Major Arcana cards of the *Ryder-Waite Tarot Deck*.

Cartomancy is extremely popular and has moved on from the sole use of common playing cards and tarot to the array of animal oracle cards you can find on sale on many websites and in magic shops. And here is an idea: why not make your own? With the help of this book you could pick out a number of animals which have a meaning for you – enough to create your own oracle. Generally speaking, oracles like the runes, witches' runes and Ogham include around 10-25 subject staves, to cover wealth/harvest, beginnings, endings, ordeals/enemies/bad luck, love and attraction, career and opportunities, messages, journeys, inspiration, sudden good luck, celebrations, health, the home and family, and sometimes death. Pick out the creatures you feel speak of these things for you and meditate on them until you are sure they have the correct meaning for you. Then use their images on cards or small tiles. Don't worry if you are not artistic – they will be just as beautiful if you cut out pictures you have found in magazines or on the internet and stick them onto your medium (be sure to protect it with a couple of coats of varnish or some of that clear sticky film used to cover books, or you can laminate cards). Keep some spare cards or tiles in case you feel later that you need to add a few more divinatory images.

Every creature on Earth has meaning associated with it. In the next section, you will find a gazetteer that is as comprehensive as possible, both in terms of the creatures listed and their magical and divinatory meanings.

CHAPTER FOUR

Dreambeasts

When I started to compile a list of animals, I took the decision to make it as far-ranging as possible, and then was astonished at the number and variety. Some sources online list every known breed of animals such as sheep, dogs and aquarium fish, every subspecies of tiger, of snakes, of sharks. My own work does not list these unless the different types are special in some way. Dogs, for instance, are an unusual species in that many different body shapes and sizes can all belong to the same species and can interbreed, even though they might bear no resemblance to one another and might not appear to be the same species of animal at all. Because a German shepherd and a Chihuahua evoke very different images and associations, I have made distinctions between types, where appropriate. I have also not included some obscure or rare hybrids, creatures like the zonkey (a cross between a zebra and a donkey), or ligers and tigons. For extinct animals, see the next section; and for animals from myth and story, see the section after that.

In the following magical bestiary, the magical and divinatory information on each animal comes from traditional belief or from my own intuitions gained through working, meditation and study. Elemental correspondences are included for each animal, and also any connections with deity.

Always remember that messages from animal divination can be very personal: even though there may be a traditional meaning for the creature you see, it may have a newer cultural meaning (I have cited, for example, the computer game figure, Crash Bandicoot, who has little to do with natural living bandicoots, but may still bring his own message into a vision or a scrying message) and, for most people, many creatures will have strong personal meanings derived from their personal lives, their early memories and their favourite books and films that would not be the same for others.

It is also important to note what the animal is doing in the dream, and to adjust the message you receive accordingly. A black cat sitting purring on your knee will have a different message from a large black cat attacking you savagely, or even a black cat walking away with its tail in the air with that "sod you, mate" body language cats do so well. Generally speaking, if the animal in the dream is friendly then take that as a good omen, even if the animal is not from a friendly species or one with good associations. An animal that speaks of bad luck which appears in your dream being friendly and licking your hand speaks of ill luck that is passing. On the other hand, an animal that is generally good-omened running away from you speaks for itself, and any animal attacking you speaks of some misfortune.

Aardvark

(*Orycteropus afer*)
Element: earth.
Deities: as with the anteater, some have associated the God Set's unusual animal head with the aardvark.

We start with an animal that is little known to most people, except as a source of jokes about dictionaries. This strange little creature is a natural winner and a fortunate animal to stumble on in a pathworking or a dream.

Although its name translates as "earth-pig" (Afrikaans) this beast is not related to pigs; in fact, it is a species on its own, its closest relatives being elephant shrews, and it is distantly related to elephants themselves, and to some marine mammals. It is not even related to other species of anteater.

Deeply grounded in the earth where it digs for ants and termites and rests in a cool burrow during the hot sub-Saharan African days, the aardvark is further tied to the element of earth by its preferred hour for activity: midnight.

In **dreams and visions**, "dig", says this symbol, "uncover what you seek." Seeking and digging are the superpowers of the aardvark, so it may speak of buried secrets, of things worth digging for, of industry and its rewards. The appearance of the aardvark as a message urges you to go off by yourself and get on with the job, reconnect to your work and set aside distractions. If there is small print, read it, and make sure you dig deeply into the subject before committing yourself. It may represent an ancestor from the distant past, or it may represent a contemporary who has the qualities of the animal: its solitary, curious, industrious nature.

As a **totem or power animal**, it brings good fortune and success, the ability to concentrate on the job in hand, ignore distractions and carry on until the reward is achieved; plus the connection with the earth and the ability to ground oneself thoroughly. Its tough skin will make you harder to injure, emotionally, and its nose will sniff out falsehoods and insincerity, uncovering truth. The solitary nature of the creature points to self-reliance or a need for this, along with the need to work alone until the goal is achieved (and shared with no one).

Aardwolf: see **Hyena.**

African Wild Dog: see **Wild Dog.**

Albatross

(*Diomedeidae spp*)
Elements: air and water.
Deities: Diomedes, Kanaloa and Kane (Hawaiian myth), Japanese pantheon generally.

"Instead of the cross, the albatross about my neck was hung ..." Coleridge's *Rime of the Ancient Mariner* gave this bird a new meaning, but it has always symbolised beauty, purity and freedom, and sailors in past times would never harm them as they believed them to be the souls of drowned sailors come to guide, bless or protect them. The veneration of flying birds as dead souls is widespread in many cultures, and white birds particularly have inspired these types of beliefs. Alternatively, the birds were believed to carry the souls of dead mariners to heaven, or to come seeking to aid living ones by steering them to land and safety.

One of the largest flying birds, the albatross can have a wingspan approaching 12ft (3.6 metres) and their size and wingspan means they need a run to achieve take off and flight, just as an airplane does. They are very long-lived, commonly reaching 50 years of age or more. Their mastery of gliding means they can travel hundreds of miles across the ocean in a day with minimal effort. It is believed that these amazing birds are even able to sleep on the wing.

In **dreams and visions**, this bird can have a wide range of meanings and the person will have to take other elements of the dream, or the feeling of the dream or vision into account to find the message. Travel and finding your way is certainly one meaning of the albatross, as well as general good luck, freedom and happiness. But such a spiritually significant and evocative creature may not speak of simple travel, as other birds, but suggest something more sacred, more numinous – travel through other realms, religious pilgrimage, contact with the ancestors or other spirit beings or progress on your spiritual path. It may appear as a messenger or guide through other realms.

The poet Coleridge gave the albatross an altogether different meaning when he wrote of it in his well-known poem in 1834. Although this is a relatively modern influence, it is already deeply embedded in our cultural consciousness and needs to be taken into account as well. In this case, the albatross becomes a burden, specifically one of guilt; a curse brought down on one's head by an evil deed. The Ancient Mariner shoots the benevolent bird from sheer wickedness, thereby ultimately causing the deaths of his entire crew, and the dead bird is hung by them around his neck to remind him of his crime.

As a **totem or power animal**, the albatross confers the gift of always finding your way, whether on a hill walk or through the intricacies of office politics. It gives you the freedom to rise above everyday annoyances and be yourself, as you were always meant to be.

Alligator

(*Alligator mississippiensis and sinensis*)
Elements: earth and water.
Deities: Zipacna, also the Ancient Egyptian Crocodile God Sobek.
I always felt that alligators and crocodiles were essentially interchangeable – beasts that are so similar it takes specialist knowledge to tell them apart, and thus they probably have the same meaning. Not so. They are so far apart genetically that they cannot interbreed (as, for example, lions and tigers can)

and they have different spiritual and magical meanings. Alligators inhabit the southern parts of the US and Mexico and parts of China, and prefer fresh water; whereas crocodiles prefer briny water, especially the enormous Australian saltwater crocodile. Alligators are smaller, darker in colour and less aggressive than crocs. Their faces are a different shape, with a broader snout and their teeth are hidden when their mouths are shut.

This ancient beast (alligators have been on the Earth for 37 million years) is one species that is not endangered, although it was listed as such in the US in 1967. Alligators were hunted for their skins to the point where their numbers began to fall, but the US Endangered Species Act of 1973 came to their rescue, and just 20 years later they were declared out of danger. Today they are farmed for their meat and skins, and contribute to the tourist industry.

In **dreams and visions**, the alligator is all about threat, an enemy, even just someone with a big mouth who can make you miserable with bullying and criticism. Someone you are afraid to approach, yet who might sneak up on you at work and just get on your case over something very trivial – because they can. If you have suffered workplace bullying from a superior, you will understand this imagery.

As a **totem or power animal**, the 'gator brings the gift of patience and waiting, of knowing that what you want will come to you. It is a powerful creature with many gifts, of fierceness, of invulnerability, of alertness, of energy and of the ability to go for what it wants with no holds barred.

Alpaca
(*Lama pacos*)
These big-eyed mini-llamas have become very popular in the UK over the last few decades, both as animals farmed for their wool and as pets. As they have so much in common with llamas, I have included them together under Llama.

Ant
(*Formicidae spp*)
Element: earth.
Deities: not many deities are associated with ants, though Zeus took the form of an ant to seduce Eurymedousa, mother of Myrmidon.
"Go to the ant, thou sluggard; consider her ways." This quote from the Bible, Proverbs, Chapter Six calls attention to the famed industry of this tiny creature. Like the bee, the ant is known for labouring away for the common good of the nest, not considering its own needs but working for all until the day it dies. There is no honey in the life of most ants, just toil and the occasional fight to protect the nest. Honeypot ants in Africa and Australia are a rather different case. The ants do not produce honey; they feed liquids and food to some workers until these poor creatures are hugely distended with it, like living storage jars. When the food is required, other ants stimulate the honeypots, usually by stroking their antennae, until they regurgitate

some of the nourishment. Honeypot ants have become part of the human diet in these countries, and ants are covered in chocolate and eaten in many countries.

Ants are formidable; as well as stinging, biting jaws, they are completely implacable and will not stop attacking until either the threat has passed or their entire nest has been exterminated. Their sheer strength is amazing, each insect being able to carry many times its own weight for long distances. Army ants live on the march, without a permanent nest, and eat all small creatures that fall in their path: insects, worms and even small vertebrates, although the tales of them attacking and consuming large animals and even humans are fanciful.

In **dreams and visions**, ants speak of self-sacrifice, total loyalty, duty, co-operation, single-minded focus, resilience, endurance, strength, hard work … and its rewards. They share many messages in common with bees, but with perhaps more emphasis on physical toil, strength and perseverance, rather than on the rewards that ensue. Dreaming of ants may indicate your workplace or career, or may speak of the community of which you are a part, or it may be telling you that you feel overcrowded in the place you live. The ant may also be suggesting that you feel undervalued in your job, or in a position where your abilities are not used to the full.

As a **totem animal**, the ant brings all these qualities and good luck as well. Someone with an ant totem may be a person of great self-control, of regular habits, of good sense in management and the ability to budget, manage and work towards a goal, always doing the right thing. But they may have to guard against their sense of duty and their work ethic overcoming all their more interesting personality traits, which could make them humourless and even a little … boring!

Anteater

(*Vermilingua spp*)
Element: earth.
Deities: The Ancient Egyptian Chaos God Set may be based on an anteater. Archaeologists have not been able to identify for sure what creature forms his head, with its drooping snout and square-tipped ears.

There are four species of anteaters alive today: the collared, the giant, the northern and the silky anteater – though unrelated species are sometimes given the name anteater. While the silky anteater is a pygmy around the size of a rat and the collared and northern are cat-sized, the giant anteater is an impressive animal weighing up to 50kg with a 30cm-long snout, a 60cm tongue and strikingly patterned fur. Its forepaws are armed with large digging claws and its size means it lives on the ground, in contrast to the other species which are tree-dwellers. Anteaters feed on small insects, including ants and termites, which they access by digging into their nests and then scooping them up with their sticky tongues very quickly to avoid most of their bites.

In **dreams and visions**, the anteater speaks of self-reliance and self-sufficiency. He may look like a big cuddly toy and have no teeth, but he has four-inch claws on the end of those furry legs, and can see off a jaguar. Even the smaller species know how to look after themselves. This is a creature which has been on the planet a great deal longer than *Homo sapiens* and its lifestyle has served it well.

As a **totem animal**, the anteater gives the gift of coping in poor circumstances. This is a creature which makes a living out of tiny poisonous insects which it grubs from the earth. As he eats them, they sting him as often as they can but he carries on regardless, tough as old boots, inured to their stings. He can make a feast of very little, live high on the poorest fare and in the humblest of circumstances – and is content with what he has.

Antelope

(While the term "antelope", loosely used to describe many cloven-hoofed species which do not fit into other categories, is in fact a "wastebasket taxon", the taxon does include many species of true antelope. These include the Thompson's gazelle and the gnu or wildebeest, which looks more like a skinny bison than an antelope. Gazelles are included in the group; they are usually smaller members of the antelope family. There are 91 species in the group altogether, and the larger part of the group inhabits Africa.)

Elements: fire and air.

Deities: Astarte, Attar, Chandra, Ea, Isis, Satet, Set, Shiva, Soma.

The word "antelope" seems to derive from the Greek words for flower and eye, meaning a flower-eyed or beautiful-eyed creature – appropriate for an animal that seems to embody beauty of form and grace of movement. As well as beauty, speed and agility are also associated with these animals, the ability to swiftly remove themselves from the scene of danger, and even to make it look enjoyable while they do so – the playful-looking *jinking* they do while running is in fact believed to be a way of demonstrating their fitness and energy, thus persuading the pursuing predator to turn away and seek an animal less capable of outrunning it.

They vary in size from the eland, which can achieve six feet at the shoulder with towering two-foot horns to the West African royal antelope, which is under a foot tall.

In **dreams and visions**, the antelope speaks of foreign places and travel, but also of beauty and grace, perhaps an ideal lover whose personal charms may make you hesitate to approach or be anything but an ardent admirer. Obviously, the class includes many different antelopes – and a wildebeest, for example, may not evoke this meaning – so some meditation may be required as to the exact meaning of some antelopes appearing in dreams. The wildebeest speaks of travel and the eland is a much less fragile and vulnerable antelope which can defend itself with its long spiral horns and has been known to push over trees to get to the foliage.

As a **totem animal**, the antelope gives swiftness and freedom, perception and alertness, a sense of fun and physical wellbeing, as well as grace and elegance. Antelope people are gentle, empathic and considerate, as well as perceptive of others' pain or unhappiness, and have excellent instincts they can trust.

Ape: see **Bonobo, Chimpanzee, Gibbon, Gorilla** or **Orang-utan.**

(Order: primates. The apes divide into two families. The great ape family consists of gorillas, orang-utans, chimpanzees and bonobos, and humans, which are tailless (unlike monkeys) and of higher intelligence. The lesser apes are made up of the 20 species of gibbon.)

Elements: earth and air.

Deities: Gekhre, Ngi, Pan.

If ever an animal enjoyed mixed images, it is the ape. The word is commonly used as a term of abuse, implying stupidity, vulgarity, subhuman aggression, lack of intelligence and gracelessness. Yet the other great apes in our hominid family come very close to us in intelligence and have even been taught to communicate with people, using actual words by pressing keyboard buttons (they are not capable of actual speech, as their vocal tracts are different to ours). Their non-verbal language of gestures has been found to be very close to our own. Their very resemblance to us seems to have made the apes the target of all kinds of opprobrium, such as the popular belief that gorillas are savage monsters, when actually they are gentle and shy.

Aphid

(*Aphidoidea spp*)

Element: water.

Deities: none identified.

These little insects probably need little description for most people: they are a common sight on rose bushes and other garden plants, tiny egg-shaped bugs clustered along the tender parts of stems to suck the sap. They may be green, black or other colours, have wings or not (within the same species), or even be woolly. They are also known for parthenogenesis – the ability to reproduce without mating.

Gardeners may have their own reasons for having unpleasant **dreams** about greenfly, but for most people they signify a nuisance about to happen, a process of being used by someone else or a feeling of uncleanliness and regret, perhaps for something you have done which is now felt to be beneath you.

The aphid, as **totem animal**, has the meaning common to many insects of rebirth and transformation, due to its lifecycle involving many sheddings of skin and physical changes.

Armadillo

(*Cingulata spp*)

Elements: earth and water.

Deities: the armadillo is associated with Mayan deities that have no discoverable names, Goddess I and God L.

These cute little armoured vehicles, of which 21 species exist, range in size from the adorable pink fairy armadillo, which is about 15cms long to the giant armadillo, which can achieve 180cms in length. Apart from one species, the nine-banded armadillo, which is native to the US, they are confined to South America. These animals live on ants and other insects and worms, which they dig out with their large claws, and they will also eat fruit.

They are a fascinating and varied family. Some can curl up into a ball like a hedgehog, one species screams like a banshee to scare away enemies and they are generally good swimmers. The shells have been used to make bowls and musical instruments.

In **dreams and visions**, this animal speaks of a need to protect oneself, but otherwise shares many meanings with the unrelated aardvark.

As a **totem animal**, the armadillo (whose name means "little armoured one") gives the quality of self-sufficiency, quiet assurance and confidence in one's own abilities. Armadillo people go their own way, allowing unkindness and insults to fall off them like the proverbial water off a duck's back, interested only in their own affairs.

Avocet
(*Recurvirostra spp*)
Elements: air and water.
Deities: no deities are officially associated with the avocet, yet the Egyptian God Thoth may be invoked as the patron of this bird, due to its resemblance in shape and habits to His sacred bird – the ibis.
The four species of this elegant wading bird are found in Europe, Asia, the Americas and Australia, and its outline is known in the UK as the emblem of the Royal Society for the Protection of Birds (RSPB). Avocets spend their time grubbing with their curved bills in shallow water and mud for the insects and small water creatures that make up their diet. Their simple nests consist of a few strands of plant material and twigs, providing nothing but the minimum outline to stop the eggs from rolling away.

In **dreams and visions**, the avocet speaks of a search, perhaps one that has gone on for a long time but will reveal results in the long run.

As a **totem animal**, the bird brings its own qualities of being satisfied with very little: its simple nest is created in muddy ground and its diet is taken from the same area. Yet this small bird will courageously attack any creature that moves towards its nest and its young, and others in the area will also come to its aid to drive away the predator, showing spirit far beyond their size.

Axolotl: see **Salamander.**

Aye-Aye
(*Daubentonia madagascariensis*)
Element: earth
Deities: Gods of death and the underworld. Crone goddesses.

This funny little creature, native to Madagascar, has been variously classified as a squirrel and a rodent (its front teeth grow throughout its life) before being identified as a primate. Its hands are long and spiderlike and, in case they needed to look any creepier, they boast an extra-long bony finger that has been likened to "the finger of death." Combined with the aye-aye's strange penetrating eyes, this goes a long way towards counteracting the animal's overall cute appearance and setting it apart, image-wise, from other lemurs. It has been described as unlucky and an evil omen. A whole mythology about this lemur has been developed for the animated series *The Legend of Korra* character Huan.

The aye-aye has developed an unusual method (for lemurs) of finding food. Like a woodpecker, it taps on tree boughs with its lengthened finger until it senses grubs beneath the bark, then gnaws with its front teeth before pulling out the insects with its long finger.

In **dreams and visions**, the aye-aye may mean some ill luck coming your way. In fact, the spooky appearance of the aye-aye has led natives in the past to kill it on sight as a ghoul or harbinger of bad fortune and it is now critically endangered. The appearance of the aye-aye in a dream warns you to protect yourself and take precautions.

As a **totem animal**, it brings fearlessness and the love of wandering, a love of mystery and dark places and an ability to find what you are looking for through inventiveness.

Baboon

(*Papio spp*)
Elements: fire and air.
Deities: Baba, Hapi (Canopic God), Thoth.
These large, striking monkeys are native to Africa and the Arabian Peninsula and eat just about any food they can get their hands on, including plant material, fruit, seeds, insects, fish and shellfish, carrion and live animals. The genus is at least two million years old and comprised of six species, which all share the close-set eyes and the long doglike muzzle that has earned one type, the yellow baboon, the species name *Cynocephalus* (dog-head). They are also known for their coloured cheek pads and large, hairless, padded behinds, which give them a comfortable seat and in the case of the females become red and swollen when they are ready to mate. They live in groups called "troops", which are now sometimes also known as "flanges" – a term coined in the BBC TV comedy series, *Not the Nine O'clock News* – which has since been generally adopted, even by the scientific community!

Baboons are formidable animals with long doglike teeth which they bare in aggressive display when threatened, and the larger males can achieve large dog size at over 80lbs (the females are smaller). They are clever, opportunistic, ruthless beasts which will raid people's homes given half a chance, steal crops and even try to take food from humans if they see them eating. Although they will not readily attack humans, they can be very dangerous if provoked or threatened, and are known for throwing faeces.

In **dreams and visions**, baboons will often be about curiosity and the seeking of knowledge, or they could be about your social life and your family.

The Ancient Egyptians revered this animal as a personification of Thoth, the God of Wisdom and Learning, and they are often pictured in Egyptian art saluting the Sun.

As a **totem animal**, they bring intelligence and an inquiring mind, a greed for knowledge even, along with bodily confidence and excellent social skills, and parenting abilities. The association of Thoth with the underworld and the judgement of the dead may add to these qualities of judgement, integrity and balance.

Badger

(*Mustelidae spp*, particularly *Meles meles*, the European badger)
Element: earth.
Deities: Brigantia, Moritasgus.
Although many of the animals classified as badgers look very much like little bears, they are more closely related to stoats, weasels, otters and mink. They are stocky, powerful creatures known for their burrowing habits, for hibernating through the winter and for their nocturnal lifestyle and shyness, and also for their distinctive facial markings, usually in the form of black and white stripes. These are believed to help these short-sighted creatures recognise one another at night. The many species are found across Europe, North America, Asia and Africa. Badger meat has been eaten within living memory in the UK and still is in Russia, and the thick hair is used for shaving and art brushes.

Most British people will associate this animal with the Kenneth Grahame character in *The Wind in the Willows*, and indeed Mr Badger does personify most of the traits of this creature, its home-loving nature, its shyness and even its hospitality: badgers are known to live peaceably with rabbits and even foxes sharing their setts.

In **dreams and visions**, badgers speak of tenacity: their jawbones are unique in the animal kingdom in that they remain locked to the upper part of the skull even after the soft parts of the body have decayed, and they are equipped with powerful muscles which can deliver a dreadful bite. When the badger has clamped onto its victim, there is nothing much that can cause it to let go. The badger may speak of defence of the home and family, of seeing off intruders or unfriendly persons, of endurance, patience and refusal to give up.

As a **totem animal**, the badger brings these same qualities: of tenacity and the ability to hold on through hard times and under attack, of quietly ferocious courage without needless aggression. Badger people may be slow-moving and slow to anger, but beware if you do succeed in getting under their thick skins!

Bandicoot

(*Perameles spp*)

Element: earth.
Deities: Ka-Ro-Ra (Aboriginal).
Bandicoot is the name for a number of species of small mouselike marsupials with long, pointed snouts, big ears and strong kangaroo style hind legs. The family, which is native to Australia and New Guinea, includes the ultra-cute bilby, but is not related to the bandicoot-rats found in Asia, which belong to the rodent order. Shy, solitary and nocturnal, bandicoots have a great many tiny sharp teeth and drill for worms and insects with their long snouts, leaving characteristic little holes which are known as "snout-pokes".

The animal's name might be better known today through the computer game character Crash Bandicoot, a resistance fighter dedicated to thwarting an evil scientist. Does he bring meaning to the appearance of the animal in dreams? That depends on the dreamer, and whether the character has any meaning for them. Remember that our cultural experiences always colour our understanding of divination and messages.

In **dreams and visions**, bandicoots are said to be associated with reincarnation and phenomena such as "recognising" people from a former life.

As a **totem animal**, the creature brings its qualities of shyness, keeping out of the public eye, doing its work unhurriedly and thoroughly, without fuss or ostentation, going deeply into every issue before moving on to the next.

Barb
(*Barbus barbus*)
Elements: water and fire.
Deities: any sea gods and goddesses.
There are almost 2,000 species of the barb – freshwater fish popular with aquarium owners because of their range of bright colours, which can range from plain silver through oranges, yellows, golds and pinks to deep red, which may change again when the fish's breeding season begins and may also include brilliant patterning of stripes and spots. Their name, Latin for "beard", comes from the barbels found around the mouths of many species. They are also very adaptable and will survive changes in their environment, such as temperature variations and even acidity changes. Though they are quite small, they cannot be housed with smaller species, as they are extremely aggressive and will eat other fish.

In **dreams and visions**, this little fish may represent someone whose courage and style you admire, or it could be someone you have less respect for owing to their vanity or aggression – other details of the dream, or the feeling you have on awakening, will tell you which.

As a **totem animal**, the barb brings courage beyond its size, audacity and greed for life. No one will stop this individual from enjoying life to the full, and they may also be extremely aggressive and territorial about their home, their family and their friends.

Barnacle

(*Cirripdeia spp*)

Elements: water and earth.

Deities: Amphitrite, Poseidon.

It is surprising to learn that these non-mobile creatures, which look so very much like shellfish, are actually crustaceans and closely related to crabs and lobsters. They are free-swimming only during their larval stages. Our ancestors didn't quite know what to make of them either, and once believed the goose barnacle (*C. thoracica*) was the larval form of the barnacle goose – a bird!

Barnacles cling tightly to rocks, the submarine surfaces of ships and even to large marine creatures such as whales, either by a stalk or by gluing their shells directly to the surface. They are famously difficult to detach, and ships, boats and submarines are obliged to dock at regular intervals so the barnacles can be scraped off, as their build-up will affect the smooth passage of the vessel. Barnacles feed in the same manner as corals, filtering small organisms and particles from the water with feathery cirri.

In **dreams and visions**, barnacles represent either the dreamer's strong desire to cling to something, perhaps an outmoded habit or way of life or even a relationship which has run its course, or a difficulty caused by someone else with this determination. Either way, the dream tells you that you are stuck for the time being.

As a **totem animal**, this marine clinger gives sticking power without equal. Barnacle people like it just where they are and will not move, whether the place is an actual location, an attachment to another person, a habit or a point of view.

Barracuda

(*Sphyraena spp*)

Element: water.

Deities: Morgan le Fey and other war goddesses.

29 species make up this genus of streamlined, colourful and beautiful fish, which can vary in size from 60cms to around two metres in length and are known for their fearsome tooth-lined jaws and aggressive behaviour. They have been known to attack human swimmers and divers, but their danger to humans is not confined to their behaviour. The US CDC lists the barracuda as the most dangerous fish to eat because it can carry the deadly marine toxin Ciguatera, which affects at least 50,000 people annually. Although they resemble the freshwater predator fish called pike, they are unrelated.

Found in warmer seas around the world, barracudas are seen as bringing ill luck in some cultures (possibly due to their vicious bite), but in others have been seen as the embodiment of knowledge and wisdom, much as the salmon has been seen in Celtic culture. Polynesians see them as the spirits of great warriors who died in battle. Other people have simply admired their strength, their power, their speed and their ability in catching their prey.

In **dreams and visions**, a barracuda is likely to mean a situation (or more likely a person) that you should avoid. It tells of danger, threat, spite, personal conflict. In dreams where you yourself *are* the barracuda, it is telling you that you will overcome all negative situations and triumph through your own innate power.

As a **totem animal**, this fish brings strength, beauty, determination and huge power, and barracuda people may have to exercise restraint as they can be aggressive and overpowering. It is a very lucky creature to have as your power or totem animal.

Basilisk Lizard: see **Lizards**, also **Basilisk** in next section.

Bat

(*Chiroptera spp*)
Elements: earth and air.
Deities: Camazotz, Evaki, Hades, Hecate, Lilith, Leutgitupa'itea, Murcielago, Persephone, Tzinacan.

Bats immediately evoke an emotional reaction in most people: loathing, fear and phobia, delightful creeps or even love. These ancient animals with their strange demon-like faces go back in the fossil record at least 48 million years and are only very distantly related to all other species on Earth. There are around 1,200 species of bat, the second largest number of species of mammals after the gigantic rodent order. These range in size from the flying foxes, which can have a wingspan of nearly two metres to the tiny two-gram bumblebee bat of Asia.

A lot of misinformation is held about bats: they are not blind, for example, but have perfectly adequate eyesight. Many women (and some men) are terrified of having a bat get entangled in their hair, but the astonishing accuracy of the bat's bio sonar system (which enables them to catch tiny insects on the wing in the dark) means that this should never happen.

Even before the publication in 1897 of Bram Stoker's horror novel, *Dracula*, bats have enjoyed, if that is the right word, a close association with vampires, witches, monsters and devils in people's minds. Their nocturnal habits and strange appearance – many have leaf, horseshoe or other odd shapes on their faces – and their colonies in deep, dark caves have made them the subject of much superstitious belief. And that's before you get to the vampire bats (*Desmodontinae spp*) which live on small amounts of blood sucked from other animals and humans while they sleep. Bats can indeed be dangerous, but this has less to do with their sharp teeth and more to do with the diseases they carry, such as Ebola, SARS and rabies, which can transfer to humans that come into contact with bats or their faeces.

They are also strongly associated with mental illness: we say someone "has bats in their belfry" or is "bats" or "batty" – an expression dating from the beginning of the twentieth century and possibly referring to the way bats flit about, seemingly without purpose.

In **dreams and visions**, while dreaming of a vampire bat sucking your blood can mean you are being used or exploited; dreams of bats otherwise can mean something much more mysterious. These creatures are entwined with the dead and the mysteries of the night in our cultural consciousness, and speak of necromancy, magic and communion with the dead. They speak of deep-seated fears, superstition and nightmares.

As a **totem animal**, bats bring good fortune and spiritual awareness, with an ability to steer a straight course through nonsense and confusing information to find the goal. Deeply gregarious, bat people get on well with others but do not put themselves forward or indulge in ego-driven behaviour.

Bear

(*Ursidae spp*)
Element: earth (Polar bear: earth and water).
Deities: Artemis, Artio (and Arthur), the Cailleach, Callisto, Ildiko, Mielikki, Odin, Thor.

Eight species of bear are still alive today, from the polar bear to the threatened tree-dwelling smallest species; the sun bear. At 700kg, the polar bear is the largest of the Ursidae and the largest land carnivore on Earth, closely followed by the brown bear, to which it is closely related: these two species may be considered brown or white forms of the same kind of bear and can interbreed. In North America, the brown bear is known as the grizzly bear. Other species are the Asian and American black bears, the spectacled bear, the sloth bear and the iconic giant panda. A Canadian subspecies of the black bear is the Kermode bear, often called the spirit bear because such a large proportion of them are pure white.

Bears have been feared, admired and worshipped throughout human history, and a lot of beliefs are attached to them. Native Americans saw the bear as a brother, partly because of the appearance of the animal when dead and skinned: it looks strangely human! Although the bear is one of the deadliest carnivores, it nevertheless has a cuddly appearance, and has been feted in children's books, cartoons and as toys down the years. Its slow and deliberate movements have been seen as evidence of wisdom and judgement, and in many cultures it is honoured as a symbol of these qualities, as well as of strength and ferocity. Bears can also symbolise grumpiness and bad temper, as the terms "bearish" and "bear with a sore head" demonstrate.

In LGBT culture, a "bear" is a term for a big, hairy, gay man.

In **dreams and visions**, bears can have many meanings. Which facet of them have you dreamed of? Their fierceness? Their strength? Their apparent cuddliness? Maybe you have connected them with greed, with their love of rich foods such as honey and salmon and their layers of body fat, or maybe with their habit of hibernating through the winter. They may speak of a person or a situation which seems peaceful and safe, yet can suddenly erupt.

As a **totem animal**, the bear brings strength and self-reliance, the ability to live through difficult times. Bear people do not look for trouble, but when trouble comes knocking, they are more than ready to respond. They can go from relaxed and quiet to a roaring fury that will cow any attacker in a heartbeat.

Bearcat
(*Arctictis binturong*)
Element: earth.
Deities: no deity is specifically associated with this animal, but those associated with bears would be appropriate.
This Asian tree-dwelling creature is a species on its own, with no closely related species, although it closely resembles the bear and weasel families. Very endangered, it enjoys an omnivorous diet, eating fruit, seeds, leaves, insects, eggs, meat and fish. Its powerful, stocky shape may have been the inspiration for its name being given to a range of armoured vehicles.

In **dreams and visions**, this animal indicates comfort, both in yourself and with your surroundings and the life situation in which you find yourself. You can take care of yourself, wherever you are.

As a **totem animal**, the bearcat brings ease of manner, playfulness and freedom from stress or fear. Go with the flow, says this spiritual guide. Life is good, and if it isn't – it's what you make it.

Beaver
(*Castor canadensis*, the US beaver and *C. fiber*, the Eurasian beaver)
Element: water.
Deities: Capa, Gods of work and industry, such as Völundr or Wayland. Some sources cite Castor, the brother of Pollux, because of his name, but this seems a little far-fetched to me.
These fascinating and beautiful creatures are now being reintroduced into the wild in the UK and I had the privilege of visiting a Cornish beaver colony one night and observing these large rodents swimming and moving about on land by the red light of a night-adapted torch. They had completely transformed the landscape, damming the river at various points to create a series of small lakes, beside which their *lodges* were built, and thus not only rendering the area more wildlife-friendly, but protecting it from flooding. The lodges are cunningly built with underwater entrances, to foil predators. With climate change, flooding is a real concern for many areas and beavers have been suggested as one line of action.

The other thing that struck me was their size: after the gigantic capybara of South America, they are the largest rodents, up to 120cm in length (the Eurasian beaver being longer than the American species) and with a weight up to 66Kg of muscular body, which is needed to lug around the tree trunks they have cut down with their big, razor-sharp incisors to build their dams. The rubbery, paddle-like tail alone is 35cms long in the smaller species and up to 50cms in the Eurasian one.

Gentle and retiring, they are still up to defending their families, and the guide at the reserve told us they would unhesitatingly attack a dog that came near their young.

In **dreams and visions**, as you might expect, the beaver indicates industry and diligence, whether this is required of you or something you are already doing. Given the lifestyle of the animal, this will have the special meaning that all you do is for your family or your community, and that it is very worthwhile.

As a **totem animal**, beaver people are work animals! They enjoy nothing more than *beavering away* at a chosen project, often one connected with home improvements, and have the ability to keep at the job until it is finished to their satisfaction. This totem brings a lot of energy and staying power and the ability to work well and harmoniously with others.

Bed Bug

(*Cimex lectularius* and *hemipterus*)
Elements: earth and fire.
Deities: none, though there are deities connected with insects generally.
A nasty subject and one that most might think was relegated to the grubby bedrooms and hotel rooms of the past, before effective washing machines and hygiene-awareness. Not so: bed bugs are found across the world and infestations are on the increase, probably due to increased global travel. The insects are tiny, dark brown and their bites cause a blotchy rash that may lead to more serious health implications such as allergic reactions and infections.

In **dreams and visions**, bed bugs may appear as a warning that someone (perhaps within your own home) is using you, or doing you harm behind your back – for instance, by spreading unpleasant rumours. They may be telling you that you are unhappy in the situation you are in, whether that is a relationship or a job, and that you should try to change things at once. They may even be a sign that you are under psychic attack, while dreaming about crushing and killing the bugs means you are on your way to changing the bad situation.

If anyone is unfortunate enough to have this creature as a **totem animal**, it will bring bad luck.

Bee

(*Apis spp*)
Element: fire.
Deities: Aphrodite/Venus, Diana of the Ephesians, Pan, Parvati, Ra, Zeus/Jupiter.
Where to start with this magical creature, which has been close to mankind from the dawn of time? Beekeepers will tell you their bees are like family members, and even today many will go and "tell the bees" about any changes within the family: of births, marriages, deaths and changes in fortune. The old belief was that the bees would feel snubbed if they were not kept in the loop and would stop making honey, leave the hive or even die. The belief is widespread across the UK and Europe, with each region having its own preferred method of addressing the bees. In Flora Thompson's wonderful autobiographical book, *Lark Rise*, she describes an elderly neighbour telling the bees of her husband's death by tapping on the lid of each hive and saying,

"Bees, bees, your master's dead, an' now you must work for your missus." Other traditions may have special names to use to address the bees (such as "Little Brownie") or believe it is unlucky to use bad language in the bees' hearing. After the death of Her Majesty Queen Elizabeth II, as I was writing this book, John Chapple, the Royal Beekeeper, reported that he had indeed kept the palace bees informed of events, telling them about the Queen's death and the accession of King Charles III in the approved manner.

Bees themselves are known to be excellent at communicating. It has been suggested that the insects have a kind of common "hive mind" – a theory inspired by the way the hive seems to function smoothly without any need for communication. However, modern technology has allowed man to pry into the inmost recesses of the hive and observe "waggle dances" and "round dances" that indicate to other bees where the richest sources of nectar are currently to be found. The dances are surprisingly sophisticated, giving the other bees the direction, distance away and even height off the ground of the food source. The functioning of the bees and the hive is also managed by pheromones, which tell the bees when to go out and look for honey, how to spot intruders and how to care for the eggs and larvae produced by the queen, some of which will need special treatment in order to mature into new queens and drones.

In **dreams and visions**, bees speak of industry and co-operation, leading to the gain of wealth and happiness: the gold of the bee's body and the gold of the honey both speak of wealth and good fortune, gained through hard work by the deserving. Keep your head down and get on with your work, says this animal. Work closely and humbly with others: if you are not working for the common good, you will not gain your desire. Dreaming of bees may indicate that you are worried about not fitting in in some way, perhaps at a new workplace or with your in-laws, that you need to be accepted, to be part of a team.

The bee also speaks of strength in numbers, the power of people working together, how they can achieve far more than one individual, of loyalty, even of patriotism and national pride. The bee can speak of courage and self-sacrifice: shown by the way all the workers will unhesitatingly attack any creature, including things many times larger than themselves, to defend the hive. And in the act of stinging the intruder, they lose their own lives, as their sting is torn from their body, causing irreparable damage.

As a **totem animal**, the bee brings good fortune and an excellent work ethic, but also strength: this is a creature that can fly for miles, soar above troubles and, if troubles insist on troubling it, the bee has its sting at the ready! It offers a pleasant life, one of working amongst attractive places to gather sweetness and wealth, but never one of indolence or non-productivity. The bee is also a creature of great courage and self-sacrifice, willingly giving its life to defend the hive and seemingly not afraid of anything.

The bumblebee shares the attributes of the honeybee, and also acts as a harbinger of the spring, whereas the honeybee is firmly tied to the summer.

Beetle
(*Coleoptera* order)
Elements: varies with species.
Deities: Cerambus, Khepra, Tithonus.
The beetle kingdom, comprised of some 400,000 species, is alive with beauty and colour: bright hues, spots and stripes, glowing wings, metallic and opalescent wing-covers and, in some species, phosphorescence, as in fireflies and glow-worms. Some can fly and some cannot, some have big staglike horns or huge jaws. From the common household black beetle to the exotic white scarab (and every colour in between); they inhabit every continent except the Antarctic and range in size from the 120mm Goliath beetle, which weighs as much as a small apple, to the almost microscopic featherwing beetle. Beetles can be useful or inimical to man: from the pretty ladybird that clears away greenfly from our gardens to the notifiable Colorado beetle, which can decimate potato crops; and species like the Emerald ash borer beetle, which is in the process of attacking our native ash trees.

One beetle, the Egyptian scarab (a dung beetle), has inspired worship, becoming a central part of the iconography of the Ancient Egyptian gods and pharaohs, as its breeding behaviour was thought to mimic the Sun (it collects a ball of manure and lays eggs inside, rolling the ball about to a place of safety).

In **dreams and visions**, beetles suggest the work environment, business and financial affairs.

If you have the beetle as your **totem animal**, it will bring you business acumen and good fortune, as well as compassion for others.

The scarab beetle may mean more, especially if you have some knowledge of Egyptology: its name *khepera* meant "to rise, to be reborn", and it may suggest new starts, new hopes, the dawning of a new time.

As a **totem animal**, it can bring you quite magical powers, with good luck and an ability to rise beyond bad situations and continually reinvent yourself.

Binturong: see Bearcat.

Birds
(Class: *Aves.*)
Elements: generally air.
Deities: see individual species.
For more detail, see individual species. Birds are a gigantic class of some 10,000 species of warm-blooded creatures, some with flight and some without, all now considered to be living theropod dinosaurs and the only dinosaurs now extant. They are found across the world in all habitats, and range in size from the tiny bumblebee hummingbird to the ostrich, which can be almost three metres tall. In the past, birds reached enormous sizes, the largest being the half-ton elephant bird of Madagascar, distantly related to the kiwi.

In **dreams and visions**, birds can have a huge range of meanings, even where the species being dreamed of is not clear. Different coloured birds can mean different things. For example, white birds and black birds may both speak of death or ill fortune, blue birds may speak of freedom, caged birds are self-explanatory, and birds inside the house may mean good luck. A flock of birds may speak of your friends and family, your workmates and anyone within your social group, while being attacked by a bird may mean you owe someone something and should make sure you pay it back. Do not forget that meanings and associations can migrate and change with cultural events. Thanks to Alfred Hitchcock's classic horror film, the image of a flock of birds can now also have a very threatening meaning in dreams, perhaps indicating that you are feeling or being ganged up on.

Birds of Paradise
(*Paradisaeidae spp*)
Element: air.
Deities: the Bennu and Ra.
These exotic creatures comprise 44 species found across the Australasian and Indonesian areas, notable for their stunning multi-coloured plumage, including showstoppers like Wilson's bird (a very dull name for a bird that looks like a living stained glass window) and the golden-and-black lesser bird of paradise (surely lesser in the sense of size only, as it is one of the most gorgeous creatures on Earth). In many species, only the males have the bright hues – the females being drab and coloured to blend in safely with their habitat. Sadly, the beauty of these creatures led to their being captured and killed by the thousands for their feathers, which were used on ladies' hats, and the birds themselves were often stuffed and displayed under glass domes in Victorian homes.

In **dreams and visions**, if you're dreaming of a bird of paradise then you are thinking of someone who has caught your eye, someone very attractive, flamboyant even, someone who is not usually your type at all, and yet … Spiritually, the meaning of this bird is a yearning for higher things, for improving yourself and casting away old habits.

As a **totem animal**, it brings total confidence in yourself, especially in your looks, but can also mean a certain shallowness of outlook, vanity and a tendency to judge others on their appearance.

Bison
(*Bison bison* and *bonasus*)
Element: earth.
Deities: Achelous, Utu-Shamash, White Buffalo Calf Woman, Wi.
Confusingly, the North American bison, *B. bison*, is often referred to as a buffalo, although it is not in fact a buffalo. Both this and the European bison, *B. bonasus*, are in the Bovidae order and related to the domestic cow, closely enough that the two species can interbreed.

The bison is closely associated in many people's minds with the early Native Americans, who followed the herds across the plains, killing the animals for their meat and skins, but respecting them and taking only what they needed. The white settlers infamously slaughtered millions of the animals during the nineteenth century, bringing them near to extinction in an attempt to starve out the indigenous peoples – part of a historical genocide that is said to have been larger in scale than the Nazi Holocaust. The bison is not endangered today, largely because of its growing popularity as a farmed animal, bison meat being very similar to beef but lower in cholesterol.

These usually gentle giants can be aggressive, and their sheer size makes them challenging prey for all but the largest and most determined predators.

In **dreams and visions**, an individual bison can mean strength and power, or a herd of them may refer to the Native American view of them as a resource and indicate self-sufficiency, riches, stock … enough for your needs.

As a **totem animal**, the bison is about power and protection, about physical strength and contented fearlessness, just as it represented for the First Nations peoples.

Bittern: see Heron.

Blackbird

(*Turdidae turdus*, specifically *T. merula*)
Element: air.
Deities: Athena/Minerva, Rhiannon.

A common sight in gardens, this bird is pretty widespread across the world and its chinking alarm cry is very familiar to anyone who has walked in woods or just stepped quickly out of the back door into the garden. It also has a very pretty warbling song. The male is the black bird but the female is a dull brown, though they both have the bright yellow beak. Children know this bird early in their lives from the nursery rhyme, *Sing a Song of Sixpence*, in which four-and-twenty blackbirds are baked in a pie – which refers to the once common practice of eating garden birds such as blackbirds, rooks, thrushes and sparrows.

In **dreams and visions**, black birds often refer to mysteries or even to a death, and the blackbird is no exception. However, if the "flavour" of the dream is light and happy, it may speak of tricks and pranks. It can also speak of "finding your voice" – whether that be making up your mind to speak on a matter, or literally discovering your singing talents.

As a **totem animal**, it brings seriousness and serenity.

Bobcat: see Lynx.

Bonobo

(*Pan paniscus*)
Element: air.
Deity: Pan.

Sharing an astonishing 98.7% of their DNA with humans, the bonobo and chimpanzee are our closest living relatives. Yet these two apes, so similar in appearance, are quite different in their habits. Bonobos are the hippies of the ape family, relaxed and laid back, practising free love and peace, man. While the chimps are aggressive carnivores that will sometimes steal, kill and eat one another's babies, the bonobos are far gentler, possibly due to their social structure: where most gregarious apes have a male leader, bonobos have a female one. Both species have high intelligence.

Smaller than chimps, bonobos can also be distinguished by their dark faces (whereas chimps typically have light ones) and their leaner body shapes.

Dreaming of bonobos is about your social life, for (like chimpanzees) they represent other humans, other people. It is difficult to separate them from chimps in terms of spiritual meanings, because the two creatures are so similar and because our consciousness defaults to "chimp" because they are better known to us than bonobos, which were not recognised as a separate species until the 1950s.

As a **totem animal**, it can be seen as similar to the chimpanzee, but with a gentler, more peaceable vibe, bringing contentedness, relaxation and compassion.

Booby

(*Sula spp*)

Element: air.

Deities: none identified.

The booby is a large tropical seabird closely related to gannets, and gets its unfortunate name from its clumsy behaviour on land, as well as its silly habit of landing on ships and putting itself at the mercy of seamen, who in the past might catch, kill and eat it! We derive the term "booby trap" from this practice. I remember as a child, being helpless with laughter while watching a TV wildlife programme featuring footage of boobies taking off and landing: their antics are extremely comical. Some species have brightly coloured feet and beaks, not for breeding displays but due to their taking in marine pigments from their diet of seafood.

However silly they may appear, the boobies are all successful species, and all are listed as "Least Concern" by the International Union for Conservation of Nature.

As with other birds, the meaning of a booby in your **dreams or visions** will depend on its behaviour. A booby attacking you obviously speaks of a person you do not have a lot of respect for getting on your case, whilst a peaceful booby sitting beside you may direct your attention to someone you are not giving enough attention to and do not value as much as you should.

As **totem animal**, booby people enjoy their lives more because they don't worry overmuch about how other people see them. They are happy to clown about – for their own enjoyment rather than that of others – and are relaxed and delightful souls to know.

Budgerigar

(*Melopsittacus undulatus*)

Element: air.

Deities: no deity is specifically associated with budgerigars, though there are many general bird deities. The iconography of the Goddess Meenakshi shows Her holding a parrot.

Although the common budgie is simply a small parrot, it has won the right to a section of its own here through its importance to man. As a pet, it ranks third in popularity globally after dogs and cats, and has famously been the sole companion of many a lonely elderly person, singing its cheerful songs, whistling and mimicking human speech. Instantly recognisable for its zebra-striped wings, pastel plumage and curved, flattened bill the budgie has been bred to produce a range of colours and patterns.

Dreaming of a budgie can have a range of meanings, and the rest of the content of the dream or vision would have to be examined to determine the message. Like all caged birds, it might mean a feeling of being trapped or hunted, but the friendly domestic feeling of the budgie would more likely indicate a memory from one's childhood home, or may by association evoke memories of a relative who had such a pet. Dreaming of a budgie is fortunate, though the meaning may also depend on the colour of the bird. It speaks of childhood dreams coming to pass and old happiness revisited.

In common with other parakeets, the budgie as a **totem animal** brings happiness and content, the wisdom to be satisfied with what you have and to be cheerful and friendly to all.

Buffalo

(*Bubalina spp*)

Elements: water and earth.

Deities: Hsi-Ho, Varahi, Yama.

Although the term buffalo is sometimes used for bison, the true buffaloes are species of wild cattle found principally on the African continent and Asia, although they have also been introduced into Europe, Australia and America. Unlike the bison, they have large backward-curved horns which can form a bony bracket across the top of the head and generally lack the bison's characteristic long shaggy hair. The Asian water buffalo has been a domesticated animal, used for transport and farming and for its milk and meat.

In **dreams and visions**, the appearance of this animal speaks of hard work and its rewards, of the slow building of financial security through labour and the power of patience.

As a **totem animal**, it can bring a deeply spiritual, almost monk-like aspect, with feelings of humility, gratitude and willingness to serve and work at a humble level.

Bull: see Cattle.

Bushbaby (also bush baby, galago.)
(*Galagidae spp*)
Element: water.
Deities: no deity appears to be associated with the bushbaby, but deities who protect and nurture babies and small children would be appropriate in this role, such as Bes, Hera, Isis, Frigga, Juno-Lucina, Ta-Urt.

The eyes have it ... easily the most prominent feature of this small creature, which is also blessed with very sensitive hearing, acute enough to track insects in the dark. These nocturnal primates are found in sub-Saharan Africa, where they live in trees: local tradition has it that although they will venture down onto the ground, they are never found there when dead as they build themselves a deathbed of branches. Their name may derive from their eerie childlike cries, which may have inspired legends of a creature that steals human babies and takes them away into the forest. They are highly intelligent, curious animals which, despite their appealing appearance, do not make good pets; in fact in many states it is illegal to own one.

In **dreams and visions**, the bushbaby represents innocence, playfulness, childhood and vulnerability, as well as new concepts and events. Its huge sad eyes recall the legends of the lost children and, by extension, all lost children. Therefore, its appearance in a dream may be speaking of a deep grief connected with a child, perhaps that of a childless woman grieving for the children she so desperately wants.

As a **totem animal**, it brings a childlike quality, the ability to live in the moment and enjoy the smaller, simpler things in life, but also with a degree of sadness – childhood can be pretty sad, after all.

Bustard
(*Otididae spp*)
Elements: earth and air.
Deitiy: Artemis.

This handsome and impressive bird was once my neighbour. When I lived on Salisbury Plain there was (and still is) a conservation project devoted to repopulating great bustards (*Otis tarda*) on the plain, importing them from Eastern Europe and Russia. They are rather like beautiful turkeys without all the red wattles, though some species have throat sacs and the larger species have the distinction of being the heaviest of flying birds. They lay their large eggs in a shallow scratch in the ground, easy for predators to find, which may account for their becoming extinct in Britain in the nineteenth century.

Seeing a bustard in **dreams and visions** is interesting. There is a generally accepted dream-meaning for the bustard: a greedy rich person who will not help others. But the subconscious mind may be transferring the term "bastard" from a person to the bird. Either way, the same definition seems to work well!

As a **totem animal**, the bustard gives competitiveness, to the point of foolishness perhaps, but still a capacity for strength and speed.

Butterfly

(*Lepidoptra* order)

Elements: air and fire.

Deities: Freyja, Iris, Psyche and all deities associated with death and rebirth.

Some of the most beautiful creatures in nature, butterflies flit peaceably from flower to flower, sucking up nectar and displaying the glowing colours on their wings. They harm no one and give pleasure with their beauty and grace, as well as pollinating countless plants. The same cannot be said of their larvae: caterpillars, which munch their way through garden vegetables, flowers and crops, attack hedges, bushes and trees and are generally less than appealing to see, wriggling wormlike in their structures of web and faecal matter.

This dichotomy echoes the twofold character of the butterfly in human folklore and legend. For some, it is a ridiculous creature, flitting around aimlessly and never settling in any one place or achieving anything; for others, it is a powerful symbol of transformation. Christians have seen it as symbolic of the journey of the soul: released from the body (like the chrysalis) at death, it wings its way heavenwards, transformed from a creature of earth into one of glory. In the same way, the caterpillar may be seen as a creature of promise and potential (but perhaps not by gardeners).

In **dreams and visions**, butterflies speak of your spiritual progress and of transformation, and the message will depend on the content of the dream. Does the insect land on you, or flutter in your face or just fly by? If you dream of caterpillars, they may speak of your struggle to transform yourself in some way, whether that is a spiritual struggle or just that of a teenaged girl who thinks she is plain and wants to change her look.

As a **totem animal**, the butterfly is surprisingly powerful, giving an ability to change oneself, to soar above problems and to dazzle others with wit and beauty. One should take care, however, to curb the habit of flitting from one interest to another without learning or gaining anything.

Buzzard

(*Buteo spp*)

Element: air.

Deities: Nekhbet and other vulture gods.

The term buzzard is used for a number of related species of birds of prey, including *B. buteo*, the common buzzard, which is has a wide range across the northern hemisphere, and migrates into the southern hemisphere as far as South Africa. This species is the most common daytime bird of prey in Europe, with a population of millions. But the name buzzard is also applied to the American turkey vulture, *Cathartes aura* – an unrelated species – although both the European buzzard and the turkey vulture will feed on carrion (*Buteo* is primarily a bird of prey, feeding on small mammals and birds, insects and earthworms).

In **dreams and visions**, buzzards share with most birds the meaning of freedom, being able to rise above it all, get away from it all. In common with many other birds of prey, buzzards are occasionally mobbed by smaller birds, and this happening in a dream alerts you to attacks by others, perhaps lesser minds who are jealous of your success. It signifies the upward struggle, of learning and spiritual development, of the cycle of birth, death and rebirth.

As a **totem animal**, the buzzard's grace and beauty brings good fortune and an ability to soar, knowing when it is time to let go of a lost cause and fly away without regrets, on to the next challenge.

Caecilian

(*Gymnophiona spp*)
Element: earth.
Deities: none identified.
The caecilians are a large family of limbless amphibians that look like snakes, worms or eels, but are not related to any of these, being more closely related to newts, salamanders and frogs. They have very long, featureless bodies, no tails (the anus is right at the posterior end), no limbs and often no discernible eyes, although some species do have a long fin along their backs. One species is even lungless, breathing instead through its skin. The one feature they do all have is a set of small tentacles near their snouts, which probably help them smell or taste their environment. They live in tropical and subtropical wetlands, burrowing in the ground and in the mud of streams.

As unlikely as these obscure creatures are to appear in **dreams and visions**, they can be seen as a reference to one's secret life, the private concerns which are not shared with others (the hobby of which one is slightly ashamed), the quarrels or silly habits which go on between husband and wife and which are no one else's business.

As a **totem animal**, the caecilian brings a sense of fertility and renewal, of being a vital part in the scheme of things, and also a desire for secrecy and preserving mystery.

Caiman

(*Caimaninae spp*)
Element: water.
Deities: Sobek and Zipacna.
These are small crocodilians, apart from the black caiman, which can achieve a scary four metres in length and has been known to attack and prey on humans. They inhabit the Americas, living in swampy areas and feeding largely on fish.

In **dreams and visions**, seeing this creature warns of being too trusting; you must proceed with caution and with your eyes wide open. Watch where you walk and take nothing for granted. There are enemies on all sides.

As a **totem animal**, the caiman has many of the qualities of the alligator and crocodile, bringing power, patience, alertness and speed along with a complete mastery of one's own habitat, whether that be the office or the golf course!

Camel
(*Camelus dromedarius, C. bactrianus* and *C. ferus*)
Element: fire.
Deities: Allat, Arsu, Hanuman, Momai Maa, Pabuji.

With its comical shape, beautiful eyes and dour face, the camel is one of the strangest of animals, almost mythical in its ungainliness, its talent for survival and its legendarily grumpy personality. Its characteristic gait (if you have ever ridden one, you would be prepared to declare it was walking on three legs) carries it effortlessly across deserts and fertile lands alike, and it seems able to carry enormous burdens. Its most prominent feature is its hump (one in the dromedary, two in the Bactrian), a mound of stored watery fat that enables the animal to travel for long periods in arid conditions.

The camel has a wide range of behaviours towards humans; it can be gentle and friendly, or it can be aggressive and dangerous. When annoyed, it may spit a gobbet of evil-smelling mucus at you.

If this ship of the desert has a superpower, it is travel, for it has migrated all over the world from its North American origins in the Eocene era, and is now chiefly associated with North Africa and with the huge feral populations that have sprung up in Australia. Its relationship with man goes back to earliest times; it was probably domesticated during the 3rd millennium BCE. Today, almost all camels on Earth are domestic animals or feral, with only a small and threatened population of truly wild camels: *C. ferus*, the wild Bactrian, surviving in the Gobi Desert.

Camels have been kept as transport animals, and for their milk, meat and wool or hair. Seen on the animal, this last often has a patchy, mangy appearance and does not seem a promising material, but it is prized for outerwear: camelhair coats are an expensive, luxury item.

In **dreams and visions**, this animal indicates travel, perhaps for a prolonged period and maybe under less-than-ideal conditions, but with the assurance that patience and preparation will see you through. A camel coming towards you may speak of gifts and riches coming your way, or powerful friends. It is a very lucky animal to encounter.

As a **totem animal**, the camel brings its own brand of eccentric power, courage and the ability to survive many things. Camel people may be long-lived and have the patience and other qualities to endure all kinds of ordeals; they prefer to do things their own way in their own time – which is not the same as being lazy or awkward!

Capybara
(*Hydrochoerus hydrochaeris* and *H. isthmius*)
Element: water.
Deitiy: Pachamama.

This giant guinea pig is the largest rodent on the planet and divides its time between the land, forest and waters of South America, where it lives in large family groups. The animal stands around 60cms at the shoulder and can weigh up to 66kg, although the lesser capybara *(H. isthmius)* is smaller.

A vegetarian, it lives on grass and water plants, diving for the latter and holding its breath underwater for up to five minutes. Like many rodents and rabbits, it processes cellulose from plants by eating it twice: then it produces faecal pellets which are ingested again to extract the sugars. Although killed for their meat and skins, they are not endangered. A popular creature on the internet, it has its own meme, "OK I pull up".

In **dreams and visions**, capybaras are often about your social life, whether it is prospering or not doing as well as you would like. A visit from a single creature could mean you are about to meet an influential new friend, while dreams of capybaras moving away from you could mean your social circle is breaking up.

As a **totem animal**, it gives a friendly and sociable vibe which draws others close and helps forge lasting friendships. Capybara people are relaxed and often in a holiday mood, though they can also be nervous and lacking in confidence.

Caracal
(*Caracal caracal*)
Element: fire.
Deities: Bast, Mafdet, Pakhet, Sekhmet.
The most noticeable feature on this beautiful wild cat is its flamboyantly tufted ears – the tufts can be almost as long as the ears themselves. It is a medium-sized cat, slender and long-limbed with a deep reddish coat and the black "tear-line" markings of the cheetah. Although its usual prey is small animals, it also feeds on birds and it can leap an astonishing ten feet into the air to catch them! Two species of caracal are found in Africa and one in Asia.

They have been domesticated: the Ancient Egyptians kept them as pets and in Ancient Persia and India they were used for coursing and for hunting, in a similar manner to the cheetah. They are still kept as pets today (as many internet videos and photos testify to) and appear to make perfectly good, affectionate companions.

A caracal appearing in **dreams or visions** can be about secrecy and solitariness, as this nocturnal animal keeps itself to itself and avoids attention at all times.

As a **totem animal**, it brings a desire for secrecy, privacy and solitude, with a delight in one's lifestyle for these very reasons. You won't find caracal people posting on social media every detail of their lives, from what they had for breakfast to what time they are going to bed. They love to play alone, enjoying doing things their way without anyone else to overlook or judge them.

Caribou
(*Rangifer spp*)
Element: earth.
Deities: Beaivi, Elen of the Ways, Meandash, also winter deities like the Cailleach, Frau Holle, Skadi, Ullr, Vili.

As the bison was to the First Nations of North America, so too is the caribou or reindeer to a number of peoples of the northern hemisphere: a resource so important it became sacred. Six species are known across the land masses all around the North Pole, including Russia, Northern Europe and the regions in and around Canada. The Sami, the Ostyaks, the Chukchi and the Inuits, among others, have historically followed the herds as they migrated, using the animals for meat, skins and for transport, their destinies woven tightly together. Shamans of these deeply spiritual peoples interacted with the reindeer and with other wild creatures on shamanic journeyings, seeing the deer as helpers and protectors.

Today, reindeer remain an important part of the economy in Russia and Scandinavia, being farmed like cattle for their meat, milk and skins.

These iconic animals are the only species of deer in which females generally grow antlers, and in most Western minds they are inextricably bound up with Santa Claus and Christmas. As with most deer species, the antlers are grown every year, and the males shed them in early winter. The females, however, keep their antlers until they have calved, giving rise to the popular speculation that Santa's reindeer must all be female, including Rudolf!

Perfectly adapted for both swampy and snowy conditions, these large deer have wide, spreading hooves with sharp edges that act like snow-chains, preventing them from slipping on the ice.

In **dreams and visions**, the reindeer may speak of natural resources and natural cycles, of the importance of keeping to traditional ways and preserving traditional knowledge in the face of "progress". It can also indicate travel, including turning to a migratory lifestyle. Of course, to many Westerners it can also indicate matters around winter and Christmas, and all the traditions associated with these.

As a **totem animal**, the reindeer is rich in strength and endurance, in the ability to adapt to any situation and survive all hardships, whether by sticking it out or by knowing when to move on to a better place.

Carp

(*Cyprinidae spp*)
Element: water.
Deities: Ebisu, HatMehit.
This deep-bodied freshwater fish comes in all sizes, from 100kg monsters to the goldfish in the bowl in your home. Important to coarse anglers, it has also been a staple protein for people down the ages and forms the basis of soups and stews across the world. At one time, no mediaeval estate or monastery would be without its carp pond, though it is less popular now in the West as better-flavoured sea fish have become more available (like many freshwater fish, the carp can have a bland, rather muddy flavour and it is very bony).

Carp are also bred for their ornamental value in garden ponds and in lakes and large ponds on estates and in parks. The larger breeds of ornamental carp, known as Koi, which come in a range of colours and sizes, can be very valuable. The common goldfish is also popular in indoor aquaria and in garden ponds and also ranges in colour from the typical bright orange to black, silver/white, grey, yellow and brown.

Nearly all fish are about emotions when they crop up in **dreams and visions**. In Japan, they symbolise heroic feelings, courage, endurance and confidence. While, in the West, they are more likely to indicate prosperity, a windfall, or good health or some other change for the good – even the humble goldfish is likely to have this meaning, its bright gold scales symbolising riches.

Having a carp as a **totem animal** brings good fortune, good health, longevity and prosperity.

Cassowary

(*Struthio casuarius*)
Element: earth.
Deities: none identified.
This primitive-looking bird with its heavy, flightless body and colourful head is the second largest bird on Earth today, going by weight. It is the third tallest, after the ostrich and the emu. It has also been described as "the world's most dangerous bird" – it is capable of severely injuring and even killing a human being, using not its large blunt beak, but the largest of its three toes, which is armed with a long, sharp claw. Yet it has been and continues to be kept as a domestic fowl and even as a pet. Probably its most prominent feature is the huge horny crest on its head, which really causes it to look like a dinosaur. Scientists still do not really know the purpose of this crest, though it may protect the bird from branches while it is running through the forest.

The cassowary loves rainforest habitats, although it is also found on grasslands and other areas in the New Guinea region. There are three species: the southern, the northern and the dwarf. These birds live chiefly on fruit, but will eat insects and worms, small lizards, mammals and birds if they get the chance, and also any carrion they happen to find.

In **dreams and visions**, this bird warns of danger, especially if you dream of being attacked by one. Is there someone scary in your life, from whom you can expect trouble? Prepare yourself, it may get nasty!

As a **totem animal**, the cassowary brings huge strength, power and confidence, but combined with a love of solitude it makes cassowary people very self-reliant, and they may be seen by others as aloof and unfriendly, as well as stubborn and prideful.

Cat

(*Felis catus domesticus*)
Element: fire.
Deities: Artemis/Diana, Bast, Freyja, Hecate, Sekhmet.
It is difficult to know where to begin writing about this animal, which is so hugely important in folklore, in magic, in story and simply as one of

mankind's favourite animals on the planet. Cats have been part of the human household for thousands of years and have been loved as pets, employed as destroyers of vermin, bred for showing, worshipped as gods and tortured and killed as the demonic servants of witches. Modern cats are descended from the wild cats who approached human settlements around nine and a half thousand years ago, drawn by the rats and mice which fed on the stored grain of very early farmers. These people very quickly discovered that it paid to have cats around the barns, and then fell under the spell of these beautiful, graceful, intelligent creatures and allowed them into the house as working pets.

Around 60 varieties of domestic cat are known today, ranging from the common "moggy" (the British shorthair), which comes in a range of colours to the enormous Maine coon, which has been mistaken for a lion at a distance – and more exotic breeds like the curly-haired and naked cats, including the sphynx, and the dwarf cat.

Today, you can hardly boot up the internet without seeing a picture or a video of cats, and this obsession was shared by our pre-tech forebears. While the Ancient Egyptians went the whole hog and worshipped cats as gods (passers-by would set upon and kill anyone who caused the death of a cat, even accidentally), many other cultures ascribed all sorts of powers to this animal. In Japan, it was seen as a supernatural creature, and the Maneki-Neko (possibly the forerunner of Hello Kitty) is found everywhere in the country. Its origin was the story of a magical cat which saved a man from a lightning strike by raising its paw. The cat yokai Bakeneko is another figure in Japanese folklore: the yokai are supernatural beings which roughly align to the Fae in British lore.

In England, the cat is said to have nine lives and to always land on its feet, and there is a whole raft of superstitions surrounding black cats, often contradictory: it is lucky to meet one, it is unlucky if one crosses your path, it is lucky if it crosses from left to right, black cats protect sailors at sea, black cats are the evil companions of witches. ... This last is such a common belief that cat rescue organisations report that it is actually harder to rehome black cats!

Cats appear often in **dreams and visions**, but explaining their meaning can be problematic. Right at the root of this problem is the attitude of the dreamer towards cats: sure, most people love them, but many people hate them or are afraid of them (ailurophobia) to the point where they will not enter a room where they know a cat to be. The next problem is the huge body of myth, folklore, belief and story touched on above: any story you have read that has impressed itself on your memory will likewise affect how you see a cat when it shows up in a divinatory message. From the Cheshire Cat to Jim Davis's Garfield, they will have influenced you. As a very brief guideline, cats speak of sensuality, relaxation, intuition and magic (especially black cats), and also of home and family, but the context of the dream is what should guide you. Dreaming of kittens could mean you have a subconscious desire for children, or it could mean you have someone vulnerable you need to protect.

As a **totem animal**, cats bring a range of positive things: confidence, an untroubled belief in your own rightness and superiority, energy, intelligence, alertness and curiosity. Cat people will be night people, who are on their toes just as others are settling down in front of the telly before turning in, and they love to go off and enjoy themselves on their own, finding their own pleasures and answerable to no one, comfortable in their own skins.

Caterpillar: see Butterfly and Moth.

Catfish
(*Silurus glanis*)
Element: water.
Deities: HatMehit and a series of unnamed catfish-headed Gods in Ancient Egypt, Namazu and Takemikazuchi.
This very successful fish is found on every continent on Earth except Antarctica, even in Britain, where the Wels catfish was introduced in the nineteenth century by fishing enthusiasts. It can achieve enormous size, even in the UK, where a 66.7kg (10 stone) specimen was caught in Essex in 2021. The Mekong giant catfish has been recorded at 293kg (the weight of at least three big men at 46 stone!), making it the largest of all freshwater fish.

Named for its catlike "whiskers", which are sensory filaments similar to a cat's and help the animal navigate its habitat, the catfish includes about three dozen families, but this number is on the increase as taxonomic changes are made by scientists, and fish not previously classified as catfish are reclassified.

In **dreams and visions**, catching a very big fish, and also eating it, means sudden prosperity, a windfall, or the perception of yourself as suddenly gaining in importance (we speak of "a big fish in a little pool"), but the catfish itself may indicate a person who is deceiving you, who is not who they pretend to be.

Catfish **totem animal** people are deep and mysterious, the sort of people you might look at and think, "what's going on in there?" They don't see any reason to share their inmost thoughts with others, but go their own way, cool and unflurried and self-sufficient.

Cattle
(*Bos taurus*)
Element: earth.
Deities: (Cows) Hathor and Isis, Indra, Krishna. (Bulls) Agni, Apis, Dionysus, Hadad, Osiris, Poseidon, Ra, Serapis, Shiva.
Man's relationship with cows goes back into the distant past, when they were a hunted animal, as cave wall art testifies. Eventually, the cow was domesticated and is now an integral part of the food industry, providing meat and dairy products, gelatine and also leather for clothing and other uses. Ancient cattle looked a lot different to our modern hornless, sanitised

milk-machines; for one thing they sported huge sharp horns, which have been bred out of many types of cattle today for convenience and safety. Most people are probably more familiar with the modern breeds developed specifically for meat or for dairy. The black-and-white Holsteins, for example, have been selectively bred to produce the highest milk yields of any cows: 22 litres a day per animal is the average, while the "black stirk" (the Aberdeen Angus) has been bred to produce the finest beef. Hides and leather are by-products of cattle farming and are used in a variety of goods, and even their dung is a resource in Third World countries, where it is burned as a fuel and can be used as a building material. In India, the cow is seen as sacred by Hindus and its meat is not eaten, nor is the animal harmed or even incommoded as it goes about its business on the busiest street. This relationship with cattle has led to milk and ghee (clarified butter) becoming very important in Indian cuisine. The expression "sacred cow" has come to mean a tradition that cannot be broken or even questioned.

Wild cattle are known, and all are so closely related to bison that they can interbreed, producing offspring known as "beefaloes". The zebu (humped cattle) and the yak are also in this family, and all are ruminants; that is, they chew the cud and digest plant material in stages through four stomachs.

This is one animal which throws up different answers according to the gender seen. A gentle, lowing, milk-giving cow has very different meanings from a violent, rampaging bull! Throughout time, bulls have been seen as the ultimate symbol of masculine fertility and aggression, more frightening because they are unpredictable – a bull can be docile one day and aggressive the next. Cows, however, have always been a symbol of feminine docility, maternal devotion and gentleness. The zodiac sign Taurus the Bull is ruled by Venus, and speaks of physical beauty and love (perhaps it is really a cow).

Dreams and visions featuring bulls are about power and competitiveness, about using force and willpower to achieve goals, regardless of whether they are right for you or the correct thing to do.

As a **totem animal**, bulls deliver this feeling of being in the right, and having the right to shout others down, even bully them, which has to be guarded against.

Cows in **dreams and visions**, on the other hand, speak of family and love and gentleness, of nurturing children and providing for them. Dreams of cattle generally also speak of fertility and riches, of prosperity coming your way. The Norse rune Fehu (riches and fertility) says it all about cows: they have long been a symbol of wealth and comfort.

As a **totem animal**, the cow brings solid loving patience and a desire to nurture one's family and provide for them, and to build relationships based on respect and gentleness.

Dreaming of an ox, which is usually a castrated bull used for pulling vehicles or a plough, speaks of strength and patience, of waiting for the right moment and, as a **totem animal**, it gives these qualities.

Centipede

(*Myriapoda chilopoda*)
Element: earth.
Deities: Sepa-Osiris.

The name of this prince of creepy-crawlies means "hundred-footed", but even if you could count them on this wriggly creature, you would find it has any number between 30 and 300, and always an odd number of pairs, too – so 100 is not accurate. Just in case it needed to be any creepier, all species of the centipede have a poisonous bite. While in the UK centipedes are relatively small at around 3cms, they can be much larger in warmer climates, up to a 30cms (one foot long) monster found in South America, which is large enough to eat lizards and small mammals (ugh!).

In **dreams and visions**, it is easy to dismiss the centipede as a nightmare, but it does have a range of meanings, and mostly ones of good fortune. The creature represents an obstacle in your path, one that is down to your own fears and imaginings, and is actually really easy to get around. So, welcome this sign if you have something that has been troubling you about your career, your personal or your spiritual life. But the animal can also speak of your problems with managing your money, cautioning you to be careful instead of spending freely.

The centipede is actually very lucky, although people with this **totem animal** can be filled with self-doubts, particularly about their attractiveness.

Chameleon

(*Chameleonidae spp*)
Element: fire.
Deities: Agemo, Iris.

Everyone knows what the chameleon can do! Although other reptiles and amphibians, including the common frog, and many sea creatures can do this trick to some extent, the chameleon is probably the best colour-change artist. Pop him on a green branch, he turns green; let him climb on your navy coat, he will turn navy: all round camouflage in the blink of an eye. And speaking of eyes, he also has a pretty extraordinary pair of those as well: eyes that not only have a strange, diaphragm-shaped eyelid but can swivel independently, allowing him to take in a 360-degree view of the world around him. His other distinctive features are specialised feet that can grip branches like a spring clip and a very long tongue with a sticky end which he can shoot out at speed – bringing a sticky end to any tasty insect! Most chameleons also have decorative or protective features as well, which increases their resemblance to some dinosaurs: facial and cranial horns, spines and crests.

Actually, the reptile's ability to change colour (which is not shared by all the 202 species of chameleons) is only partly about camouflage, and its main function seems to be communication and as a reaction to environment. A chameleon will change colour if it is frightened or cold, and it will use its colour to attract a mate.

A chameleon appearing in **dreams and visions** is telling you of the need to fit in, to adapt yourself to the people around you rather than sticking out like a sore thumb, that you can do this and it will lead to a more comfortable life for you. Or it could be telling you of someone in your life who is not appearing *in their true colours*, who is effectively lying to you and others about who they really are.

People with a chameleon **totem animal** are ultra-adaptable and make life easy for themselves wherever they go by fitting in with others. Ever met someone who just walks into a room and in minutes is chatting with everyone, completely at home? They can do this, or they can stand out as very different as well – they are in very good control of their lives and emotions.

Chamois

(*Rupicapra rupicapra*)
Element: air.
Deities: Artemis/Diana, Dali.
This small member of the antelope-goat family is renowned for springing about on mountain tops and inaccessible hillsides, quite happy in places where other creatures would probably fall to their deaths. It lives in the mountainous areas of Europe and Turkey, the Pyrenees and the Caucasus. There are also introduced populations in New Zealand.

Although the wild chamois does not look much like the logo on the Babycham bottle, it is a graceful and sturdy creature with a coat that ranges from blond through to dark brown, and the characteristic prong-like horns. The chamois is hunted for its meat, but probably better known to most people for chamois leather, often called shammy leather, an ideal material for polishing windows and car paintwork.

In **dreams and visions**, a chamois speaks of freedom and joy, of effortless ability, of being at the top of your game without trying and the ease and pleasure that brings. Soar and be free to be yourself.

As a **totem animal**, it gives strength, courage, effortless ability and grace in the face of all challenges. Chamois people may be shy, but they do not walk away from any challenge.

Cheetah

(*Acinonyx jubatus*)
Element: air.
Deity: Mafdet.
This beautiful long-legged cat is famed for being the fastest land creature on Earth: in short bursts, it can run as fast as your car, thanks to its super-lean body, long legs, well evolved heart and lungs and flexible spine. Large dog-sized, it has some characteristics in common with dogs, including non-retractile claws (unlike almost all other cats, which can retract theirs), a longer snout, a greyhound-like body shape and tough paw pads. It hunts by day, relying on eyesight rather than scent.

Baby cheetahs look a little different from their parents, as they have long greyish manes or capes growing along their backs which can make them look more like a honey badger than a cheetah. It is thought this is a disguise or camouflage to keep them safe from predators.

The cheetah is seldom aggressive towards humans, and in fact has been domesticated since ancient times and used like a hunting dog, its speed making it very useful to bring down swift prey like antelopes. Unfortunately, the custom of keeping cheetahs has continued into the present century, with wealthy people acquiring them as status symbols. They are delicate creatures and very prone to health conditions which make them unsuitable as pets.

Dreaming or having a **vision** of a cheetah is about speed, and is calling your attention to some aspect of your life in respect of this: are you rushing things in a relationship? Are you running away from something that perhaps you should be running towards? Are you going too fast or too slow in some aspect of your life?

Lucky is the person who has the cheetah as a **totem animal**; they have energy, alertness, a quick mind and a strong, healthy body. Cheetah people can stand up for themselves without being aggressive, and know how to extricate themselves from trouble.

Chicken

(*Gallus gallus domesticus*)
Element: earth.

Deities: Alectryon, Anu, Demian, Eostre, Kuzma.

These birds are kept all over the world for their meat and eggs, and owing to the hen's obliging habit of laying infertile eggs when no cockerel is present, even vegetarians can enjoy the eggs without feeling guilty, though the chicken industry does destroy surplus male hatchlings. The hen lays almost every day, and modern birds have been bred to lay all year round to supply the enormous demand for eggs. The chicken outnumbers all other birds on the planet because of its popularity as a farmed creature, and sad abuses occur because of the demand for its meat for fast food, although many supermarkets have now agreed to stock only free range or deep litter eggs. They are easy to keep, as long as foxes can be kept out of the runs, and will eat almost anything. In the past, it was common for rural households to keep a "chicken bucket" for scraps, which would be collected gratefully by the local chicken farmer. A cockerel or rooster – known for its crowing from early dawn – is the name for the male bird, while the female is a hen and an immature female chicken is a pullet. A capon is a neutered cockerel. Centuries of breeding have produced chickens in every colour and size, with the Jersey giant being the largest breed and bantams and silkies being the smallest.

The importance of these birds to the human race is reflected in their appearance in folktales and fables going back to the earliest times, and including substantial works of literature like the *Canterbury Tales* and Shakespeare. They have also had an influence on the English language, with all kinds of chicken-based expressions common even today: something to crow about, an old boiler, she's no spring chicken, counting your chickens before they've hatched, broody, hen party, mother hen, etc.

Sadly, their importance to us has also been marked by abuses: battery farming, cock fighting and the killing of male chicks are just a few. They have also been a favoured choice for animal sacrifice, and continue to be so today in the Voodoo streams.

Seeing a single chicken in **dreams and visions** might be a message that you are being cowardly ("chicken"), although the appearance of many chicks or chickens may be indicating a piece of good luck and monetary gain, though they also speak of frivolous social gatherings and gossip.

A cockerel may indicate male pride and the need for conflict, and this meaning goes on into the **totem animal**, which brings a confident and fearless nature, also a rather pugnacious one. The chicken also gives great adaptability and a love of home and family.

Chickadee: see **Tit.**

Chimpanzee
(*Pan troglodytes*)
Element: air.
Deity: Pan.
Commonly known as chimps, these intelligent apes are so human that they have even appeared in a TV advertisement for tea, drinking the beverage genteelly at the table, and the chimp generally has a long and respectable career in Hollywood, often completely upstaging its human co-stars. They are closely related to Bonobos but, despite their resemblance, they have a darker side to their natures. Simply put, chimps go in for aggression, murder and cannibalism. Bonobos also eat meat, but chimps will gang up on a female of their own group and take her baby to eat. There have even been cases recorded of chimps attacking and killing humans.

In **dreams and visions**, chimps speak of family, particularly extended family, tribe, social groups, workplace acquaintances and friends, your community and the relationships you have with individuals in these settings, whether good or bad. They can also be about ego, usually that of the dreamer but sometimes that of another person within their circle, perhaps someone out to make trouble.

As a **totem animal**, they bring a very sociable nature, and the need to fit in within one's community and to stand out in some way, to have respect and even power.

Chinchilla
(*Chinchilla chinchilla* and *C. lanigera*)
Element: water.
Deities: none identified.

And you thought bunnies were cute! The chinchilla looks like a rabbit, but clothed in soft grey velvet and with lustrous dark eyes and a habit of clasping its forepaws before it as though in supplication. Aww! The two species (*C. chinchilla* is short-tailed and *C. lanigera* long-tailed) have the densest fur of any creature on Earth after the sea otter, which has sadly led to their being hunted and killed for their pelts, and *C. lanigera* is now on the verge of extinction in the wild (western South America). They are very popular as caged pets and sadly have been used as laboratory animals.

In **dreams and visions**, seeing this cuddly gregarious animal means you are thinking of your social life, your friends and acquaintances, in a friendly and loving way, perhaps seeking to help others and improve life for those around you.

As a **totem animal**, it gives sensitivity to the needs of others and a friendly, warm personality, making for a person who cares and worries about their friends and family, and often puts them first.

Chipmunk
(*Tamias* and *Eutamias spp*)
Element: air.
Deities: Medb, Odin and Ratatosk.
This little creature is a cartoonist's dream, with its big eyes, cheeky personality and squirrel-like cuteness, and animated screen chipmunks have been traditionally given helium trebles by speeding up the soundtracks of the actors supplying their voices. Most chipmunk species inhabit North America, but the Siberian chipmunk is found in Asia. All of them have the familiar reddish coats and bright lateral stripes, with a smaller version of a squirrel's tail and an upright sitting posture, like that of the squirrel, which is a close cousin, adopted to eat or watch the world. These little creatures exist on a diet of nuts, seeds and fruit, supplemented by green stuff and occasionally insects, eggs or worms.

Seen in **dreams and visions**, chipmunks are about friendliness, sociability, charm and curiosity, but can also be about housekeeping: about saving and making plans, putting aside something for a rainy day. Is your dream drawing attention to your need to save and plan? To fill the freezer ahead of Christmas or set aside cash for future plans?

People with a chipmunk as their **totem animal** have lots of energy, a sense of humour and a gentle, playful character, but may also be timid and retiring.

Cicada
(*Cicadoidea spp*)
Element: air.
Deities: Apollo, Dionysus, the Muses (especially those associated with music and recitation), Tithonus.
You probably wouldn't know this insect if it came and sat on your hand, but you would recognise its iconic song from a million movies set in warmer

climates: the hero leans moodily on a gatepost, smoking a cigarette and staring up at the heroine's window, and around him the night is alive with the atmospheric chirping song of these often very colourful insects. In Britain, their only relatives are the froghoppers, the little bugs that create *cuckoo-spit*, a white frothy substance often found on green plants, in which the larval stage is protected from predators. Cicada larvae live underground, for up to nine years, one of the longest larval stages of all, but emerge as adults which then typically live less than a couple of months. The song is produced by the males only in most species and is made by a sound organ below the abdomen. The females have this organ as well, but for them it functions just as an ear, so they can hear the males' mating calls. Some cicadas also stridulate, like grasshoppers.

In **dreams and visions**, the cicada has something in common with the butterfly, in that it speaks of transformations after long periods of work or preparation – but it is particularly associated with finances, career, resources, where the butterfly might speak primarily of your spiritual life. Hearing the cicada's song in your dreams may also speak of a desire for change or a feeling that you are unsatisfied creatively or artistically.

People with the cicada as a **totem animal** are creative and articulate, and not afraid to express their opinions. This is the person who, in a room of muttering, discontented people, is the one voice that pipes up and speaks for all, resolving the problem where others have been afraid to speak.

Civet

(This name is used chiefly to refer to the species *Civetticus*, *Viverra* and Viverricula, but other species are also referred to as civet.)

Element: air.

Deity: Hecate.

Although several different species of small carnivores go by the name civet, what they have in common is their musk – a scented secretion produced in the perineal glands of both males and females – which is used to mark territory and attract mates. Unfortunately, as with any animal product seen as desirable, this has resulted in civets being caught and stressed by handling and squeezing (though not usually killed) in order to harvest the secretion, or being kept confined in cages. Asian palm civets are further abused through their relationship with one type of coffee bean, which is prized for its flavour when it has passed through a civet's digestive tract. This has led to the animals being kept for their scent but fed only on coffee cherries, leading to malnutrition. In the wild, civets are omnivorous, favouring meat and insects but also eating fruit and seeds.

These attractive little creatures are sometimes called civet cats; they are in fact more closely related to mongooses and hyenas as their lengthened snouts testify.

In **dreams and visions**, the civet, because of its association with the perfume industry, can speak of profits gained through running a business, but also of sexual magnetism.

As a **totem animal**, it brings the love of solitude and a preference for your own space, but also the ability to influence others when you do emerge to interact with them, giving confidence but also the wisdom of knowing when to retreat.

Clouded Leopard
(*Neofelis nebulosa*)
Elements: air and water.
Deities: Bast and HatHor, Mafdet
This incredibly beautiful Asian wild cat (not a leopard) has coat markings reminiscent of decorative mosaic work in shades of brown, grey and cream, and very long canine teeth that have caused it to be called a "modern day sabretooth." Loving the seclusion of dark rainforests, it leads a solitary life, feeding on small to medium animals and birds which it carries up into the branches of a tree to eat.

In **dreams and visions**, this creature speaks of shy beauty, perhaps calling to mind an attractive friend who is always afraid to make the first move and maybe needs help getting out there to socialise or find romance – or it could be you who has this problem. Secrecy and shyness are key words with this animal, so its appearance may mean you have secrets to keep, perhaps for a very long time – or secrets are being kept from you. Secrecy is also a watchword of the clouded leopard as a **totem animal**, bringing a love of solitude and a close-mouthed nature to anyone with this totem or power animal.

Clownfish
(*Amphiprion ocellaris*)
Element: water.
Deities: all sea deities.
This is the *Finding Nemo* fish, which would probably never have intruded on anyone's dreams before the 2003 Disney animation, but is now much more in the human imagination. The little reef fish, with its striking stripes of white, blue-black and goldfish-gold (although black-and-white forms are also common) is also called an anemone fish because of its symbiotic relationship with sea-anemones. It nestles among the anemone's stinging tentacles with impunity, safe from predators and feeding on microorganisms, while eating any parasites or other creatures that could harm the anemone, and its faeces drift down to feed its host. This fish is a species in which dad takes over the job of bringing up the young, guarding the eggs and fanning water over them for several days until they hatch.

In **dreams and visions**, fish are usually about emotions, and this beautiful and colourful fish could be about sexual attraction or fears for your relationship. Look at the details of the dream for clarification: does the fish seem happy, does it seem distressed?

As a **totem animal**, the clownfish gives great adaptability: it can move from seawater to fresh water without ill effects and has a childlike innocence and playfulness as well. It gives social ease and an ability to naturally slot into any group or community, even with difficult or aggressive people.

Coati (also known as coatimundi.)
(*Nasua* and *Nasuella spp*)
Element: earth.
Deities: Hanapu and Xbalanque.
Four species of this relative of the raccoon live in the Americas in a variety of habitats (unfortunately becoming quite endangered in some areas), and England. Did I say England? Yes: a number of coatis have apparently colonised wooded regions in Cumbria, having escaped from captivity – and their numbers are increasing.

All species of coati have the characteristic very elongated doglike snout, and many have striped tails like the ring-tailed lemur. Unlike their cousins, the raccoons, coati are active in the daytime, eating a varied diet of small mammals, birds, insects and worms, eggs and vegetable matter.

In **dreams and visions**, this animal warns of the danger of getting involved with the trivial, instead of working towards your goal. Put down your phone and stop playing games and get to work, or you will miss out on your goal!

As a **totem animal**, the coati gives an almost magical ability to find what you are looking for in unlikely places, through serendipity and luck. Curious, intelligent and friendly; coati people are capable of achieving much – if they don't get sidetracked.

Cobra
(*Naja naja* and other *Elapidae spp*)
Element: earth.
Deities: Buto/Wadjet, Mehen, Nehebkau, Shiva, Vishnu.
This most distinctive of snakes conjures up a number of images for Westerners, not least the hooded snake rising from a wicker basket as a snake-charmer performs his act. The name cobra is given to a number of species of the *Elapidae* family, especially the *Naja* species (or true cobras) which includes *N. Naja* – the Indian cobra which features in so many Kipling stories. Not all snakes referred to as cobras have a hood, but all are poisonous. Some, like the coral snakes, have vivid markings to warn off would-be predators, and some rear up in a threatening manner (spreading their hood if they have one) to frighten away enemies. One hooded snake, the false water cobra (*Hydrodynastes gigas*) of South America, is not related at all, though it does resemble real cobras.

The largest species (and the longest venomous snake on Earth) is the enormous King Cobra or hamadryad (*Ophiophagus hannah*), which can achieve a length of almost six metres.

Cobras are important in Indian culture, and many temples care for these snakes, allowing them to live under the building and putting out milk for them to drink (although there is some suggestion that this harms them, as their digestive systems are not adapted to digest milk). These snakes are also worshipped during Hindu festivals. The Indian cobra's striking "spectacles" mark on its hood is said to have been placed there by Lord Shiva, who is sometimes depicted with a cobra around His neck. The Ancient Egyptians saw them as sacred also, and the pharaoh wore the head of a cobra on his crown, next to that of a vulture: these creatures symbolised the Goddesses of Lower and Upper Egypt.

Snakes are creatures of earth, fertility and healing, and they are also connected to sex in our subconscious, so a cobra in **dreams and visions** may be about your sexual partner or the person with whom you desperately want to have a physical relationship. Always look at what the animal is doing in your dream: if it is threatening to bite you, this could mean you know the relationship is a mistake that will bring you grief. If it is not attacking, but merely scaring you, it may speak of the need for healing, of a poisonous situation in your life that needs to be sorted out.

As a **totem animal**, the cobra brings deep knowledge and understanding, with the ability to react quickly and always to defend yourself: remember that Canadian Black Watch heraldic symbol of the snake biting the foot that is crushing it and the motto *"Nemo me impune lacessit"* (no one harms me and gets away with it).

Cockatiel: see **Parrot.**

Cockatoo: see **Parrot.**

Cockroach
(*Blattodea spp*)
Element: earth.
Deity: Tithonus.
There are thousands of species of cockroaches in the world but only a few species cause a nuisance by invading human homes and eating establishments and spreading germs and disgust. However, these roaches are the ones that have come to human attention, and are the ones that may crop up in dreams.

Roaches have a typical shape, like a beetle (though they are not beetles, but more closely related to termites and praying mantises) with very long antennae. Although they have wings, most species are not capable of flight. They are not usually very large (except in *Men in Black* movies), although two giant cockroach species in Australia and South America can reach a length of eight centimetres and weigh up to 35g. With a few exceptions, they are brownish in colour and their adaptability to all temperatures means they can live in the Arctic, as well as in the tropical regions they prefer.

Cockroaches are gregarious and follow one another to food sources, almost like bees and ants. They are also quite noisy: some make grunts and chirps and even hiss. Humans have a love-hate relationship with them: while in most Western countries they are seen as disgusting, unhygienic pests, they are eaten in some Eastern countries, used in laboratories, bred for Oriental medicines and even kept as pets. One cockroach was even sent into space!

In what world could **dreams and visions** of cockroaches be positive? You would shudder yourself awake – and indeed this creature indicates misfortune and disappointment, the need to go into hiding, even.

On the other hand, as a **totem animal**, it indicates great positivity. The cockroach brings the ability to get through any ordeal, to live very frugally, to survive anything. There is an urban myth that these animals could even survive a nuclear holocaust; whether this is true or not, they could certainly survive almost anything else!

Coelacanth
(*Latimeria chalumnae* and *menadoensis*)
Element: water.
Deities: none identified.
This famous fish is known as a living fossil: believed extinct for millennia, it was rediscovered in 1938 by a museum curator who was told of a strange fish caught by fishermen in East Africa. This large (up to two metres in length), colourful fish was supposed to have died out in the Cretaceous period. It has a broad body which does not taper as it becomes the tail, and sturdy, leg-like fins which show its relationship to lungfish. It escaped discovery for so long because it is a deep-sea fish, feeding on bottom-dwelling fish and squid. Unusually in fish, it bears live young. It is almost inedible due to the chemical composition of its flesh.

In **dreams and visions**, this animal speaks of things returning from the past to haunt you, of finding things you thought were lost forever. One source felt it could mean a divorce: probably this could be the case if your own misbehaviour, or that of your partner, caught up with you!

As a **totem or power animal**, the fish gives great calmness and a slow deliberate way of proceeding. Nothing fazes this animal as it drifts at great depth on its own affairs – it never hurries, nor feels anxiety.

Condor: see Vulture.

Coot
(*Rallidae fulica*)
Element: water.
Deities: Anthus, all water deities and bird deities.
The coot, and its close cousin, the moorhen, are so similar in appearance, habit and meaning that I have lumped them together in one section: a lot of people would struggle to tell the difference between them. The coot has a white beak and a whitish knob on its forehead above the beak: this may explain the expression "bald as a coot." The moorhen (*Gallinula chloropus*) has a bright red beak and red forehead; otherwise these two black, medium-sized water birds of the rail family look very much the same.

The moorhen is found across Europe and Asia, while the coot species are found across the Americas as well, and can look quite different from the common coots found in the UK. A moorhen called the common gallinule is also found in the US. Both live on a wide range of water plants, algae and small animals and they will also take eggs.

In **dreams and visions**, these water birds share some of the humour of the duck, but also speak of lucky finds and new good fortune.

As a **totem animal**, either of them brings a happy-go-lucky outlook, a sense of fun and adventure, and a readiness to explore and take chances.

Coral

(*Anthozoa*)
Elements: water and fire.
Deities: Aphrodite/Venus, Hina/Sina, Hermes, Thalassa.

Although the beautiful branching coral structures look like plants, they are merely homes for the colonies of coral polyps, the tiny animals that build them – though many do obtain nutrition by playing host to organisms that use photosynthesis to produce food. Most familiar are the stony corals, those that build the intricate structures, branches, leaves and whorls of the coral you see on a scuba dive, but there are also soft corals, which do not produce these structures. Stony corals have changed the topography of the ocean, creating coral reefs, such as the Great Barrier Reef, which provide a habitat for many other species, but many corals are now at real risk due to global warming.

Coral jewellery is made from the stony structures created by the polyps, and not from the animal itself, but does involve the destruction of the coral, which is also plundered for aquaria and even mined for building materials.

Corals are often armed with stings, which they use both to capture prey and defend themselves from enemies. They reproduce both sexually and asexually, through division.

Seeing coral in **dreams and visions** is about beauty and sanctuary, perhaps something you have been longing for, a wonderful holiday when you are stressed and exhausted, a quiet, beautiful place to go and recuperate. Coral is deeply bound up with isolated, exotic faraway places in our minds – coral islands with white sand and blue skies.

As a **totem animal**, the coral brings self-reliance and imperviousness; it stands up to anything except stress, its stony secretions guarding its body from harm.

Cougar

(*Puma concolor*)
Element: fire.
Deities: Toho Kachina, Viracocha.

Also known in different regions as the mountain lion, puma and sometimes panther, this large cat is native to the Americas, from southernmost Chile all the way up to Canada – a huge range of habitats. Although it is the fourth largest feline on Earth (after the tiger, the lion and the jaguar) and can weigh 100kg, it is more closely related to smaller cats like the cheetah. It has a small, round head, a lithe, muscular body and long tail, and its colour is an overall light golden-brown, with black tear-marks on either side of its nose. A powerful predator, its diet includes large animals such as deer and cattle, though it will also take smaller creatures such as birds and rabbits. Although solitary and shy, it is by no means timid and has been known to attack and even kill humans.

In **dreams and visions**, the cougar speaks of physical power and fitness, perhaps telling you that you need to improve yours in order to improve your life in some way. Perhaps you are a bit flabby and the opposite sex is not impressed; perhaps your weight is taking its toll on your health, or is even impinging on your career in some way. The dream may also speak of another type of cougar, viz the relatively new term for a sexually predatory older woman: remember these slang terms soon take hold in our subconscious mind, bringing their own meanings.

As a **totem animal**, the cougar brings great power and influence over others. This is an animal that most people are afraid of meeting, an animal that does not hesitate to attack and has weight and strength behind it. It does not flinch from any situation; it is the animal's enemies that flinch and give way to it. Yet the totem does not encourage bullying, rather wisdom backed by strength and experience.

Cow: see **Cattle.**

Coyote
(*Canis latrans*)
Element: fire.
Deities: Anubis and Wepwawet, Huehuecóyotl.
From Native American creation myths to the Looney Tunes character, Wyle E Coyote, this creature (sometimes called the prairie wolf) has stirred the imagination. People have a love-hate relationship with them, admiring their intelligence and beauty on the one hand – even keeping them as pets – and cursing them the next for their inroads on livestock and pets. This handsome creature of the wolf and jackal family is found throughout North America and Canada, where it lives on a wide range of animals and birds (including roadrunners!), carrion and plant matter. It is an opportunist feeder and will not only attack livestock but will also come rooting through garbage cans and even bird feeders. It has been known to attack humans, but this usually happens when the animal is cornered or feels threatened or has young to protect.

The coyote appears as a trickster figure in Native American tales and has always been connected with mischief, humour and trickery.

The most common meaning of this creature in **dreams and visions** is trickery and deception. This may be as harmless as someone playing a mischievous prank on you, or teasing you endlessly, but it can also mean downright lying – and one particular meaning can be that you are deceiving yourself, perhaps about your relationship. The rest of the dream will have to be examined for more particulars.

As a **totem animal**, the coyote brings a great sense of fun and an ability to get the most out of life through a humorous and relaxed outlook. Coyote people have sharp, active minds and can always rely on their own cleverness to get them out of trouble and even come out on top, despite everything.

Crab

(*Brachyura* and *Anomura spp*)

Element: water.

Deities: Amphitrite, Hera, Karkinos, Krios, Luna and Selene, Mayan God N-, Neptune/Poseidon, Tihtipihin.

Well-known to anyone who was ever on a beach in childhood with a bucket and an inquiring mind, crabs inhabit every ocean on the globe, as well as some freshwater habitats, and even venture onto land. They are easily recognised by their hard shells, their sharp pincers and their habit of walking sideways. The true crabs, the *Brachyura*, have their own shells, whilst the hermit crabs in the *Anomura* group famously go house-hunting for empty shells left by other shellfish – and have even been seen making themselves at home in manmade objects, such as tin cans.

Crabs are also a part of the human diet in most parts of the world, from the familiar Norfolk crab with its compact shape and shorter legs to the spider crab eaten on the Continent and the gigantic king crab popular in Asia. The cooking of crabs (as with other shellfish) is an upsetting thought for non-meat eaters, as it involves either plunging the animal into boiling water or placing it in cold water which is then brought slowly to the boil. Unfortunately, crabs that are already dead are too toxic to eat, as they decay so quickly.

Seeing crabs in **dreams and visions** speaks of something or someone who bridges different realities, just as the crab happily scuttles about on the sand, though its home is the water. It can be about antisocial habits: are you "crabby" and prefer your own company, and should this be changed? It can speak of the need for protection.

To people with an interest in astrology, the crab will immediately suggest the star sign Cancer, which begins with the entry of the Sun into this constellation at the summer solstice around 21st June.

Cancer is about emotion and the love of the home, and people with a crab as **totem** can be expected to aspire to traits similar to those of Cancer star sign people, who can be true stay-at-homes with no desire for a social life.

Crane

(*Gruidae spp*)

Element: air.

Deities: Annwn, Apollo, Hephaestus/Vulcan, Nugua, Xianhe Tongzi. In Chinese belief, they were said to fly between Earth and Heaven as messengers for the gods.

These large and often colourful birds have made a huge impact on art, mythology and folktales all over the world and have been seen as sacred in many cultures. In Europe and other places, it is common for them to nest on chimney pots, which is seen as bringing good luck. Some cranes have strident calls, some dance and most species have a naked forehead which can change colour and even inflate to communicate with other cranes. Some have impressive crests or crowns of feathers. Like flamingos, they often stand on one leg while at rest and the Ancient Greeks believed that sleeping cranes appointed one of them to stand guard. This watchman would hold a stone in his raised foot, so that he would drop it if he fell asleep, and thus wake himself. The Japanese, who love to paint this bird, see it as a bringer of good luck and long life, and the Native Americans also see it as a very good omen.

Varying in size from the tiny, 30cm-tall demoiselle crane to the sarus crane which, at 150cms, is the tallest flying bird in the world – cranes are found across the globe, with the exception of Antarctica and South America. They can easily be confused with the heron, which is unrelated, but cranes fly with their necks straight, whilst herons tuck their heads back towards their shoulders when they fly.

Cranes are good-omened birds, and seeing one in a **dream or vision** speaks of good luck coming your way. If the crane is white, it may also mean new beginnings or even a birth in the family.

As a **totem animal**, the crane brings good luck and good health, but also happy relationships and the integrity that often helps these to be achieved. Crane people are serene, graceful and agile and are said to enjoy a great deal of success in life.

Cricket

(*Gryllodeia spp*)
Element: air.
Deities: Apollo, Saki Yama Hime, Tithonus.
"No fibbing, now! You know you're not supposed to tell lies. A lie only grows and grows, 'til you get caught! Plain as the nose on your face!" Everyone knows what a cricket looks like because of Walt Disney's famous character (though they tend not to wear waistcoats and top hats). This sweet-voiced insect came close to man as soon as homes became warm and dry, and has been important to many of us ever since. It has cropped up in literature regularly, from *Pinocchio* to Dickens's, *The Cricket on the Hearth*. Crickets are valued for their cheery, comforting sound and encouraged into the home in some countries, or even kept in cages; they are sold in pet shops in Japan. Whilst in most countries it is seen (or heard!) as lucky, in some regions of Brazil it is thought the cricket announces illness or death. The exclamation "Jiminy Cricket!" (which predates Collodi's children's book and the Disney animation) is an old expression commonly used in place of the name of Jesus Christ, which as an exclamation was regarded as blasphemous.

Sadly, like most creatures that live in close contact with humans, they are exploited, being used for cricket fighting and as part of the human diet in

Asia, where they are fried or ground into flour to be added to other foods. In other countries, they are bred as food for pets, such as snakes and spiders.

The song is produced by males hoping to attract the attention of females, by rubbing together textured sections of their wings. Most female crickets do not stridulate.

The information above should be considered when interpreting the appearance of a cricket in **dreams and visions**: your own cultural background may well dictate a different meaning for you, than for someone else from a different culture. If you consider crickets lucky, then that is what the dream indicates. Don't forget that even more modern influences will colour how you see an animal, so in this case the vision may be speaking directly to your conscience!

As a **totem animal**, the cricket brings good luck, sensitivity and an ability to let others know exactly how you are feeling.

Crocodile

(*Crocodylidae spp*)

Elements: water and earth.

Deities: Sobek, Zipacna.

With their sinister half-submerged shapes and toothy smiles, crocodiles have always held our imagination and have featured in many a story, notably in Peter Pan, whose piratical villain Captain Hook has lost his hand to a persistent croc. There are 18 species of true crocodiles, from the huge (up to seven metres long) Australasian saltwater croc, or "saltie", to the Osborn's dwarf – the smallest species at around a metre long. But what they all have in common is the characteristic ridged "dinosaur" back and the ferocious sharp teeth, which are always on display as, unlike alligators, crocs cannot hide them when they close their mouths.

In **dreams and visions,** crocodiles speak of hidden but deadly dangers, and counsel extreme caution when entering a new situation. These animals are stealthy and beguiling: we say "crocodile tears" when speaking of someone who puts on a show of false emotion to further his or her own ends, and they can speak of living surrounded by people who lie and deceive. See **Alligator** for further meanings.

People with the crocodile as a **totem animal** are filled with power, strength and energy, and are top rate at what they do. However, this does not always include being compassionate or supportive to others.

Crow and Raven

(*Corvus spp*)

Element: air.

Deities: Apollo, Babd, Bran the Blessed, Hecate, Macha, the Morrigan, Odin, Shani.

Not a beautiful bird, with its jet-black, often raggedy plumage and its hoarse croaking cry, the crow has yet captured the imagination as a magical and portentous bird. The term "corvid" applies to a huge number of species, but

I am using it here for the European and Asian carrion crow *C. corone* and analogous birds in other regions. People know what a crow is. The term raven is used for larger members of the crow family, with which they are interchangeable in terms of divination and magic. In Europe, we have the common raven *C. corax*, but it is simply a larger species of crow.

This is an ill-omened bird: storm-crow, its name often used as an insult to black-robed clergy or older women. Superstitious fears have clung to it down the millennia. The appearance of crows and ravens to feast on the dead of battlefields throughout history has forever associated them with death and warfare, but they also appear in many stories as wise and benevolent creatures, and attract respect and recognition as sacred birds and servants to the gods. They are holy to a number of deities in many cultures.

Odin has His ravens, Huginn (thought) and Muninn (memory), which fly all over the world and bring Him news. Corvids are among the most intelligent of birds and some can be taught to speak, like parrots.

In **dreams and visions**, these birds may speak of a feeling of being ganged up on (especially if you see them attacking you), and they also speak of death and of illness, though ravens may also speak of healing. Shameful secrets, guilt and inner fears are also some of the meanings of these birds. If you are a pagan, and see them as sacred to a god or goddess, however, they may have quite a different meaning for you – a message from your deity which can be positive as often as negative – and ravens can also be a symbol of kingship. Look at other components of the dream for the message meaning.

As a **totem animal**, the bird brings a strong and sharp mind, wit and knowledge, or the ability to pick up and retain knowledge. Crow people are self-sufficient without being solitary, adaptable and ready to understand any problem and deal with it.

Cuckoo

(*Cuculidae spp*)

Element: air.

Deities: Hera, Kamadeva, Zeus.

Unpleasing to the married ear … the cuckoo has long been associated in British culture with the act of adultery and illegitimacy, probably due to the bird's curious habit of laying its eggs in other birds' nests and obliging them to bring up her offspring as their own. The term "cuckoo" has also become a slang term for mental abnormality or comic stupidity (Laurel and Hardy's iconic theme tune is called *The Dance of the Cuckoos*).

The *Cuculidae* family includes the common cuckoo *Cuculus canorus*, but also many other species across the world, some of which breed in large communal nests – and true to the cuckoo paradigm, hens may be observed turfing out other eggs in order to lay their own. The family also includes the roadrunner.

Hearing the first cuckoo of spring (it is a migratory bird) has superstitions associated with it: turning over the money in your pocket is one, as this will ensure you have plenty of cash in the coming year (not sure how this works with credit cards).

Dreams and visions of a cuckoo are not likely to suggest infidelity to the modern mind (unless you are a keen Shakespearean scholar) but can speak of someone who has wronged you making amends in some way. It can speak of unusual behaviour, eccentric or bordering on insane (cuckoo), or of someone you consider slightly odd.

As a **totem animal**, the bird brings a pleasure-loving and mischievous spirit. These are people who are fun to be with ... in good times – but they would not hesitate to take advantage of another if the need arose.

Cuscus: see Possum.

Cuttlefish
(*Sepiida spp*)
Element: water.
Deities: Kanaloa and all sea deities.
Anyone who has kept budgies will be familiar with the inner skeleton of these amazing and diverse creatures which inhabit temperate and tropical seas all over the world. The delicate, chalky cuttlebone is given to caged birds to sharpen their beaks and ensure they have calcium in their diet. Closely related to squid and octopuses, they share many of the same characteristics, including green, copper-based blood, well-developed eyes, tentacles, ink, sharp beaks and the ability to change their colour. Like its cousins, the cuttlefish is eaten as a delicacy, and its ink was once used for dyeing cloth.

In **dreams and visions**, the cuttlefish speaks of the work environment, and may indicate failure in some area. But it also gives you the message that you are capable of adapting your strategies to reverse the situation, if you look deep within yourself.

As a **totem animal**, it gives the ability to change and adapt, to camouflage oneself into any situation in which you find yourself.

Damselfly: see Dragonfly.

Deathwatch Beetle
(*Xestobium rufovillosum*)
Element: earth.
Deities: Kronos and Saturn.
The resonant name of this greatly feared pest refers to its ticking sound, which can only be heard in an infested building when all is quiet, as would have been the case with people sitting with a dying person or watching over the body at night. The frog-shaped beetle bores into the timbers of old buildings until they are weakened – even to the point of collapse (modern houses are usually safe because they are constructed with softwood beams, which the beetles do not like).

Unlike other beetles, **dreaming** of the deathwatch beetle can be unsettling, for it carries ominous meanings, including ill luck for your home and family, or even a death in the family. Many people believe today that hearing the ticking of the beetle means a death.

As a **totem animal**, it has none of the fortunate gifts of other beetles, but brings a restless spirit and anxiety.

Deer

(*Cervidae spp*)
Element: earth.
Deities: Artemis, Cernunnos, Daal, Diana, Elen of the Ways, Finn, Flidais, Freyr, Herne, Pan, Rohanitsa, Sylvanus.

Embodying grace and beauty, the 43 species of deer evoke a wide range of human emotions, from awe and love to the urge to destroy. Deer have been kept as pets and park creatures, painted onto heraldic devices, hunted for sport, eaten at banquets, their horns and skins used to adorn ancient halls and their images used in animated entertainment for children. To neopagans, they are sacred to the Horned God.

Deer range in size from the moose (the largest deer at two metres high) and the not much smaller elk (*C. canadensis* in North America; however, in Europe the term "elk" is used for the moose) to the tiny dik-dik, and are found across all inhabitable areas of the planet.

In **dreams and visions**, deer represent the better side of human nature: gentleness, nobility, compassion, shyness and modesty, positivity, grace and innocence, combined with vulnerability. But because not all deer are the same, the beast seen in the dream must be considered on its own merits. A huge roaring stag coming at you with antlers aimed for your heart will have quite a different meaning from dreaming of an innocent fawn or its gentle mother. The former vision might cause you to wonder which normally calm and kind person you have upset with your own bad behaviour, while dreaming of an innocent doe and fawn may speak to you of family and close, beloved friends. The word "deer" has nothing to do etymologically with our English term of affection "dear", yet they speak to one another, as well as sounding the same.

As a **totem animal**, the deer brings gentleness, nobility of character, physical grace and great sensitivity: deer can look out for themselves with their finely-tuned senses and attunement to their environment.

Devil's Coach Horse Beetle

(*Ocypus olens*)
Element: earth.
Deities: Hades, Saturn, Tithonus.

This little beast looks like a common black beetle until you bother him; then he rears up his tail end and suddenly looks twice his already impressive 30mm size. If you get close enough, he will also spray you with a nasty-smelling fluid or chomp on you with his massive jaws. Fortunately, he is more likely to be found in the garden than the house. Also known as the devil's coachman and the devil's footman, this beetle earns his fearsome reputation by preying on invertebrates larger than himself. They are found across Europe and North Africa, and have also made it to the Americas and Australia.

Deeply associated with the Devil, the beetle was believed to be able to curse people when it reared up its tail.

In **dreams and visions**, it may bring bad omens, but the body language should be observed, as a rearing, threatening beetle will have a different meaning from one just scurrying away.

As a **totem animal**, it brings great strength and self-sufficiency; it fears no one.

Dhole
(*Cuon alpinus*)
Element: fire.
Deities: Anubis and Apuat, Cerberus, Fenrir, Garm, Kitsune.
Kipling fans may remember "Red Dog" from one of the scarier Mowgli stories in which a seemingly unending pack of this Asian wild dog invades the wolf pack's territory, killing anything that falls in their way. Actually, this handsome fox-like dog hunts in packs usually no larger than a dozen or so and is considerably smaller than even the small Indian wolf. Known for its whistling call, it is now an endangered species, with perhaps as little as 2,500 animals left alive.

In **dreams and visions**, the dhole speaks of a need for freedom but not isolation: do you long for that group holiday with your friends, or feel that you and your colleagues are being repressed and held back by a difficult regime at work?

As a **totem animal**, the dhole brings guidance and independence, as well as courage and motivation. It has many meanings in common with the wolf.

Dik-Dik: see Deer.

Dingo
(*Canis familiaris* or *C. lupus dingo*)
Element: fire.
Deities: Anubis, Bau, Cerberus, Fenrir, Gaiya, Hecate, the Morrigan, Set, Upuat, Xolotl.
This beautiful wild dog is an interloper in its own land, Australia, for it is not a marsupial. It is believed to have been introduced to the continent about 8,000 years ago by humans, but it has certainly earned its green card. Far from impacting badly on indigenous animals, it does its bit towards keeping down recent immigrants which have caused so much damage to the wildlife of the continent, such as rabbits, deer, foxes, feral cats and dogs and even some of the larger man-introduced animals, such as horses, donkeys and camels.

Dingoes are not a threatened species except through interbreeding with feral and domestic dogs, with which they are genetically identical. The proportion of purebred dingoes is now down to less than one-third of the population, and in 2018 the International Union for Conservation of Nature reclassified the dingo as a feral dog and removed it from the Red List. Pockets of purebred dingoes are still found and maintained in some areas.

Since the media frenzy surrounding the disappearance of baby Azaria Chamberlain in 1980, dingoes have become inextricably linked with this tragic case, though it remains unproven conclusively that a dingo took the child. Dingoes are known to attack humans rarely, usually when trying to take food from them, and as large animals with sharp teeth they can be dangerous.

This cultural reference will impact on the meaning of dingoes when seen in **dreams and visions**. Dingoes represent snatching freedom from routine and toil, going off on a jaunt or a well-deserved holiday with friends and family and leaving your cares behind. Sacred historically to the aboriginals, it was associated – like the wolf in Europe – with shapeshifting. However, the negative association with the abducted child must now be taken into account – consider the "taste" of the dream to see if this is relevant.

As a **totem animal**, this powerful, beautiful dog gives independence and a love of travel and adventure, an ability to look after oneself and one's family.

Dog

(*Canis lupus familiaris*)
Element: fire.
Deities: Anubis, Ares/Mars, Artemis/Diana, Bau, Cerberus, Fenrir, Garm, Gula, Hecate, the Morrigan, Set, Upuat.
Perhaps no other animal on Earth has been so closely associated with man, so loved and domesticated, so tailored to our needs and so influential as Man's Best Friend. Its closest relative is the wolf, but it is hard to imagine that when you look at some of the more genetically modified breeds: the Chihuahua, for example, or the Shih Tzu – dogs small enough to be carried in a handbag. Other dogs may even be larger than wolves, like the English Mastiff and the Great Dane. The dog is unique in the animal world in that its form can be so diverse, while genetically it remains a single species.

Dogs greet us and comfort us, guard our homes and other premises, act as helpers to the blind and deaf, warn of medical emergencies, search for lost people on moors and mountains and sniff out murder victims, work with hunters, shepherds and farmers and perform countless other functions for people.

Going into the meaning of dogs in **dreams and visions** is a major enterprise, for each kind of dog may have a different meaning for the dreamer. Dreaming of a snarling Alsatian will mean something quite different to a dream of a small, cuddly cocker spaniel, and you will have to examine the tone of the dream and your own personal associations with the dog you saw. However, as a general guide, a dog represents friendship, loyalty, protection, home, family and love. Each breed of dog will layer its own meanings onto these, however, and then you must consider the cultural references. If you dream of a corgi, is it to do with the Royal family? Does a collie make you think of the countryside and farming? Does a Dalmatian make you think of love and marriage and a big family? Black dogs are in a case of their own, as they speak of misfortune and health troubles, especially mental health issues such as depression, and feelings like guilt, as well as issues like addiction and criminal records.

As a **totem animal**, the dog embodies total loyalty and devotion, either to a person or a situation, but also to a spiritual path. Dog people make the best of every situation and stick to what they believe in; they do not take offence easily or hold grudges, but they will snap if someone repeatedly targets them with nasty behaviour.

Dolphin (for killer whale, see **Orca**.)
(*Cetacea spp*)
Element: water.
Deities: Aphrodite/Venus, Amphitrite/Salacia, Apollo, Ganga, Melicertes, Neptune, Poseidon, Triton.

Four nations of the Earth have now ruled that dolphins are "non-human people" who should be accorded equal respect due to their extremely high intelligence, rather than abused or exploited as other animals are. Although gauging their intelligence is challenging, given their physiology and marine environment, brain size has been held to show that cetaceans are second only to humans in intelligence. They have a complex language of sounds and have been observed teaching their offspring to use tools.

Although they can be aggressive, dolphins appear very benign towards humans and other mammals and have been seen to circle protectively around swimmers when sharks were in the area, and to protect other cetaceans, including one instance of a dolphin guiding a stranded whale and her calf away from shallow water. Dolphins in Brazil work with local fishermen, driving fish towards their nets and being rewarded with some of the catch.

Sadly, humans have repaid dolphins' benevolence with abuse – killing dolphins for their meat and accidentally during fishing for other species, forcing them to perform as tourist attractions and incarcerating them in tanks. Dolphins have also been used in scientific experiments and as working animals by the military. Climate change is a threat to dolphins, particularly river dolphins, and the Yangtse river dolphin has recently been declared functionally extinct.

Dreams and visions of dolphins speak of fun and adventure, friends and parties, but some of our cultural influences may also cause these meanings to include help, protection and someone coming to our aid. Dolphins also have a strongly sexual meaning, due to their phallic shape and their known tendency to interact sexually with humans – female trainers at dolphinaria report that male dolphins will attempt to mate with them.

As a **totem animal**, the dolphin brings great happiness and fortune, a sense of fun and love of adventure, plus great kindness towards weaker creatures. It brings harmony, intelligence and sociability.

Donkey
(*Equus asinus*)
Element: earth.
Deities: Kalratri, Priapus, Set-Typhon, Shitala, Silenus, Vesta.

> *With monstrous head and sickening cry,*
> *And ears like errant wings,*
> *The devil's walking parody*
> *On all four-footed things.*

GK Chesterton's cruel lines are one end of the spectrum of images associated with this animal; at the other it forms an integral part of imagery associated with Christian mythology, standing by the manger at Bethlehem and carrying Christ into Jerusalem. As Christian tradition avers, the donkey does indeed have a cross on its back, a ridge of black hair that runs along the spine, with the crosspiece running down the shoulders. The animal was known as the ass until around the end of the eighteenth century, when the word donkey (of unknown origin) became generally used.

Christ's choice of transport harks back to the ancient world, in which the ass was seen as a symbol of lust, as the goat is to this day. It has also been seen as a symbol of stupidity (to this day, we call a foolish person an ass). Christ riding on this animal symbolised his triumph over the lower instincts.

Donkeys are also known for stubbornness; they will get it into their heads that they don't want to move, and nothing can make them. Yet this is probably a survival instinct: a donkey is not easily frightened, but it will refuse to proceed towards what it sees as peril, nor will it bolt like a horse.

Donkeys crop up regularly in literature, from Apuleius's Golden Ass to AA Milne's Eeyore. Sadly they are still killed for their meat in some countries, and are used for transport, and the glue derived from their hides has also made them a commodity.

In **dreams and visions**, a donkey speaks of a mixture of positives and negatives: its patience, its strength, its toughness and its ability to survive suffering on the one hand, and its alleged stupidity and stubbornness on the other. Dreaming of a donkey may indicate someone in your life who has been causing you trouble by their own foolishness, or it could mean you yourself are the ass.

As a **totem animal**, it confers gentleness, simplicity and integrity, with an abundance of inner strength to survive anything life can throw. There is an innate goodness about donkeys; they are not vicious (beyond the odd kick) and endure much with stoicism.

Dormouse

(*Gliridae spp*)
Element: earth.
Deities: Bride, Morpheus and Somnus.
Sleeping is the favourite occupation of this small rodent: its name comes from the root of the French verb *dormir*, to sleep, for it does just that, for at least half the year. Lewis Carroll's Dormouse in *Alice's Adventures in Wonderland* cannot keep awake at the tea table, probably because dormice are nocturnal. They are found across most of Europe, Asia and Africa and look very like the common mouse, except that their tails are furry. The Romans were fond of eating them, cooked in honey. The Chinese saw them as a good luck symbol, though they have also been associated with death and the dead.

In **dreams and visions**, the little beast has few meanings, but some have seen it as a symbol of regeneration – as a good night's sleep will enable.

As a **totem animal**, it gives the ability to regenerate and reinvent oneself.

Dove: see Pigeon.

Dragonfly

(*Anisoptera spp*) ـ
Element: air.
Deities: Freyja, Ixchel.
Next to the butterfly, this is surely the most beautiful of insects, and has inspired artists, glass-blowers, sculptors, jewellers and poets down the millennia. Ancient creatures going back to before the dinosaurs, the 3,000-odd species alive today often feature vividly colourful wings, coloured eyes and metallic-hued bodies with swift and graceful flight.

Their close relatives, the damselflies (*Zygoptera spp*), are also gorgeous but distinguished by their habit of folding their wings to their bodies at rest, like a butterfly. Both are found worldwide on or near wetlands, lakes, ponds and rivers where their young, or *nymphs*, may remain for months or even years before emerging as adults.

Dreams and visions of a dragonfly or damselfly can speak of an exciting event on its way, an adventure or a chance to shine at what you do. They can also speak of rebirth and regeneration (like butterflies), of meeting someone who will be important to you, and of enjoying life in the here and now.

As a **totem animal**, they bring grace, courage and adaptability.

Duck

(*Anatidae spp*)
Elements: earth, water and air.
Deities: Ehecatl, Nganuleima, Penelope, Yemaya.
An air of comedy surrounds the duck...why do we find it so amusing? Is it the stubby orange beak, or the waddling walk or the funny croaking cry? These birds, a huge family of many different shapes and colours, have

been important to man since the dawn of time, being hunted and their eggs gathered well before they were domesticated. In our modern culture, they are very close to children, whose toy boxes, stories and even bedroom wallpaper may be populated with ducks, often wearing sailor hats like Disney's Donald Duck to celebrate their watery lifestyle.

In many areas of Britain, particularly the Midlands, "duck" is a term of endearment, like "dear", and seems to derive from the mediaeval habit of calling people by birds' names, like "hen" and "goose", perhaps because these birds were seen as a valuable part of the household. The word "duck" is found in many common expressions: a "sitting duck", "out for a duck," a "lame duck", "water off a duck's back," a "dying duck in a thunderstorm."

In **dreams and visions**, a duck or ducks can have a very wide range of meanings, and these will obviously be impacted by your own cultural take on the duck, which children's books you read when you were small, whether you have hunted with guns or been a farmer, etc. Generally speaking, the appearance of a duck means a blessing or gift with the promise of more to come – for ducks lay eggs! Because the mind is so strange and complicated, "duck", whether spoken in your dream or appearing as an actual bird, can be a warning to take care – to "duck" – as there may be danger. Plural ducks may speak of travel, especially if they are in flight.

As a **totem animal**, the duck brings humour, happiness, lightness of heart and an ability to open yourself to your own feelings.

Dugong: see Sea Cow.

Eagle
(*Accipitridae spp*)
Elements: air and fire.
Deities: Eagle Mother, Hebe, Horus, Huitzilopochtli, Jupiter/Zeus, Nekhbit, Ra, Vishnu.
Next to the lion, the eagle is the most popular heraldic beast, being the national symbol of many nations across five continents. In Britain, we are privileged to have the magnificent golden eagle, and in the States the bald eagle is the national bird, but eagles are indigenous and admired in almost every corner of the Earth.

The term "eagle" is given to 68 species of large birds of prey in the *Accipitridae* family, in four groups: booted eagles, fishing eagles, harpy eagles and snake eagles. Their size, their beauty and their grace in the air have made them sacred in many traditions, notably the Native American peoples, who to this day are permitted to collect eagle feathers – although the bird is protected in the US – for their spiritual practice.

In **dreams and visions**, eagles signify truth, nobility and courage, which virtues they also bring to people with eagle as a **totem animal**. If you dream of being attacked by an eagle, it could be that your conscience is not at ease and you feel you have wronged someone by indulging in less than righteous behaviour. Dreaming of killing an eagle could mean you are considering some dubious behaviour and fighting with your conscience. An eagle carrying you may mean freedom or moving on to a higher position, fulfilling a dream.

Earthworm
(*Annelida spp*)
Element: earth.
Deities: Akka, Eir, Ur, Xol and Yul (the five worm gods of Sumerian culture), Iörmungandr and Nidhöggr.
Thinking on these slimy wriggly beasts may well make you shudder, especially when you learn that there are species in the US and in Australia which can reach three to four metres long! "Worm" is a term of abuse often used towards people we consider to be sneaky, creepy or cowardly. Yet we owe these creatures so much. In fact, it is not an exaggeration to say that without them we could not exist.

Earthworms are the dustmen of the planet and a lot of their time, as with human refuse collectors, is given over to recycling. Dead leaves, dead animals, faeces and other organic matter is grist to their mill, and all is passed through the worm and returned as clean, fertile soil in which plants can grow. They can even recycle themselves! The US scientist Gordon Gates found that it is possible to chop a worm in half and grow two new worms from the pieces. However, don't try this at home: not all species are capable of doing this and it is cruel.

The other thing a lot of people know about earthworms is that they are hermaphroditic and can reproduce by a process of parthenogenesis – without mating.

Not very promising creatures spiritually, or so you might think. Actually, in **dreams and visions**, they bring all sorts of good news and they align very closely with the aims of many pagans and other "green" people. Worms mean answers to problems, new starts, regeneration, transformation and the achieving of high aims, though they also bring the message that a lot of hard work might be involved in getting where you want to be.

As a **totem animal**, the worm also gives this ability – to dig deep, work hard and achieve your aims, whilst remaining realistic and unassuming.

Earwig
(*Dermaptera spp*)
Element: earth.
Deities: none identified.
Don't despise creepy-crawlies just because of their appearance! Just as you should not judge a book by its cover, or a person by their clothes, some animals have qualities you could not guess at just by looking at them. Lady earwigs, for example, are great, caring mothers. Where most insects abandon their eggs as soon as they are laid, earwig mothers stay with theirs, seeing off any predators with those fearsome pincers on their rear ends (some species can also shoot evil-smelling liquid at foes), and even look after

the hatched babies until they are grown enough to look after themselves. Their unpleasant name comes from the idea that they crawl into human ears, and some horror stories would have you believe that they lay eggs in there and even in the brain! Not true. Although they love moist dark crevices and they may enter the ear canal, they do not lay eggs there, nor do they carry any diseases harmful to humans.

The 2,000 or so species that make up the order *Dermaptera* are found across the world, except in very cold regions. Their usual habitat is tiny crevices, in wood, brick or stone, and their flat bodies make it easy for them to creep into these. Although most species have wings, they do not usually fly.

Despite their loving behaviour towards their young, earwigs in **dreams and visions** speak of unhappiness within a family, of bad news concerning the family, of plans disrupted and also of being stalked by someone you do not like.

As a **totem animal**, the earwig presents as someone who can take care of themselves and their nearest and dearest, thank you very much, and needs no one to protect them.

Echidna

(*Tachyglossidae:* four species.)
Element: earth.
Deities: Echidna, Gaia, Typhon.
The spiny anteater is a native of Australia and New Guinea, but is not a marsupial. It is a monotreme like its close cousin, the duck-billed platypus (a mammal that lays eggs). It has large claws and a thin, snout-like beak with a long, sticky tongue with which it feeds on ants and termites, but it is not related to the true anteaters. When these timid animals are alarmed, they curl up into a ball, like a hedgehog, protected by their spines.

Echidnas are not good news when they crop up in **dreams and visions**. If you see one, it means you may have a fight on your hands – with an enemy or someone at work, or even a member of your family.

As a **totem animal**, however, it brings many good qualities of resilience, wisdom, knowledge and the ability to protect oneself. As always, bear in mind cultural references: for example, Knuckles the Echidna, a close pal of Sonic the Hedgehog, who goes after the bad guys with his enormous mailed fists.

Eel

(*Anguilliformes spp*)
Elements: water and earth.
Deities: Atum, Farmea, Hina/Sina, Riiki, Te Tunaroa.
These snaky-looking creatures are actually long, thin fish and they come in a huge range of sizes and shapes, from the teeniest little mud eels to the fearsome 1.5 metre conger eel. They are found across the globe in fresh water and seawater, and freshwater species are known for returning to

the sea to lay their eggs, so that the small elvers are then obliged to return to their natural home in the rivers and streams by swimming upstream, jumping weirs and other obstacles. Many species are believed to journey to the Sargasso Sea, in the North Atlantic, to breed.

I remember seeing a conger eel in a fishmonger's window when I was a child: the inventive shopkeeper had labelled it "Loch Ness Monster". I wonder if he sold much of it: people were not as open to trying strange foods then, and this fish has a firm, very strong-flavoured flesh. But eels are and always have been a food source in many cultures and were once popular in the UK, both fried and as "jellied eels".

Like snakes, eels in **dreams and visions** are often about sex, or about a male person to whom you are attracted or, in the case of the conger eel, of whom you are a little afraid – or both. Do you have a male person in your life that frightens you or even bullies you? Look at the context of the dream for the message, for it will be about this person.

As a **totem animal**, the eel brings security, for it is a slippery customer who can wriggle out of any bad situation and is also prepared to travel extensively to get what it wants.

Egret: see **Heron.**

Eland: see **Antelope.**

Elephant
(*Elephantidae spp*)
Element: air.
Deities: the Buddha, Ganesh, Girimikhala, Indra, Janus.
The largest animals on dry land, elephants are known for their wisdom, their legendary memory and their occasional gentleness – though they can be very dangerous if provoked. Many writers have been inspired by these strange creatures with their huge size and startling body parts: the trunks, the tusks, the flapping ears, the tree-trunk legs and bare but tough skin set them apart from many mammals. Three species exist today: the African bush elephant has a single dome on top of his head, enormous tusks and huge ears, while the Indian elephant has a two-humped dome on his head, smaller ears and much smaller tusks. The African forest elephant is the smallest species, though at around seven feet tall, it is hardly little.

Their use in circuses and zoos is increasingly frowned on by many, especially in circuses as they are often trained by cruel methods. An implement a little like a pickaxe called an ankus has been used by owners and trainers on elephants in Asia.

Used for centuries as working animals in Asia (the African elephant is much harder to domesticate, although it has been used), the animal has inspired much folklore and many sayings: we speak of a white elephant, meaning something expensive and useless, due to the habit of Asian monarchs of gifting this animal to nobles who had annoyed them (the ceremonial upkeep demanded for a white elephant would then bankrupt the nobles). We use the word "elephantine" for anything of giant size, and "the elephant in the room" is the subject on everyone's minds that no one has dared to mention. Elephants have also featured in fiction, especially children's books and movies, notably Jean de Brunhoff's *Babar the Elephant* series and Disney's 1941 animation, *Dumbo*.

Perhaps the most famous historic incident involving elephants is Hannibal's crossing of the Alps with 37 of them to march on Italy in 218BC, a campaign that sparked the Second Punic War.

In **dreams and visions**, it is good luck to see an elephant, which speaks of strength, stability and intelligence. The elephant also brings luck for the family, and may even speak of a new baby.

As a **totem animal**, it brings strength, power and intelligence, good memory and an emotional nature, plus the ability and the inclination for hard work.

Elk: see Deer.

Emu
(*Dromaius novaehollandiae*)
Element: earth.
Deities: this bird is important in Aboriginal belief.
People my age immediately think of a giant bird puppet which often seemed to get the better of its hapless puppeteer, Rod Hull, who claimed he was not to blame when Emu had a go at guests on his TV show and that the bird had a mind of its own!

Real emus are not nearly so aggressive, unless people approach their young, and there have only been two documented cases of them attacking humans. The second tallest bird after the ostrich, as tall as a man, the emu is a cuddly-looking brown bird with beautiful red-gold eyes. It loves woodland and water, is very curious and lays an enormous malachite-green egg. It is considered the national bird of Australia, where it lives.

The emu was once eaten by Aboriginals, who also used its fat for medicinal purposes and as a lubricant for tools, and later on it was eaten by Europeans who arrived on the continent. It is still farmed for its meat, fat and leather. Its name derives from the male's mating call.

In **dreams and visions**, the bird speaks (as does any bird) of freedom but, in the case of the emu; it can centre on the problems and joys of single parenthood.

As a **totem animal**, the emu brings playfulness, curiosity and self-sufficiency, with gentleness and a sense of honour and justice.

Ermine: see Stoat.

Falcon
(*Falco spp*)
Elements: air and fire.
Deities: Apollo, Charon, Circe, Freyja, Horus, Ra.
Many people's minds will wander to the ancient art of falconry – a form of hunting for sport in which a bird of prey was kept hooded so it could not see, on the handler's gloved wrist, until the quarry bird was spotted. Then the hood would be removed and the falcon was freed to chase the prey. Many different types of birds of prey were used in falconry, even eagles, and there was an elaborate system of rules about who was entitled to carry which species of falcon. A modern use of hawks and falcons is at airports, where they are employed to keep other birds away from flight paths.

Falcon is a group that embraces about 40 species of falcons, kestrels and hawks – birds that are distinguished from eagles because they kill their prey with their beaks instead of their feet. They are not actually closely related to eagles. Falcons range in size from the magnificent gyrfalcon to the tiny Pygmy falcon, and the Peregrine falcon is the fastest creature on Earth, having been recorded at 240mph in flight.

In **dreams and visions**, these beautiful birds speak of the ability to anticipate, and can be a warning to keep your wits about you, as danger – or opportunity – may be coming, so you need to "watch like a hawk." The birds were deeply sacred to the Ancient Egyptians, who associated them with the Sun Gods Horus and Ra, and with the pharaoh (who was considered divine), but they were associated with the Sun and sky in other traditions as well.

As **totem or power animals**, they bring strength, vision, courage, integrity and clarity of thought.

Ferret
(*Mustela furo*)
Element: air.
Deities: Alcmene, Galinthias and Hecate.
There is something very British about ferrets: they go well with jokes about pubs and farmers and trousers. Yet they are known across the world, and in some countries they are the subject of strict legislation. In Australia, for example, it is illegal to own one as a pet in some areas, and their breeding and sale is illegal in New Zealand because of the dangers they cause to the existing wildlife, which is already compromised by the importation of cats, dogs, rabbits and other creatures.

Very closely related to the wild polecat, ferrets look a lot like these animals – unless they are albinos (white with pink eyes), which many ferrets are. They have been used for many centuries for hunting, the typical technique being to net runs in a rabbit warren, introduce a ferret and stand by to catch the panicked rabbits as they run into the nets. Like many of the *Mustelidae*, they have a characteristic strong ammoniac smell.

In **dreams and visions**, the playful but stealthy ferret can mean someone is playing a practical joke on you, or stealing from you or mocking or teasing you in some way.

As a **totem animal**, the ferret brings cunning, stealth and resourcefulness, as well as a sense of adventure and fun … but usually it knows when to stop.

Finch
(*Fringillidae spp*)
Element: air.
Deities: Aphrodite/Venus, Bragi, Ostara.
Found pretty well all over the world, these small, colourful birds are valued as garden visitors for their beauty and song. Small passerines, they typically have short, thick beaks for eating nuts and seeds, and brightly coloured feathers that typically include a "cap" and "bib" marking. The family includes familiar British wild birds like the bullfinch, greenfinch and chaffinch, but also the canary, the grosbeak and the siskin. Some of these birds are very exotic indeed, and could compete with birds of paradise for colour. Some birds in other families are known as finches – for example, the famous Galapagos Darwin finches – and some common birds are closely related, such as the sparrow.

In witches' runes – a system much less known than Norse runes – there is a stone called "the birds" which means messages and communication: from the type of gossip that goes on over garden gates to emails, letters, phone calls and postings on social media. This is how you should see the small passerines when they appear in **dreams and visions**, as a sign that news or a communication is heading your way and that, from a party invitation to a job offer, it will be good news. Their meaning may also be to do with friends and family, and their appearance in a dream symbolises good friends, people who mean us well. The goldfinch, sacred to Ostara, especially tells of good things to come, its golden feathers being associated with sunshine and golden riches.

As a **totem animal**, these small birds mean sociability, good luck and the contentment of always having enough for one's needs, although they may also bring riches.

Firefly
(*Lampyridae spp*)
Elements: fire and air.
Deities: the Fae, Kitumu, Loki.
Many beetles and their larvae in this family glow, emitting a greenish or yellowish light from their rear ends by bioluminescence, either to attract a mate or to warn off predators (they taste very nasty, due to the chemicals in their bodies). Widespread globally, there is one species in Britain known as the glow-worm. They are particularly appreciated in Japan, where entire parks are given over to space for viewing these beautiful creatures doing what they do best.

It is wonderful to see fireflies or glow-worms in **dreams and visions**: they speak of enchantment, romance and creativity, of adventures beyond the everyday world. They can also symbolise bright ideas arriving in large numbers, and are a generally good omen for any project you are thinking of undertaking.

As a **totem animal**, the firefly brings inspiration and an ability to connect to otherworldly beings such as the Fae. It is associated with a strong spiritual path and abilities with psychism and magic.

Fish
Element: water.
Deities: any sea deities such as Aphrodite/Venus, Manannan, Neptune, Njördr, Nun, Pontus, Poseidon, Yemanja.

People (setting aside fishermen and marine biologists) generally do not recognise different species of fish, because they do not usually come into contact with them, other than as plastic-wrapped frozen food portions. Perhaps they might recognise some aquarium fish, sharks, tuna, sturgeon and the clownfish made famous by Disney's animated feature, *Finding Nemo*, otherwise a fish is just a torpedo-shaped marine animal.

Bony Fish
(*Osteichthyes: bony fish*)

95 per cent of fish today fall into this category: bony fish. These are the fish that need boning if you eat them; they have sharp ribs and hard spines and a proper bony skull. This is an enormous group of fish, taking in all shapes and sizes from tiny aquarium fish, like neon tetras, to the two-ton ocean sunfish. Some bony fish inhabit fresh waters; some live in the sea but visit or spawn in fresh water.

Cartilaginous Fish
(*Chondrichthyes spp*)

The older types of fish on the planet do not have proper skeletons, but a rubbery spine and a softer skull. This order, including all sharks, dogfish, rays, sawfishes, huss and skate, were the first vertebrates on Earth. If you ever had "rock" or "rock salmon" from the chip shop, you may remember the soft rubbery bones, for rock salmon is actually a member of the shark family.

Sharks are one exception to the remark above that people do not recognise fish species: a huge number of marine horror films (originating with Peter Benchley's classic novel, *Jaws*) and our own instinctive, possibly genetic fear make sharks instantly recognisable the instant that triangular dorsal fin appears. This incredibly successful group, known to our forebears as "sea dogs", were swimming in the seas 450 million years ago, long before any land animals were alive. Probably the most iconic shark alive today, the great white, descends from megalodon – an ancient shark the size of a whale, but now extinct. However, not all sharks are flesh-eating monsters: three species of very large shark are gentle, harmless baleen-mouthed plankton eaters: the whale shark, the basking shark and the megamouth shark.

Generally speaking, cartilaginous sharks are found in the sea, but there is a group that are found in fresh water, and one which can move between rivers and the sea. See under **Shark** for more details.

In **dreams and visions**, fish often speak of emotions and sex, but this will be generic fish, and not necessarily a species of fish that you recognise and whose name you know – for these, see under their specific names. Seeing fish in dreams speaks of hope, good luck and prosperity – a good "catch" of some kind – of fertility, even of pregnancy, and of the relationship that may lead to it. The phallic shape of most fish has caused them to be associated with sex and love, and dreaming of eating commonly served fish, such as haddock, cod and hake may have a sexual meaning. It is also now associated with Christianity due to its ancient use as a secret symbol for persecuted Christians to recognise one another (Ichthys = Iēsoûs Khrīstós, Theoû Huiós, Sōtḗr = Jesus Christ, the son of God, Saviour). The flying fish speaks of travel, and going out of your comfort zone, but finding it much easier than you expected.

As a **totem animal**, the fish brings tender, gentle, compassionate feelings, with quick reflexes and great curiosity.

Flamingo
(*Phoenicopteridae spp*)
Elements: water and fire.
Deities: Ra and Thoth.
As a member of the baby boomer generation, I can't see this beautiful bird without starting to hum Manfred Mann's *Pretty Flamingo*. And it is pretty: one of the most colourful birds of all, yet its hue is not natural; it is due to the bird absorbing carotenes (the micronutrients which make carrots orange) from the invertebrates, particularly shrimp, that it feeds on. I was delighted to learn that a group of flamingos is known as "a flamboyance"! They have become an icon for the LGBT community.

There are six species of flamingo, which all look quite similar: the pink of their bodies is more intense on their wing-feathers, particularly the large primaries, they have long necks and long legs (and like to stand on one with the other tucked up under their bellies) and a large, trowel-shaped bill for digging around in the mud for food. They are found in the Americas (it is the national bird of the Bahamas), Africa, Asia and Europe, and also as ornamental birds in parks and zoos.

The colour pink has usually been associated with love and romance in the West; and so, in **dreams and visions**, the flamingo may speak of a new love interest coming into your life, or just of meeting exciting new people, possible partners or not. It speaks of fun and flirting, travel and adventure, and a bright future.

As a **totem animal**, the bird brings a huge sense of fun, also artistic creativity and a willingness to take risks for their own sake, to experience and to enjoy life to the full.

Flea

(*Siphonaptera spp*)

Element: fire.

Deities: none identified.

Big fleas have lesser fleas, on their backs to bite 'em. And smaller fleas have smaller fleas, and so ad infinitum. Augustus de Morgan's little ditty has amused schoolchildren for years: it is actually called *Siphonaptera*. If you have pets, the chances are you have fleas and flea larvae in your home. There are also fleas which prefer humans, though our twenty-first century hygiene has made these a lot less common. And yes, some of them do have their own fleas as well.

Although they cannot fly, fleas are known to be able to leap 50 times their own height. They are also a suspect in the Black Death and the Great Plague; the rat flea carries bubonic plague, and when the disease has killed the rat, the fleas go in search of another host, and infects nearby humans.

In **dreams and visions**, fleas can have a number of meanings, beginning with the modern preoccupation with cleanliness, and also with being seen to be clean and tidy, or they can speak of a problem that is too small to be called a danger but is an ongoing nuisance. Fleas on another person may speak of your own distrust or dislike for them, or your feeling of superiority to them.

As a **totem animal**, the insect brings a promise of lessons to be learned, of new things to be taught and new beginnings, as well as the ability to rise above poor circumstances.

Fly

(*Diptera spp*)

Element: air.

Deities: Beelzebub, Bramari Devi, Loki, Myiagros, Nergal.

There are around a million species of fly but, for the sake of this study, this section is on the kind of flies we associate with the home and garden, the flies that buzz in our windows or circle over a dead bird or fly in our faces when we are doing the gardening. Most people find them utterly disgusting – Mao Zedong famously ordered the Chinese people to kill as many flies as they could in his ill-thought out Four Pests campaign. But even flies have their important role to play in Nature: they lay their eggs on rotting and dead matter, and the maggots then feed on this smelly substance, helping with the vital process of decomposition. The Ancient Egyptians honoured them, as they honoured all natural processes, wearing fly amulets for luck and giving their renowned soldiers and public servants fly medals.

Seeing flies in **dreams and visions** tells you that you are beset by difficulties and need to find a way out of them; not major problems, necessarily, but the kind of nuisance that can affect you for a long time if you do not find a way to resolve it. Dreaming about maggots has much the same meaning, but it can tell you a situation has reached the point of no return; that an ending has to be made, things thrown out and a new start made.

People with the fly as **totem animal** are lucky, the kind of people who can negotiate all sorts of ill fortune without losing their cool or their good humour.

Fox

(*Vulpes spp*)
Elements: fire and air.
Deities: Huxian, Inari, Kitsune, Loki, Sigyn, Skadi.
There are many species of fox across the globe, and sometimes the border between fox, jackal and wolf gets a little blurred. But the true foxes, the genus *vulpes*, are instantly recognisable as such, even the quirky species like the pure white Arctic fox and the fennec fox (*V. zerda*), the smallest fox of all… but with the largest ears! Our own red fox, which occurs across the Northern Hemisphere, is the largest species of true fox. Delicate and dainty, they seem more closely related to cats – until you take in the long doggy snout.

The fox is first and foremost associated with slyness, cunning, deceit and trickery, from Aesop's Fables through Chaucer to Beatrix Potter's Mr Tod and David Rook's *Belstone Fox*, and the English language has several expressions that reflect this: "foxy", "outfoxed", "sly fox". In songs, folktales, animations and poems it gets the better of its enemies and heads for home carrying a fat goose, or other prize. In real life, the fox is certainly a survivor and where its natural rural habitat has diminished through development, it has taken to towns and cities, where the foraging includes high-calorie takeaway leftovers and tempting garbage cans. Unfortunately, this has brought them into conflict with humans; there has been at least one account of a fox entering a home and biting a baby, and there have been suggestions that councils should actively cull or trap them. But maybe a creature that could survive – and frequently escape – the dreadful phenomenon of fox hunting with hounds ("the unspeakable in pursuit of the uneatable"), now banned by law, can survive this too.

In **dreams and visions**, the appearance of a fox almost certainly warns you of someone who is out to deceive you, perhaps to steal from you or get the better of you in some way through trickery. If the fox appears to be attached to you, or representing you, it speaks of the need for cunning and planning if you are to succeed in something.

As a **totem animal**, the fox brings great intelligence, perception, mental dexterity and the ability to plan and think things through, as well as being a lucky animal.

Frigatebird

(*Fregata spp*)
Elements: air and fire.
Deity: Oro.
Not an easy bird to miss, this magnificent creature boasts a large, bright red neck pouch which it inflates like a balloon to attract a female (the female does not have one). Found across tropical oceans, they have very light bones

and this with their enormous wingspan, nearly three metres, gives them the largest wingspan to weight ratio of any seabird. It also gives them the ability to soar for *weeks* without landing! And if this makes them seem fly-by-night characters, they devote more time to their babies than any other bird, up to nine months, so that they usually only lay their one large egg every other year. Frigatebirds, of which there are five species, are also known for robbing other seabirds of their food, swooping on them and bullying them until they drop or regurgitate their meal.

In **dreams and visions**, the male bird's scarlet neck pouch could represent your fears of a love rival, but generally the bird brings a nicer message – of freedom and fun, of enjoying life and family life and also what you do for a living.

As a **totem animal**, it brings strength and endurance, but also a sense of fun, or the ability to find fun, in whatever it is you have to endure.

Frog
(All species of the order *Anura*)
Elements: water and earth.
Deities: Aphrodite/Venus, Heket, Kek.
Cold, slimy and pop-eyed, frogs do not seem the most appealing of animals. Yet down the centuries, they have been the stars of children's stories, fables and fairy tales and later animated films and TV shows, and they have also appeared as mobile phones, bath toys and stuffed cuddly animals for young children. Where the toad has been associated with witches and evil magic, the frog appears much more lovable and friendly. Yet most people would be hard put to it to tell a frog from a toad if they found one in their garden.

Moving to other countries, frogs begin to have other associations. In some cultures they are eaten, and even farmed for their meat. In some countries they are kept as pets (it is illegal to sell them in the UK). In some tropical countries they are associated with weaponry, as the poison from their skins has been used to tip arrows and spears. Some of these tropical frogs are amazingly beautiful, with jewel-coloured skins and large coloured eyes.

Frogs – which includes the true toads of the *Bufonidae* family – have no tails, but large, strong back legs which in most cases enable them to leap long distances. Toads are classed as frogs, yet it is customary to describe any warty-skinned frog as a toad. These amphibians live mainly on land but must return to the water to lay their eggs – the familiar masses of black-spotted *spawn* seen in early spring in your pond.

They live on all larger land masses of every continent except Antarctica; some species are even adapted for life in deserts. More than almost any other creature, frogs are seen as an indicator of the dangers of climate change. Frog populations have declined worldwide, with more than a quarter of species now threatened, and there has also been a rising incidence of frogs being born with genetic defects, such as extra limbs.

Because of their sudden appearance as teeming tadpoles and baby frogs in the spring, frogs in **dreams and visions** are associated with renewal and rebirth, with new starts and fresh beginnings. If you have been thinking your life needs a reboot, the frog is telling you: now is the time.

As a **totem animal**, it gives great flexibility and adaptability, making for a sociable and practical person who can tackle problems with ease and fit into most environments, employing a dry sense of humour to deal with all problems.

Galago: see **Bush Baby.**

Gar
(*Lepisosteidae spp*)
Element: water.
Deities: none identified, but all fish and river gods.
This fish has a very distinctive body shape, with a fat, stubby tail at one end and a long, pointy snout at the other: the largest species is called an alligator gar from its size and long, toothy jaw, which apparently has led some people to mistake it for an alligator – if you ever see one in its natural habitat then you will understand why. This particular fish can grow up to 10ft (over 3m) long, although other species are small enough to be kept in aquaria. Despite its resemblance to pike, it is not related. Although there are marine fish known as gars, the true gars inhabit mainly fresh or brackish waters throughout the Americas. Gars can be eaten, but their roe is toxic.

In **dreams and visions**, it is a rule of thumb that fish will be at least partly about emotions. The gar can be about blind competitiveness and having ideas above your ability, and may be counselling you to think carefully about your real needs and interests.

As a **totem animal**, however, it is much more fortunate, bringing a co-operative nature, great strength of mind and tenacity.

Gazelle: see **Antelope.**

Gecko
(*Gekkota spp*)
Element: air.
Deities: Abas, Adnoartina.
I always imagine these colourful little lizards as speaking with a Mexican accent: perhaps I have seen too many cartoons. And they are not confined to Mexico: they are found across the world, everywhere but Antarctica.

What singles the gecko out from other lizards is not only its fondness for clinging to the ceiling, but also its voice: geckos sing! The 1,500 species of gecko include species that can click, whistle, chirrup and hiss when they are trying to attract a mate or have been startled. Often brightly coloured, geckos have sucker pads on their toes which make climbing a doddle and in warm climates, where they are common, they will happily live in human homes, clinging to the ceiling and probably welcomed, as many species eat flies.

In **dreams and visions**, these cute little creatures represent the ability to escape from peril and to hold on through difficult times. They also signify good luck in some cultures.

As a **power or totem animal**, the gecko brings great flexibility and capability, indicating the sort of person who can do just about anything but is never boastful or proud, dealing with everything with humour and resourcefulness.

Genet
(Genetta spp)
Element: earth.
Deities: none identified.
A genet is a pretty spotted beast that you might mistake for a cat, but it is neither a cat nor a member of the weasel family, although it belongs to the same order. Found in Africa and Europe, it has a catlike body and long tail, with a sharp fox-like face and a furry crest along its skull and neck which can be erected as a threat. It is nocturnal and lives on small mammals, insects and fruit. Although it is preyed upon by larger animals, it is not endangered.

In **dreams and visions**, it promises new beginnings, good luck and protection.

As a **totem animal**, it brings the ability to deal with trouble without losing your cool, and to weather periods of darkness – both real and emotional.

Gerbil
(Gerbillinae spp)
Elements: fire and air.
Deity: Artemis.
Someone once described Mongolian gerbils (that's the kind you find in pet shops) as having "eyes like a girl being kissed for the first time." With their tiny furry bodies, upright pose and clasped paws they are certainly very appealing and are a nice alternative to hamsters as a family pet, as they are not so aggressive. Almost all pet gerbils today are descendants of 46 gerbils which were brought to the USA in 1954 for use in laboratories. Sadly, they are still used in scientific research.

The rodent family *Muridae* – once referred to as desert rats – also includes jirds and sand rats which, like the cage gerbil, have an upright, kangaroo-like stance and travel in leaps and jumps. In the wild, these small animals are adapted to dry places and when kept as pets do not seem to drink at all.

Seeing a gerbil in **dreams and visions** may be about children, as their large eyes and appealingly vulnerable appearance suggests infants. Seeing two gerbils may be about romance, particularly for young people.

As **totem animals**, they give great energy, but can give a trivial mind and one without great focus.

Gharial

(*Gavialis gangeticus*)

Element: water.

Deities: Ganga, Sobek, Varuna.

Imagine a big crocodile, but with a snout stretched out long, thin and toothy like a bandsaw, and you have the gharial. Sometimes it has a big bony knob on the end of its thin snout, especially in males. It is related to the crocs, but has a few differences, including the way it will slide on dry land on its belly, rather than walking or running like a crocodile. This might make it easier to escape from ... but in the water it is a different story! Unlike other crocodilians, the male gharials help guard the eggs.

This Asian reptile was nearing extinction a few years ago, but has made a comeback, thanks to various conservation projects.

In **dreams and visions**, seeing a gharial could mean someone who has been treating you unfairly, or spying on you; while seeing more than one could speak of bad news.

As a **totem animal**, however, it is fortunate, bringing strength, patience and self sufficiency and the instinct to protect others.

Giant Panda

(*Ailuropoda melanoleuca*)

Element: air.

Deities: pandas have been worshipped as gods in China and Tibet.

Was there ever a more iconic animal? It has been the World Wildlife Fund's logo since 1961, a few years after the famous Chi Chi came to live at London Zoo, also inspiring a flood of children's toys. Chi Chi was so loved that her death was announced on the news and the nation went into mourning!

Giant pandas are true bears (unlike the unrelated red pandas) and instantly recognisable for their striking black and white coats – although a subspecies called the Qinling panda has a buff and brown coat. They are found only in China, and have been considered at high risk for many years, owing to habitat loss and fragmentation (animals cannot meet to breed if there are roads and homes in the way). But possibly an even greater problem for them is their very low birth rate: typically, one single cub every other year. They have proved very difficult to breed in captivity. However, in 2020, Chinese scientists announced that the pandas were no longer endangered as their numbers had risen to over 1,800.

Pandas live exclusively on bamboo, from which they take in over half a milligram of cyanide every day, a toxin which is dealt with by their unique digestive system.

The nobility of the panda, revered by the Asians for centuries, makes this a fortunate animal to see in **dreams and visions**, and a herald of some piece of good luck coming your way.

As a **totem animal**, it brings great power and a sense of justice, with panda people being unable to bear seeing injustices done to others, or cruelty either. They are protective and benevolent, but should not be underestimated or provoked.

Gibbon
(*Hylobatidae spp*)
Element: air.
Deities: Hanuman, Sarutahiku. Gibbons have been worshipped in Asia.
The gibbon is the only lesser ape, a sort of poor cousin to gorillas, chimps, bonobos, orang-utans and us! There are 20 species, living across Asia and Indonesia, and they look very much like some monkey species, apart from the absence of a tail. They come in a range of colours, from light beige to red, brown and black.

Gibbons are known for their song and for the ease with which they swing from branch to branch through the forest: they have unique wrist joints that enable them to do this at high speed. The singing, communication using high pitched cries and musical whoops, can be heard over a mile away (funky gibbons!).

Many sources seem to think that a gibbon in a **dream or vision** is quite a bad sign, that the animal represents low intelligence and the journey into ill health or danger because of poor choices. Take this as the meaning if you wish, but I acknowledge the Asian reverence for them and see the animal as representing exuberance, artistic expression and ability in a number of ways.

As a **totem animal**, it brings cleverness, artistic ability, honour, integrity and intuition, combined with playfulness and family affection.

Gila Monster
(*Heloderma suspectum*)
Element: fire.
Deities: none identified.
Do not get on the wrong side of this beauty! As its name suggests, the monster is a very dangerous creature, a poisonous lizard whose venom is as toxic as that of a rattlesnake. Just to let you know this, it is brightly patterned in orange and black: Nature's way of marking out poisonous creatures, and as well as being easy to see it is very slow moving.

Dreaming of monsters is common enough; dreaming of gila monsters means something different: this creature is saying that you need to value yourself more, that you have gifts and abilities that you have not acknowledged.

As a **totem animal** it brings self-reliance and an ability to regenerate oneself when all is lost and others are in despair.

Giraffe
(*Giraffa camelopardalis*)
Element: air.
Deities: the Qilin, Set.

Hide of a leopard and hide of a deer
And eyes of a baby calf,
Sombre and large and crystal clear,
And a comical back that is almost sheer
Has the absurd giraffe. – G. Dearmer.

If the habits of this amazing creature were better known, the LBGT community might jettison the unicorn and adopt the giraffe instead. Animal watchers have observed that although males fight over females, clonking one another with their long necks, they will make up afterwards and have a cuddle, often leading to sexual behaviour; and that these same-sex hook-ups are more common than heterosexual ones!

This tallest of living beasts is also one of the best known, popping up especially in the art connected to children's books and toys, poking out of the top of Noah's Ark and often used as a logo for smaller zoos. The reticulated pattern on their coats occurs in all sub-species of giraffe, and ranges from very blond to quite dark brown.

A giraffe in **dreams and visions** is telling you to keep your head up, to look all around you and be watchful; in effect, it is giving you a real heads-up. There may be something you are not seeing because you haven't raised your eyes from your book or your PC or your games console – now is the time to look!

As a **totem animal**, the giraffe brings pride, yet humility – pride without arrogance or boasting, self respect – and a certain grace and charm, combined with the gentleness of the very strong who know their strength.

Gnat
(*Nematocera spp*)
Element: air.
Deity: Tithonus.
Gnat is a general term for a number of tiny flying insects that typically fly in clouds and may bite. They have become a byword for anything tiny and insignificant, or anything which causes a nuisance but no real peril.

Dreaming of gnats means we are aware of nuisances in our lives, but do not have the strength, time or inclination to do anything about them.

As a **totem animal**, they confer great strength: that of the tiny creature that is too small and too fast for the larger one to harm.

Goat
(*Capra hircus*)
Element: air.
Deities: Agni, Artemis/Diane, Baphomet, Dionysus, Faunus, Hera/Juno, Marduk, Pan.
The goat brings a lot of mixed images with it: it is comical, it is diabolic, it is tame and a good pet, it brings healthy milk, it is a lustful animal that will mount anything, it will eat your clothes and may rush at you and butt

you. It climbs like a cat and it smells bad! Man domesticated the goat in Neolithic times and it has lived close to us ever since, but still something about this animal unsettles us, perhaps its strange, slit-pupiled eyes, with the pupil horizontal, instead of vertical like a cat's. This is a feature shared by sheep, yet most people will have noticed it only in goats, perhaps because of the often brightly coloured eyes of these animals. Where sheep seem dull, unintelligent creatures, goats are lively, curious and full of mischief. They have also been historically associated with the Devil and witchcraft, especially black goats, which are still used in Voodoo workings today.

Actually, the goat has brought many benefits to mankind, including meat, easily digestible milk and other dairy products, wool and leather. They can clear land rank with weeds and are fond of thistles, and they can also be used as pack animals and can carry quite a lot of weight. Their agility means they will seldom stumble and can be used in hilly and mountainous regions. People who keep goats tend to regard them more in the light of pets, due to their stronger personalities, whereas sheep farmers see their stock more as meat and wool on the hoof. Incidentally, where the line between sheep and goats is blurred, you can tell sheep from goat because a goat's horns grow backwards from its brow, while a sheep's typically grow sideways and outwards.

In **dreams and visions**, goats indicate good fortune and riches, despite their mischievous and often troublesome behaviour, and dreaming of a baby goat (a kid) may be hinting that a kid of your own may be on the cards! It certainly may speak of sex, perhaps someone who is being a nuisance in pursuit of you – a "randy old goat" in fact.

As a **totem animal**, this creature gives a strong and colourful personality, a huge sense of fun and an ability to surmount troubles and come out of any situation with a big smile and a positive result.

Goldfish: see **Carp.**

Goose
(*Anser and Branta spp*)
Element: earth.
Deities: Amun, Geb, Hera/Juno, Nemesis.
Rarely seen being kept as farm stock nowadays, the goose was once as important to rural economies as chickens, and it populates older nursery rhymes and fairy tales: *Goosey Goosey Gander* and *Old Mother Goose* are two famous examples. Geese are a strange mix of cuddly toy cute and savagery: the Romans famously used them as watchdogs, and many other people since have used these birds in the same way, even keeping them with chickens to protect the latter from foxes.

The word *goose* conjures up a typical farmyard goose, pure white with a yellow beak, but of course they come in many varieties, including the greylag goose (grey all over as its name suggests) and parti-coloured geese, such as Canada and brent geese.

Geese were once an important part of the diet, as chicken is now; and they remain as the source of some dishes: pâté de fois gras, the roast goose commonly served at Christmas and goose fat, which is abundant and sold for frying or roasting vegetables.

English is full of expressions which demonstrate how important and widespread this bird once was on farms and on village greens: "what's sauce for the goose," "killing the goose that laid the golden egg," "wild goose chase," "his goose is cooked" and "silly goose". A more modern expression, *goosing*, refers to the act of feeling someone else's buttocks or private parts as an act of sexual aggression, presumably deriving from the necessary posing of the fingers into a beak shape.

Seeing a goose in **dreams and visions** generally speaks to the sense of family, and protection of the family, but the aphorisms above must be taken into account if they appear to tint the dream at all. Seeing many geese acting aggressively may be a warning of family discord or a quarrel with friends, and flying geese speak of the need to leave a situation.

As a **totem animal**, the goose brings great courage and the ability to protect and nurture family. Family is extremely important in the case of the goose, a major consideration and motivation at all times.

Gopher
(*Geomyidae spp*)
Element: earth.
Deities: Gaia and other chthonic gods and goddesses.
When I first encountered this animal as Vincent van Gopher on the *Deputy Dawg Show*, I had never heard of a gopher, but they are very familiar to Americans, who probably hover between admiring their cuteness and loathing the damage they do to any cultivated ground. They are tiny rodents who create a complex network of tunnels in the earth, from which they emerge to steal vegetables from gardens or nibble at the roots of shrubs – neither activity serving to endear them to gardeners or farmers. Like their cartoon namesake, they have very poor eyesight, and rely on their sense of touch to guide them.

In **dreams and visions**, a gopher can mean you are not being well treated by friends, that you are being used, manipulated or coerced (used as a gopher, for example: an English expression for an underling based on the words "go-for"), or in some cases ignored altogether.

However, those with the gopher as a **totem animal** are extremely resourceful and can find endless ways round any problem.

Gorilla
(*Gorilla gorilla and G. beringei*)
Element: earth.
Deities: Ghekre, Ngi.
Our largest living relative, gorillas are yet another species that have suffered from misunderstanding and misrepresentation. Quiet, shy and gentle, they

are represented properly by the 1988 movie, *Gorillas in the Mist*, rather than by King Kong. The brutal-seeming chest thumping of the males and their sheer muscular size seems to have misled humans into thinking them savage and aggressive far beyond their real behaviour. They live almost exclusively on plant material, though they will eat insects; only in zoos have they been persuaded into eating meat. The adult males, known as silverbacks because they develop whitish hair on their backs as they reach maturity, are very protective of their harems and will fight to the death to save them from danger.

In captivity, these gentle giants display behaviours that really demonstrate their closeness to humans: they can be taught to "speak" using keyboards, and have demonstrated very human self-destructive conduct, including eating disorders and self-harming when stressed.

As with all well-known animals, cultural influences must be taken into account when looking at their meaning in **dreams and visions**. If you know a little bit more about them in reality then your dream may be telling you of some noble struggle you have to undertake, or of some sacrifice or other good action taken for your family, or for those you regard as family. But you may just be dreaming of someone oafish and physically threatening, and of low intelligence, for this is how we were taught to regard gorillas until quite recently.

As a **totem animal**, the gorilla brings reserve combined with inner strength, a peaceful and calm nature and a closeness to family and to nature.

Grasshopper

(*Caelifera spp*)
Element: air.
Deities: Bramari Devi, Tithonus.
This sparky little creature is familiar to any child that has played in long grass. Its buzzing chirps and its great leaps, which can carry it for up to a metre, mark it out as a close relative of the cricket, but this family also includes the dreaded locust which, in some countries, can descend in a massive flock and strip crops down to the ground in minutes.

Grasshoppers are a very ancient insect, and are also unusual for not developing through larval stages from the egg: instead of a larval caterpillar or grub, a tiny grasshopper emerges which grows, moults its skin and grows until it reaches adult size. The thousands of species across the globe come in a range of sizes and colours and most can fly as well as leap. Locusts and grasshoppers have been part of the human diet in Eastern countries since earliest times.

Seeing a grasshopper in **dreams and visions**, is held to be lucky and also to mean that you are progressing on the right course *in leaps and bounds*. It may also speak of *a leap of faith*. Although it may be the same species, seeing a locust will have a very different meaning (in a dream, you tend to know the name of what you are seeing and you should awaken with this knowledge). Locusts bring the meaning of fears for the future, fears of being ruined and destitute, or fears of someone stealing from you or preying on you in some financial way.

As a **totem animal,** the grasshopper brings energy, forward-thinking, the ability to think laterally or outside the box and to achieve what you want swiftly. The locust, on the other hand, brings reprehensible behaviours and a realisation that you need to rethink your conduct.

Greyhound
Element: air.
Deities: Anubis, Coyote, Hecate, Pollux.
I was amused to learn that these mythically speedy dogs are total couch potatoes when they leave the racetrack, and rehomed retired greyhounds sleep a lot and need much less walking than other varieties of dog! The breed is formally known as an English greyhound, but has become popular all over the world for its grace, its affectionate nature and, of course, its speed when used as a racing animal. Its speed and lean shape have inspired logos for sportswear and travel companies. A smaller dog bred from greyhounds is the whippet, and greyhound crosses are called lurchers.

The earliest archaeological evidence for greyhounds goes back some 4,000 years, but they did not arrive in the UK until brought by the Romans. It is the only dog specifically named in the Christian Bible. Greyhound racing, often seen as a "poor man's" version of horse racing, had its origins in coursing for hares and other prey, but as a track sport is relatively recent: the first professional track was opened in the US in 1919. It has come in for its fair share of criticism from animal rights groups.

In **dreams and visions**, a greyhound speaks of speed, not necessarily in MPH, but the speed of outcomes, the speed of your work and your progress in any sphere of your life: are you so fixated on outcomes that you rush work or relationships?

As a **totem animal**, it brings a certain competitiveness, but with a friendly and tranquil character that appeases rivals. It is a lucky creature to encounter in dreams, and some sources think it indicates a legacy.

Groundhog: see **Marmot.**

Grouper
(*Epinephelinae spp*)
Element: water.
Deities: all sea gods and goddesses.
This ugly and scary-looking fish is actually a seagoing success, one of the few fish in the ocean which can feed off the venomous lionfish with no ill effects, and it often pals up with moray eels to hunt. This fish is immediately recognisable, with its thick, sturdy body and massive toothy jaws. Not all groupers are very large but some species grow up to eight feet long.

In **dreams and visions**, the grouper shows tenacity and loyalty to the family.

As a **totem animal**, it brings good fortune: grouper people usually get their own way and fear nobody.

Grouse
(*Tetraonini spp*)
Element: earth.
Deities: a range of bird and hunting deities.
These attractive game birds belong to the same family as the turkey (which is covered separately), and includes the prairie chickens. They come in a range of hues, from the snowy ptarmigan to the black grouse, and have long been popular in restaurants and on shooting ranges, but who could not value them for their beauty?

Seeing a grouse in **dreams and visions** indicates that an opportunity lies before you ... or is it a temptation? The English expression *to grouse*, meaning to complain or grumble, may also enter the equation, bringing the meaning that maybe you are discontented with your lot, and thus are drawn away towards other pleasures or attractions.

As a **totem animal**, the grouse comes with great energy and resilience and a strong sense of honour and honesty, but can also show antisocial attitudes.

Guineafowl
(*Numididae spp*)
Elements: earth and air.
Deities: Artemis/Diana.
These striking birds have attractive speckled plumage which can take the form of a polka-dot pattern covering the entire body, and are especially known for their faithfulness to their one mate – like swans, they pair for life. They have long been popular as pets and park birds, and have also been kept for their meat and rich eggs, but they are also beneficial in that they keep down parasites like fleas, flies and ticks, and in their native Africa they also eat scorpions and locusts.

Having **dreams and visions** of guineafowl is a good omen, signifying that something good is on its way to you, possibly as an answer to a problem you have been having. Some sources say the bird shows you are being indecisive and need to confront your own problems head-on.

As a **totem animal**, the bird brings protection and the ability to confront dangers and ill luck with confidence.

Guanaco: see **Vicuna.**

Guinea Pig
(*Cavia porcellus*)
Element: earth.
Deity: Pachamama.

Surprising to think that these charming little creatures, often called cavies, were originally kept for their meat; as they are smaller than rabbits, there must have been scanty pickings. Brought to Europe from South America (they do not come from Guinea) by traders in the sixteenth century, they quickly became popular as pets – even Good Queen Bess herself kept them. They come in a range of colours, with long or short fur, and can be quite noisy, with a range of whistles, chirps, growls and chattering. They are extremely sociable – in some countries it is illegal to keep one in a cage by itself.

In **dreams and visions**, they are all about family and tribe, about taking care of children, showing respect to older people and considering the needs of everyone – including yourself.

People with the guinea pig as their **totem animal** are most comfortable in groups or with family and cannot bear to live alone or be alone for any length of time.

Guppy
(*Poecilia reticulata*)
Element: water.
Deities: none identified.
The humble guppy is the most popular choice for aquaria, as well as being one of the most widespread species to be found in fresh water across the world, having been exported from South America. It is also called the millionfish, presumably because of its large numbers, and also the rainbow fish because of its colourful beauty. This little creature is so adaptable that it will tolerate brackish water or even seawater. Instead of laying eggs, guppies give birth to live babies, up to 200 tiny fry at a time.

Seeing a guppy in **dreams and visions** is fortunate; it speaks of happiness, truth and the attainment of long held goals.

As a **totem animal**, it brings a greater involvement with one's feminine side, with being comfortable with one's sexuality and one's appearance.

Haddock: see **Fish.**

Hagfish
(*Myxini spp*)
Element: water.
Deity: the Morrigan.
This less than attractive creature has been called the slime eel, from its habit of gushing thick foul slime at any creature which threatens it. It is unique in the animal kingdom in that it has a hard gristly skull, but no spine. Slimy, bare-skinned and wormlike, it feeds on smaller creatures and on sea carrion, which it eats from the inside out, and will also attack larger but weakened sea animals. It is not an eel or a worm but a fish, and distantly related to lampreys. Like them, it has no jaws, but a round mouth lined with rasping quasi-teeth.

In **dreams and visions**, this nightmare creature does not have the ominous meaning you might expect. Perhaps because its skin is very loose and easily shed, it speaks of rebirth and transformation, of new beginnings. In Eastern countries, its slime is held to have medicinal properties, and thus the fish may also speak of healing and wellness.

As a **totem animal**, it brings these same qualities, with an ability to face down foes without fear.

Hamster

(*Cricetinae spp, especially Mesocricetus auratus*)
Element: earth.
Deities: none identified.
Few children in the West can have missed coming into contact with these tiny rodents, which are very popular as pets and need less attention than dogs or cats. The Syrian or golden hamster, *Mesocricetus auratus*, is the type usually sold in pet shops, although there are 19 species altogether. I was surprised to learn that the keeping of pet hamsters only dates back to 1939, when a pair of Syrian hamsters, a brother and sister, were bred in a laboratory. Even more surprising is that from this shallow gene pool descend all the hamsters in laboratories and sold as pets.

Seeing hammy in a **dream or vision** is a sign of domestic happiness, tenderness for your dear ones, of happiness in your private life and contentment with your lot, and the **totem animal** also brings these qualities into your life. They are about enjoyment, fulfilment and contentedness – strange as that may seem for a caged animal.

Hare

(*Lepus spp*)
Element: air.
Deities: Andraste, Aphrodite/Venus, Artemis/Diana, Eostre, Eros, Osiris, Weneu and Wenenut, all Moon gods and goddesses.
This is another creature, like the cat, the crow and the snake, about which there is a great deal of magical and superstitious belief. Hares have little of the commonplace cuddliness of rabbits, but have a strange, eldritch quality: they "box" and dance madly in the spring when they are fighting for mates – although modern science now holds the belief that a lot of these fights are does seeing off unwanted attentions from bucks. They gaze at the Moon with their strange eyes and have been connected with the Moon because of the marks on their coats and the shape formed on the Moon's surface by the "seas", of a seated lagomorph with long ears. They have long been associated with witches, who were said to shapeshift into hares, and in modern paganism they are sacred to Eostre, Goddess of the Spring (it is said to be the origin of the Easter Bunny in Christian tradition). The Ancient Egyptians associated them with Osiris because of a pun on one of his titles: *Un-Nefer*, the Beautiful Being – *un* being the Egyptian word for hare. In Cornwall, white hares were believed to be the souls of young girls betrayed

by their lovers. The Three Hares symbol, which depicts three hares joined in a triangle by their ears, seems to have started life as a Christian symbol of the Trinity, but has been adopted by the pagan community as a goddess symbol.

The behaviour of hares in the spring has caused them to be associated with madness, like the character in Lewis Carroll's *Alice in Wonderland*: the March Hare.

In the UK, the brown hare, brought by the Romans, is in serious decline despite its legendary fertility: the doe can conceive while still pregnant and carry both pregnancies to term. The indigenous hare, the mountain or blue hare is now confined to Scotland. In the US, hares are usually known as jackrabbits. Perhaps the most beautiful is the Arctic hare, but several species are white, or turn white in winter.

Hare meat has been considered a delicacy, especially when "jugged" – that is cooked in a tall earthen vessel with its blood, and sadly it has also been an unwilling participant in so-called sports like hare coursing with dogs.

They are not rodents but, like the rabbit, share a common ancestor with horses – easier to see in hares, which can look like little racehorses when they are running. Unlike rabbits, they do not burrow, although they may create shallow "forms" in grass in which to hide.

Hares are so entrenched in magical belief that having **dreams and visions** of them can have a number of meanings, depending on your culture. Always look at the context of the dream and see whether some pertinent context is present, such as perhaps the tale of *the Hare and the Tortoise*, which would have its own message about overconfidence or impatience. Also consider your own beliefs: a pagan would see a hare as carrying a clear spiritual message, while a Christian might not. Because of their timid nature, hares might suggest cowardice and lack of decision, or their speed might suggest a victory of some kind, perhaps even winning a race. They have also traditionally been associated with the spring and with new beginnings.

As a **totem animal**, the hare brings intuition, good instincts, wisdom and caution.

Hawk: see **Falcon.**

Hedgehog
(*Erinaceinae spp*)
Element: earth.
Deities: Abaset, Baixian, Ishtar.
This spiny little character has earned a place in our hearts from our earliest years, appearing regularly in children's literature, from *Mrs Tiggywinkle* to Allison Uttley's *Fuzzypeg* and even in Shakespeare. Harmless, snuffly and clumsy, it bumbles around our gardens at night, making enough noise to alert any predator. Gardeners bless it for eating snails and slugs, some people put out catfood and milk for it – though the latter is not a good idea: despite folk tales of hedgehogs drinking from cows' teats, they do not digest milk

easily. Unfortunately, it has no road sense whatsoever, and sad little flattened mats of prickles are all too common a sight on our roads. The hedgehog is in decline in the UK for many reasons, yet in other places, notably New Zealand, it has become so numerous as to be a pest!

Hedgehogs' closest relatives are shrews, yet there is an unrelated animal in Madagascar called the hedgehog tenrec, which is amazingly similar. The lesser hedgehog tenrec looks identical to our own spiny creature.

As well as being prey animals for badgers, and for large birds in some countries, hedgehogs have formed part of the human diet from earliest times. The Ancient Egyptians ate them, and Romany gypsies have famously coated them in clay before baking them, so that the prickly coat breaks away from the cooked meat with the coating. They are said to taste a little like pork.

Interpreting the hedgehog in **dreams and visions** can be tricky, as there are all sorts of possible meanings for this creature. Rely on your own intuition, as well as on the appearance and feeling of the hedgehog you encounter: is it relaxed and friendly, or afraid and pointing its sharp spines at you, or even running away? Although the Ancient Egyptians saw this animal as lucky (as well as a nice culinary experience), it is not necessarily so for people today. It may mean extreme vulnerability and the defences you must put up to counter this, or being let down or even attacked by others in your social circle. At best, it means you must rely on yourself and your own instincts and the defences you have put in place to defend yourself from unpleasant behaviour by others.

As a **totem animal**, it does give comfort, gentleness and curiosity, as well as the ability to take criticism from others without becoming upset.

Heron

(*Ardeidae spp*)
Elements: air and water.
Deities: Aphrodite/Venus, Athena, Frigga, Rhiannon.
Cranes are extremely rare in the UK, yet we do have a tall water bird that looks very similar: the beautiful grey heron, and also its close relatives the snowy white egret (egrets are really just white herons) and the very rare bittern. Herons are not related to cranes, but have a very similar shape. Who has not thrilled at the sight of this tall bird standing motionless in the reeds, looking for fish to catch in its dagger-like bill, or at its sudden flight across the water or over a country road? Some herons use their big wings like sunshades, spreading them over the water so they can see into the depths without the distraction of surface reflections.

In **dreams and visions**, the heron signifies the need for tact and consideration in your social life, for thought and planning in your work, and longer-term planning to achieve your goals.

As a **totem animal**, the heron brings the gift of calm thought, of forethought and planning and careful consideration before any action is taken.

Hippopotamus
(*Hippopotamus amphibius*)
Element: water.
Deities: Ammit, Ipy, Set, Ta-urt.

It is easy to see these tubby, rolling creatures as something created by Disney (like the ballet-dancing hippos in *Fantasia*); they appear good-natured, relaxed and tranquil. Two surprises: they are among the most aggressive and dangerous animals on Earth and, contrary to appearances, are related to neither elephants nor pigs – their closest living relatives are whales! Also they are alleged to sweat blood … not true, but their sweat does have a pinkish colour.

Hippos live almost exclusively in water, and their massive heavy bones – designed to support their huge bodies – allow them to sink to the bottom and walk along there. Their huge tusks, which are displayed in a "yawn" to intimidate enemies, enable them to crunch hapless crocodiles which come in their path and they will also attack small boats. Got the image of those tutus out of your mind now?

The Ancient Egyptians made a clear difference between males and females: Ta-urt, the Goddess of Pregnancy and Childbirth was a benign hippo, whilst the male hippo was associated with Set, the Chaos God who murdered Osiris.

But of course you must also have the tutus and their occupants in mind when considering hippos in **dreams and visions**, as your cultural influences must always be considered. Dreaming of a hippo signifies that your strengths are hidden, perhaps even to you, but can also be warning you about your potentially cranky, antisocial temperament and your failure to have regard and consideration for others.

As a **totem animal**, it brings some negative qualities: sullenness, irritable temper and aggressiveness, but also great strength and self-reliance.

Hoopoe
(*Upopa spp*)
Element: air.
Deities: Tusholi. It was sacred to the Ancient Egyptians.

This colourful bird with its astonishing high crown of feathers was adopted by Israel as its national bird in 2008, and there is a great deal of folk belief around it in the countries where it occurs across Europe, Asia and Africa. Related to kingfishers and bee-eaters, it is easily recognised by its headdress, its black-barred rear end and also by its brief two-note call, which sounds like its name.

The crown it bears gives this beautiful bird the meaning of royalty, leadership and pride in **dreams and visions**. Carry yourself proudly wherever you go, it says, and have faith in yourself. Face down your fears, but at the same time do not give way to arrogance and snobbery.

As a **totem animal**, the hoopoe gives great confidence and pride, but also the ability to see through others' flattery.

Hornbill

(*Bucerotidae spp*)

Element: air.

Deities: Singalang, Burong, Wubari.

This is a bird which personifies beakiness: in fact, its beak is by far the most noticeable thing about it. Gigantic and often brightly-coloured, it slopes downwards and often includes a helmet-like extension (sometimes as big again as the base beak) over the front of the head. This bird is known to form "friendships" with other animals (for example, with mongooses) and will forage for food with them and warn them of danger.

In **dreams and visions**, the hornbill signifies "putting on a brave face" in a difficult situation, or the need to do so.

Those with the hornbill as a **totem animal** are adept at doing this and owe much of their success in life to holding fast and bluffing their way out of trouble.

Horse

(*Equus ferus caballus*)

Element: air.

Deities: Aine, Ares/Mars, Athena, Demeter, Epona, Etain, Freyr, Gontia, Hayagriva, Helios, Loki, Neptune/Poseidon, Pryderi, Rhiannon, Shango, Sleipnir.

How important the horse has been – and continues to be – to mankind. Long after its usefulness as a beast of burden, it stays with us – as a pet, as a hobby, as a status symbol, as a thing of grace and beauty we cannot bear to discard as mechanised society has discarded the ox and to some extent the donkey. This creature grew into man's affections as it evolved from a tiny, rabbit-sized creature called Eohippus around 50 million years ago. Now it may stand up to 20 hands (a hand is four inches) at the shoulder and weigh 1.5 tons. No fully grown modern horse is as tiny as Eohippus, but sizes vary from the miniature Falabella, around 60cms tall, to massive shire horses like the Suffolk punch and the percheron. The extent to which it has captured man's heart can be evidenced in the number of expressions which have come from horse-husbandry: *eat like a horse, don't look a gift-horse in the mouth, work-horse, get off your high horse, unbridled, a willing horse, he's a dark horse, hoof it, win your spurs* …

Horses were sacred to many ancient civilisations and to many gods including, strangely, the Sea Gods Neptune and Poseidon. Odin had a magical eight-legged horse called Sleipnir, whose physical characteristics enabled him to run faster than any creature and to fly through the air. The horse also sired some mythical creatures, such as the unicorn, the centaur and the winged horse, which will be discussed in a later section.

Seeing a horse or horses in **dreams and visions** poses a problem because of all the nuances of meaning a horse may have. Even its colour may have significance: is the horse white? It may mean the arrival of a hero or a triumph of some kind. Is it black? This may refer to a bad guy or to the black horses that still today sometimes draw a hearse. Generally speaking, horses refer to progress and travel, strength and freedom. The Norse Futhark rune Ehwaz specifically refers to people working together, cooperating to achieve a result – a meaning which could also apply to a dream of two or more horses. Seeing an injured horse may indicate an obstruction or problem to your plans, while a dead horse may mean disaster and abandoning them altogether. A horse heavily hung with tack and painfully drawing a load far too big for it may be a message that you need to ease up on yourself and take time off work or your health may suffer. A foal may speak of a new project, of new beginnings and hope.

As a **totem animal**, the horse brings many blessings, including a stalwart personality, strength of purpose and a willingness to undertake work that needs to be done, as well as endurance, patience and confidence.

Hummingbird
(*Trochilidae spp*)
Element: air.
Deities: Huitzilopochtli.
These tiny birds, natives of the Americas, have the highest metabolic rate of any creature except insects, and are also the only birds that can fly backwards. Often brightly coloured, they live on nectar taken from flowers with their long bills, and also on insects.

Seeing the bird in **dreams and visions** can speak of joy, happiness and good fortune, or it may be a hint that you need to slow down, try to be calmer and take life more seriously: the tone of the dream will reveal which meaning is appropriate.

The hummingbird as **totem animal** brings a playful spirit, that of a person who loves life and has every intention of enjoying it to the full, experiencing every adventure, exploring every place. These are happy-go-lucky people, playful and light-hearted.

Husky
(*Canis lupus familiaris*)
Element: fire.
Deities: no specific deity for huskies, but dog deities in general (see under Dog).
Husky is a concept, rather than a breed, a term for sled dogs used in harsh weather. But the term immediately brings to mind the animals drawing the Inuit sleds, huge, shaggy, half wild and having a large dose of wolf in their genetic make-up and appearance. These dogs are known for their strength and energy – needed to draw the sleds – and for their tolerance for harsh, wintry conditions. Although these sled dogs are still used for their original purpose, they (or their crosses with other breeds) have now become sought after pets.

In **dreams and visions**, the husky is telling you of a bad situation, of hardship and maybe the ending of something – a job or a relationship. It may signify a long, hard journey, which may be actual travel or a struggle towards something you need or want.

As a **totem animal**, it presents with strength and endurance, but also with happiness and sociability, an ability to work with others, perhaps in harsh or unfavourable conditions.

Hyena
(*Hyaenidae spp*)
Element: fire.
Deities: none identified.
This is an animal with a serious image problem. Most people only know it as savage, cowardly, sneaky, that it eats only carrion and that some species laugh. Very little of this is true: "cowardly" hyenas can see off marauding lions, and almost all the meat they eat they kill themselves, rather than scavenging from other animals' kills. In fact, it is more likely to be the lion that is trying to steal from the hyenas.

There are four species of hyena still extant: the brown, the spotted, the striped and the aardwolf. All have the same general appearance, with the steeply sloping back, large jaws and rather ungainly appearance. The aardwolf eats mainly insects but the three other species are hunters and meat eaters, their jaws adapted for crushing bone. The spotted hyena is the species that "laughs", a snickering call that does sound a little like human laughter; it also growls, grunts, whoops and howls, where the other types are more silent. The striped hyena is the type most likely to scavenge, and it will also eat fruit.

Whatever the real characteristics of the animal, its meaning in **dreams and visions** will be firmly tied to what people know (or think they know) about it. The appearance of a hyena speaks of greed, cowardice and dishonesty, or resorting to unscrupulous behaviour to overcome problems or gain advantages. It can also mean a betrayal by someone you know, perhaps by spreading lies about you.

As a **totem animal**, it brings great wilfulness and selfishness, the ability to get your own way through any means, without compunction.

Hyrax
(*Hyracoidaea spp*)
Elements: air and water.
Deities: there is an African deity called Hyrax, but this is a coincidence. Elephant deities may be invoked.
This unusual looking creature (it looks like a cross between a guinea pig and a seal) is actually a relative of the elephant. Although it measures only around 60cms long, it does have some features that show its relationship to elephants, including the characteristic flat toenails, and tiny tusks. Native to Africa, it is also known as a dassie or rock rabbit. Although it retires into burrows for shelter, it does not dig them, unlike the rodents it resembles.

In **dreams and visions**, the hyrax stands for memory and ancestors, for those people in your past who have influenced the way you have grown and developed, and this can also mean ancestors of place and path, as well as ancestors of blood and family. It also means community spirit and defence of your tribe, which means a lot to you. But this wise little creature knows just when it is time to fight and when it is time for flight, so judgement is also part of its gift.

These qualities are also given by the hyrax as **totem animal**.

Ibex

(*Capra spp*)

Element: air.

Deities: Attar, Dali, Pan, Sylvanus.

This name is given to a number of species of wild goat, which is easily recognised by the mighty horns of the male, which look almost too big for its neck to support, curving and ridged in front. The female's horns are much smaller. These graceful creatures were once believed to have had wings, no doubt because of the ease and agility with which they climb mountainous terrain.

Seeing an ibex in **dreams and visions** speaks of a desire for freedom and travel, and also for someone to share that travel with you – are you looking for a mate who "gets" you and is not afraid to commit?

As a **totem animal**, it brings a sense of drive, of ambition and determination, with the instincts to manifest these practically.

Ibis

(*Threskiornis spp*)

Element: air.

Deity: Thoth.

This graceful bird with its down-curving bill spends its life poking around as though overcome by curiosity, and so became a symbol for the Ancient Egyptians of knowledge and wisdom, and the sacred bird of their God of Knowledge, Thoth – His Egyptian name Djehoti or Tehoti meant "like the ibis" and the birds were revered and mummified when they died, in His name. Sadly they are extinct in Egypt today, although the African sacred ibis is found in other African countries. Ibis come in a variety of colours, including scarlet and metallic green, but the long bill is always the same.

Sacred to the Egyptians and exotic to people in the UK, the bird is seen as a pest in other places, and in Australia is often referred to as a "flying rat" for its habit of scavenging through refuse bins. It is a monogamous species and very territorial.

Seeing the ibis in **dreams and visions** tells you that you are on the right path in your quest for knowledge, and some sources say this includes occult knowledge and magical power.

As a **totem animal**, it brings the blessings of Thoth, and not only knowledge and wisdom, but also the ability to seek out that knowledge in the right places – some would say this is even more important.

Iguana
(*Iguana spp*)
Element: earth.
Deities: Itzamna. For the marine iguana also all sea deities.
This is a big lizard, up to six feet long, with an array of spines and spikes and claws that look pretty fearsome, plus a strange scaly boss on their cheeks called the subtympanic shield. The reptile also has a very powerful bite…but it is a strict vegetarian, and the jaws are designed to mill vegetation rather than flesh. It is harmless enough to have become quite popular as a pet, particularly in the United States.

In **dreams and visions**, the iguana is about transformation of the self for the better; of losing things from your life that no longer serve you and changing habits that harm you or others. Some sources say that the appearance of an iguana is a warning against enemies plotting against you, but the general feeling of the dream will tell you which meaning is more likely. A marine iguana carries similar messages, but there will be a suggestion of travel by sea.

As a **totem animal**, it brings joy and happiness and an ability to change oneself and break bad habits. Iguana people are gentle, kind to others and do not get flustered by unexpected events.

Impala: see **Antelope.**

Insect
Dreaming about creepy-crawlies is a sign that you have unconscious fears and worries, but unless the insects you see in **dreams and visions** are indistinct, so that you can only say: "it was an insect or insects", then see the insects under their own sections.

Jacana
(*Jacana jacana, J. spinosa* and *Actophilornis africanus*)
Element: water.
Deities: none identified.
In the words of the immortal Fats Waller, one might feel like saying to this bird: *Your feet's too big*. The jacana, which can scurry across lily-pads and other weeds and hardly wet its toes, would hardly agree. This pretty bird has feet that can spread out to a width of 12cms by 20cms, easily enough to support its 30cm body on the most fragile of water weeds. There are three species, the Jacana species of the Americas and the African jacana, but they all feature the outsize toes.

In **dreams and visions**, the jacana is saying: do not fear to go where others cannot, trust your sense of balance and your surefootedness. Dare to do what others fear and be yourself. What have you got to lose? If the dream is less positive in feeling, it may be telling you of the need for more balance in your life.

As a **totem animal**, this bird gives resourcefulness and adaptability, the ability to skate over problems and reach your goal.

Jackal

(*Lupulella mesomelas, Lupulella adusta, Canis aureus* and *Canis lupaster*)
Element: fire.
Deities: Anubis, Duamautef, Kali, Upuat.

This pretty canid has suffered extremes of attitude from humans, being a god in Ancient Egypt and a metaphor for a totally vile, cowardly, unscrupulous person in many later cultures. It is a medium sized relative of the wolf and fox, often with an attractive golden-brown coat. The African golden wolf, once called the golden jackal but now reassigned to the wolf family, was the animal believed to have inspired images of the Ancient Egyptian God of the Dead, Anubis (although He is shown as a black jackal), probably one of the most familiar of their gods. Found across Africa and Asia, they are carnivores living on small mammals and birds, but will also scavenge carrion and human refuse.

Jackals are seen as tricksters in many folk tales, but above all the name is used as an insult to describe someone as a coward, a thief, a dishonourable person or someone who performs menial tasks for someone else, perhaps because they are afraid of them. Most Western people would also link the name to the movie, *Day of the Jackal* (1973), about a political assassin.

Seeing a jackal in **dreams and visions** can be difficult to interpret, but always take the "tone" of the dream as your guide. If it felt happy and well-omened then the jackal may be telling you of changes and opportunities in your life, or telling you to follow your instincts in a difficult situation. If the tone of the dream was not so good, it may signify someone taking advantage of you, using you for their own ends and taking all the credit for anything achieved.

As a **totem animal**, they bring cunning, smarts and resourcefulness, with an ability to get the better of most people.

Jackdaw

(*Coloeus monedula* and *C. dauuricus*)
Element: air.
Deities: Cernunnos, Hermes/Mercury, the Morrigan, Odin.

Highly intelligent, cheeky, handsome and thieving, jackdaws are full of personality and have been kept as pets (they can be taught to speak, like many of the corvids). They cling around human habitations, stealing from the bird table and nesting in the chimney (to the detriment of the brickwork). Both species are black with lighter markings: in the Western jackdaw these are the grey head and neck that emphasize the black cap; in the Eastern or Daurian jackdaw there are white sections on the body which call to mind the related magpie. Like magpies, they have a well-deserved reputation for stealing bright things like small items of jewellery. These noisy birds are far from endangered, in fact their numbers are on the increase.

Corvids tend to share a lot of meaning in common in **dreams and visions**; after all, they often look very alike. Many people cannot tell a rook from a crow or a crow from a raven; and a jackdaw, with its black body and grey neck, is very similar as well. These birds often have ominous meanings, and that of the jackdaw is of theft, lies and dishonesty, or of trouble at home. According to some sources, they share with the crow an association with death and disaster, but they also appear as messengers from the spirit world.

As a **totem animal**, the jackdaw brings utter confidence, cheekiness and mischief, bravura and an ease with others in all situations, as well as wisdom.

Jackrabbit: see **Hare.**

Jaguar
(*Panthera onca*)
Element: fire.
Deities: Ix-Chel, Tezcatlipoca and other Mayan gods whose names have been lost, including God L.
This stunningly beautiful cat is the third largest feline in the world and the only *panthera* species found in the Americas. Its beauty and grace inspired the century old Jaguar Car manufacturer to pinch its name for their famous, upmarket range of cars and latterly Range Rovers. Although they bear a superficial resemblance to leopards, they are larger and heavier, and their markings have a gorgeous mosaic quality with the spots having patterning within them, whereas the leopard's are generally more solid spots or rosettes. It has a large, powerful head and its bite is bone-crushing, enough to bite through the shell of a tortoise. Despite its fearsome reputation, the jaguar almost never attacks humans; in fact, the first recorded attack (on two children) took place in 2008.

Seeing a jaguar in **dreams and visions** is fortunate; it speaks of prosperity, of new ideas and inspiration which will benefit you, although the dream may also indicate that you need to be on your guard.

As a **totem or power animal**, it is very protective and brings strength and the confidence that goes with it. Jaguar people should take care not to rely on their strength too much and take on burdens and anxieties that can accumulate and weigh them down.

Jaguarundi
(*Herpailurus yagouaroundi*)
Element: fire.
Deities: none specific, but all cat gods and goddesses.
Despite its name, the jaguarundi or jaguarundi cat is not closely related to the jaguar but is closer to the cougar. It is a medium-sized wild cat with a smoky grey coat, although some jaguarundis have a red-gold colouration. Despite their similarity in appearance to domestic cats, they are too fierce to be kept as pets.

In **dreams and visions**, a jaguarundi speaks of ill feelings between neighbours, perhaps because it is believed to steal chickens and small stock animals such as lambs. It can even mean being harmed by a neighbour who does not like you.

This cat has a rather ill-natured look to its face, with narrow slanted eyes and a lowered brow and, as a **totem animal**, it is associated with an antisocial character, with grumpiness and solitariness.

Jay

(10 species of corvid, including *C. garrulus*, the British pink or brown jay)
Element: air.
Deities: Bluejay (Cherokee Trickster God), Freyja, Inanna, Odr.

Where it occurs, the jay is one of the more colourful species of birds, notably the pink jay seen in Europe and Asia and the gorgeous blue jay of the USA. It is also known for its vocalisation, as the British jay's genus name *garrulus* suggests. In fact, in old American slang, a "jay" meant a chatterbox. As well as their cawing alarm call, jays make a number of clucking, whistling and other sounds.

Seeing a jay in **dreams and visions** could be a warning to keep your own counsel instead of chattering away and revealing all your secrets – and those of other people. It may speak of a person with a rather silly character, someone who thinks a lot of their appearance and does not stop to think before they speak. With the often astonishing cleverness of the dreaming mind, it could even mean a person you know whose name begins with a J.

As a **totem animal**, the jay brings the power of persuasive speech, but also an inability to keep secrets or sometimes to speak wisely without offending others. Jay people are also full of mischief and fun.

Jellyfish

(*Medusazoa spp*)
Element: water.
Deities: Ebisu, Medusa, Ryujin.

These animals have not had a very good press. Most people see them only as frightening sea creatures that can inflict painful and dangerous stings or as the sad little gelatinous puddles sometimes found on the beach, from which children have to be steered away. Yet in their natural habitat they can be astonishingly beautiful, both in colour (some are also bioluminescent) and the grace with which they swim, and they are also a great deal older than many other species on Earth or in the oceans, at least 500 million years. They range in size from the 120ft lion's mane jelly (*Cyanea capillata*), the villain in one Sherlock Holmes story, to tiny jellies less than a millimetre across, and they are found in all oceans and some species are found in fresh water. Jellyfish blooms are also observed, when huge numbers of these animals congregate together for various environmental and behavioural reasons: they can be pretty spectacular, as various videos on YouTube will demonstrate.

In **dreams and visions**, the jellyfish may be telling you to grow a backbone, as its name has been used as an insult for a cowardly or indecisive person, or it could be telling of a hidden danger, or of someone who is more dangerous than they appear.

As a **totem animal**, it brings strength, flexibility and a sense of purpose and confidence in your own abilities.

Jerboa
(*Dipodidae spp*)
Element: fire.
Deity: Set.
These are tiny little kangaroo-like rodents with enormous ears, like something from a cheese-and-pickle dream! Living in dry sandy environments, such as deserts, they share many qualities with the kangaroo rat. Their leaping gait enables them to move at up to 15mph. See **Kangaroo Rat** for details of their meaning.

Junglefowl
(*Gallus spp*)
Element: earth.
Deities: as the chicken, with the addition of Athene/Minerva.
These colourful birds are the ancestors of our modern chickens, as a look at the male of the species will soon tell you.

Seeing them in a **dream or vision** or having them as a **totem animal** will have much the same meaning, although with added layers about independence and freedom, which the chicken does not have.

Kakapo
(*Strigops habroptilus*)
Element: earth.
Deities: Athena/Minerva, Meenakshi.
This is a parrot, but very different from other kinds; it is quiet, relatively plainly coloured and lives on the ground. It is a heavy bird, at around 3kg, and cannot fly. Where other parrots chirp and whistle and can be taught to mimic human speech, the kakapo does none of these things but makes a booming noise in the mating season and a breathy chuckle at other times. There is an urban myth that parrots live to a great age; the kakapo actually does, and has been known to reach ages in excess of a century. However, since European colonisation of New Zealand, this gentle and interesting bird has become critically endangered.

Seeing a kakapo in **dreams and visions** speaks of someone extremely shy, who perhaps only goes out at night because they are too afraid to venture out by day.

As a **totem animal**, it brings wisdom and insight and the ability to use tact in all situations.

Kangaroo

(*Macropodidae spp*)

Element: air.

Deities: none identified.

The kangaroo is such a symbol of Australia that its name is sometimes used as an adjective instead of the word "Australian", and it appears as a supporter on the country's coat of arms and as the logo of its national airline, Qantas. This amazing animal is well-known all over the world for its odd method of locomotion, its "boxing", its pouch and its super-efficient way of reproducing. Unlike many other animals, it has settled down well side by side with humans and its numbers do not seem to have been adversely affected, despite traffic accidents and its being hunted for its meat, which is also exported (it is very much like beef, but less fatty).

Four species are commonly called kangaroos (though, technically, wallabies and wallaroos are just smaller kangaroos): the red, the eastern grey, the western grey, and the antilopine. The red kangaroo is the largest of these, but they are all powerful, potentially dangerous animals – in 2022 an elderly man was killed by a western grey he had kept as a pet.

An urban myth tells that the word "kangaroo" comes from an Aboriginal term meaning "I don't know" – the response when the pioneer Lt James Cook asked a native for the name of the strange long-legged, leaping creatures he saw when he landed on the continent. Actually, the name "kangaroo" seems to have come from the Aboriginal word *gangurru*, which was their word for the animal.

Because the kangaroo is so inextricably bound up with the continent where it lives, this must be considered when looking for its meaning in **dreams and visions**. Do you have family in Australia, or ambitions to emigrate or have a holiday there? These animals have plenty of other meanings too, including the desire for parenthood, swift progress in your career, taking revenge on someone who has wronged you and the possibility of travel.

As a **totem animal**, it brings good fortune, happiness, adventure and good health, and the ability to protect yourself and your family.

Kangaroo Rat

(*Dipodomys spp*)

Element: air.

Deities: none identified, though it has been a sacred animal for some Native American tribes.

These cute little beasts hop along on their long hind legs just like kangaroos but are quite unrelated: they are rodents, while kangaroos are marsupials. Found across North America, they are nocturnal and shy, retiring to burrows during the day, which they close with a "door" of earth to keep cool. Despite their small size (35cms or less, with the tail being longer than the body), they are capable of leaping more than two metres!

Seeing a kangaroo rat in **dreams and visions** is a reminder that you should slow down a little, take thought and not rush into things. It can also speak of romantic love and hope.

As a **totem animal,** it brings resourcefulness, agility and the ability to manage your life with ease.

Kestrel: see Falcon.

Killer Whale: see Orca.

Kingfisher
(*Alcedinidae spp*)
Element: air and water.
Deities: Alcyone. They have been considered sacred in many cultures.
British people's thoughts will instantly turn to the blue-and-gold jewel that is found along streams in the UK, but kingfisher species are found in many countries and can be any colour, though they tend to be always very colourful. Small birds with large beaks for stabbing fish, they have a characteristically shaped head which is found in all species, though not all live exclusively on fish. The term "halcyon days" originates from the Greek story of Alcyone and Ceyx (who were turned into birds but granted good weather on certain days of the year) but has come to mean any prosperous or happy time in the past.

The kingfisher was said to lay its eggs on a nest built on a raft which floated on the water, but in fact these birds generally nest in holes, often unlined, though they soon become filled with bones, faeces and the bone-filled pellets the adults regurgitate after eating.

Seeing a kingfisher in **dreams and visions** speaks of hope of better times, of a let-up in misfortune, hard work or other challenging conditions, and also of coming prosperity and domestic happiness.

As a **totem animal**, it brings many abilities, including focusing on what matters and following your goals without being diverted. It brings marital happiness and good parenting skills.

Kinkajou
(*Potos flavus*)
Element: earth.
Deities: none identified.
This obscure little beast is shy, nocturnal and confined to the depths of the South American rainforests where it lives on fruit, yet its name is quite well known, in part because it has been the subject of several poems for children. Sometimes called the honey bear (though it is not a bear) or the night ape (though it is not an ape), the kinkajou is distantly related to coatis and raccoons. Attractive, with its large eyes, mouse-like face and gentle nature, the kinkajou is sometimes kept as a pet, though its nocturnal habit makes it rather unsuitable for this.

Seeing a kinkajou in **dreams and visions** is about walking into the unknown and having confidence (even though you do not know what is to come), of taking a leap in the dark or a leap of faith. It also speaks of gentleness and the need for this in your daily life, or with someone in particular.

As a **totem animal**, it brings gentleness, intelligence, calm and contentment.

Kiwi

(*Apteryx spp*)
Element: earth.
Deities: Tāne Mahuta.
Like the kangaroo, the kiwi has become a symbol, a brand, of the country in which it lives, and New Zealanders will proudly refer to themselves as "kiwis". The five species all look very similar: plain brown flightless birds with no tail (which gives them a chick-like shape) and a long slender bill. They do possess wings, but these are vestigial and concealed under their feathers. The name kiwi is said to come from their plaintive cry.

Kiwis pair for life and invest a lot in their offspring. The egg may weigh up to a quarter of the weight of the hen, one of the largest eggs in nature. While the kiwi is about the same size as a chicken, her egg is six times the size of a chicken egg. The poor hen will actually starve for the last few days before she lays, as there is not room in her body for any food! The cock bird will sit on the eggs (as the mother may be too exhausted!) and both parents then take care of the single chick.

The kiwi is easily recognised, partly because it has appeared as a brand mark. In the UK and America, Kiwi shoe polish was once found in every home. A giant kiwi carved into the chalk, like the white horses, looks down on the village of Bulford on Salisbury Plain in England. Like the nearby "Fovant Badges", it is a memorial for troops who fought in World War I, and for many years was maintained by the Kiwi Polish company.

In **dreams and visions**, seeing a kiwi is a good sign, indicating that your life will expand in some direction, probably creativity or prosperity. Bear in mind that the bird may also speak of the country of New Zealand (because that is how our subconscious minds work) and if you have relatives or friends living there, a visit may be on the cards.

As a **totem animal**, it is all about loyalty, both family loyalty and patriotism. Kiwi people invest much in their home and family and make ideal parents.

Komodo Dragon

(*Varanus komodoensis*)
Element: fire.
Deities: Fafnir, Fuxi, Hecate, Jörmungandr, Tiamat.
The Roman Emperor Tiberius is said to have had one of these scary beasties in his private zoo, and it is the closest thing to a dragon now found on Earth.

It is a giant monitor lizard – and the largest lizard alive today – growing to three metres long. The huge jaws lined with pointed teeth enable it to tear apart large prey and carrion, and it is extremely dangerous to humans as well. It is said that its bite is as deadly as a snake's, because of the bacteria in its mouth which will deliver sepsis through even a small wound, and some scientists have speculated that it may actually produce a mild venom. This endangered animal is found in Indonesia, on only three islands.

Komodo dragons may pair for life – very unusual in reptiles – though they have also been known to reproduce parthenogenetically, that is, a female will lay fertile eggs without having mated – as many insects are able to do. The offspring would then be clones of the mother. Like some crocodiles, adult dragons may eat young ones, which may form up to 10% of their diet!

In **dreams and visions**, the animal has a similar meaning to the mythic dragon, symbolising a deadly challenge, something or someone you are very afraid of but must face and hopefully overcome (although, unlike the dragons of legends, they are not connected with treasure).

As a **totem animal**, it brings huge courage and fierceness, with much wisdom.

Kookaburra

(*Dacelo spp*)
Element: air.
Deities: Eris, Loki, all trickster deities.
This bird is a member of the kingfisher family, yet it does not fish and has relatively plain plumage. It is best known for its laughing call, which has been recorded and reproduced in many movies and at animal-themed attractions. The laugh has a traditional meaning in Australia, where the bird lives: if it lands nearby and laughs at a woman or outside her house, she may be pregnant! The kookaburra is also well-known as a cheeky opportunistic bird that will swoop down and steal meat from a barbecue or picnic!

If you are aware of the kookaburra story, seeing (or hearing) it in **dreams and visions** may be a sign that you think you or your partner may be pregnant, or wish that you were. Whether or not a new family member is in the offing, the bird indicates that you should be merry, laugh, forget your worries and party (without alcohol, possibly!).

As a **totem animal**, it brings these merry trickster qualities, with a light-hearted approach to life which may verge on the mocking, but is never angry or negative.

Krill

(*Euphausiacea spp*)
Element: water.
Deities: none identified.
Krill may seem insignificant, but these are mighty little creatures which live in all the oceans and, without them, few other animals could exist. They are near the bottom of the food chain, tiny shrimp-like organisms which form

the greater part of the diet of mighty baleen whales and other animals. Living on plankton, they are themselves tiny as individuals, yet *en masse* they form millions of tons of protein, constantly replenished by reproduction every year. Humans also partake in this harvest: in some countries, the krill are eaten, otherwise they are used as fishing bait, as food for pets and in the drug industry – krill oil has proved even better than glucosamine and chondroitin at keeping joints healthy and fighting arthritis.

In **dreams and visions**, they speak of health and nourishment: we all instinctively know that seafood and seafood-derived supplements are good for us.

For **totem animal**, see prawn and shrimp.

Kudu: see Antelope.

Ladybird/Ladybug
(*Coccinellidae spp*)
Element: fire.
Deity: Freyja.
In Britain, this pretty beetle is called a ladybird, and children all learn the little rhyme, *"Ladybird, ladybird, fly away home ..."* in the nursery. In the US, the insect is called a ladybug. In both cases, the name refers to a small, round scarlet beetle with black spots, though the family worldwide includes yellow and brown beetles as well, some with stripes instead of spots, and in some species the markings are reversed, with black wing cases and coloured spots. The markings are the beetle's warning to would-be predators that they do not taste nice! Their bodies do indeed contain alkaloid toxins, and children are taught to wash their hands if they touch one.

A symbol of nature and beauty, the ladybird is the brand for a range of children's books. Gardeners also love the ladybird; a predator, it helps keep down garden pests like aphids. Its name may derive from its association with the Norse Goddess Freyja (whose name means "Lady"), and later from the Virgin Mary.

It is lucky to see the ladybird in **dreams and visions**, as it speaks of joy, happiness and freedom, also coming excitement over some happy prospect such as a holiday or a party.

As a **totem animal**, it brings many positive qualities such as kindness, community spirit, boldness and consideration and respect for others.

Lamprey
(*Petromyzontiformes spp*)
Element: water.
Deities: Echidna, Hina/Sina, Scylla, the Morrigan.
One British monarch, Henry I, famously died from "a surfeit of lampreys" in the twelfth century, so popular were these creatures on the banqueting table, and they are still eaten in some countries today. Ugh. They are not

eels, but ancient jawless fish dating back in the fossil record to the early Carboniferous Period, though they may be even older, as their boneless bodies would not easily form fossils. In place of a jawed mouth, they have a kind of toothy sucker, by which they attach themselves to their prey, rasping and sucking away blood and fluids. Yet some lampreys are vegetarians, using their unique mouths to feed on algae. When not attached to a fish or other creature, lampreys are fine swimmers, and they are found in oceans and fresh water across the world.

Though these creatures may look a little like hagfish, they are not related and do not share divinatory meanings or energies.

To see a lamprey in **dreams and visions** speaks of feelings that are troubling you, which you cannot overcome or even explain. If the fish clings on to you, it will be hard to rid yourself of these feelings, but if it is not attached then it signifies that better times are coming.

As a **totem animal**, the lamprey gives an ability to move through life without problems, attracting to you friends and protectors who will make life easy for you and shield you from annoyances. These people can be selfish and ruthless.

Leech
(*Hirudinea spp*)
Element: water.
Deities: Ebisu, Gula and all gods of healing and medicine.
These charmless creatures have long been associated with medicine and healing, and this correspondence remains, even now that we have advanced drugs and micro-surgery. Related to worms, including the common garden variety, they are typically black, with a powerfully muscular body that can elongate or contract. Many people who have waded through marshes or in lakes and ponds will have had the chilling experience of finding one or more of these small black creatures attached to them by their sucker-like mouths, and they will also attack livestock that venture into these wet areas. The attached leech can be observed to swell and grow as it takes in blood from its host, and this was the quality that made it important to historical practitioners of healing as the medicinal leech. The ancient system of the "four humours", recorded by Empedocles and Alcmaeon in the fifth century BC, supposed that an imbalance of humours caused illness. The leech was employed for an excess of the sanguine humour (blood). So strong was this connection that an Old English word for leech was used for the medic himself. Leeches are still in use in medicine today: an anticoagulant called hirudin is manufactured from their secretions.

Not all leeches are bloodsuckers; some are predators which attack invertebrates, such as slugs and snails, but it is the parasitic leech that most people know and this is the type most likely to appear in dreams.

In **dreams and visions**, it speaks of a person or a situation that is preying on you, exhausting you, draining you, whether this is a shortage of money or a stalker or a job that demands every last ounce of your strength, and this has to change or you will be so depleted you may become ill. The word "leech" is even used as a term of abuse to a person accused of preying on others or taking advantage of them. If the feeling of the dream is markedly good, then the leech may have a better meaning – speaking of healing or steps taken to improve your health.

As a **totem animal**, the leech is much more positive, bringing caring, healing qualities, though also the tendency to lean too much on people or to attach oneself in an unhealthy way to someone.

Lemming

(*Arvicolinae spp*)

Element: earth.

Deities: none identified.

This small mammal has become a byword for self-destructive stupidity, yet its legendary mass suicides are entirely the result of normal animal migration which drives these rodents to look for pastures new as a result of overpopulation or other factors. When the lemmings reach a river or other body of water, they plunge in to cross it but many do die by drowning along the way, which gave rise to the belief that they deliberately killed themselves. In older beliefs, people thought lemmings fell from the sky: in common with other rodent species, their populations can suddenly balloon, which is what drives the migration instinct.

In **dreams and visions**, lemmings speak to the sense of self-trust, reminding you to trust your own instincts, rather than those of others, about which you may be uneasy deep down. When your decision is your own, you will feel ready to take that step, that leap.

As a **totem animal**, the lemming brings independence – strangely at odds with its popular image – and the ability to see through the self-serving suggestions of others, and courage in the face of the unknown.

Lemur

(*Lemuroidea spp*)

Element: air.

Deities: none identified. It is protected by the system of taboos in Madagascar.

These quaint beasts derive their name from the Roman word for a family's ghosts – and they certainly are shy, have big luminous eyes, are seen only at night and have spooky cries. Far from being spirits, lemurs are primates, one of the families within the group that includes monkeys, apes, and...us. They are found only on the island of Madagascar, and range from the tiny 30g mouse lemur to the dog-sized indri, but much larger species (now extinct) were found on the island in the past. This family includes the iconic ring-tailed lemurs so beloved of wildlife photographers.

In **dreams and visions**, seeing a lemur or lemurs speaks of having the blessings of your family, including those no longer alive. It may be a warning that someone does not wish you well and is working against you, and it is important to see through this person and take steps to turn aside their malice.

As a **totem animal**, it brings a happy, playful vibe, with a connectedness to family.

Leopard
(*Panthera pardis*)
Element: fire.
Deities: Agassou, Diana, Dionysus, Seshat, Waghoba.
Leopards are not the largest of the cat family, and share their territories with lions in Africa and tigers in Asia – both of which will not only steal a leopard's dinner, but even make a meal of the leopard itself. They get around the former problem by carrying their kill up into the branches of a tree, where the heavier cats cannot get at them. Leopards are savage, for their size, and have been known to kill humans, sometimes in large numbers: the Panar leopard, shot in 1910, was a man-eater estimated to have killed 400 people.

In Kipling's charming story, *How the Leopard got his Spots*, the animal starts out with a plain yellow-brown coat, but acquires his spots as camouflage to help him hunt. The expression "the leopard never changes its spots" does not originate with this story, however, but comes from a verse in Jeremiah in the Old Testament.

Leopards have been sacred in some cultures, and in Ancient Egypt the priesthood wore leopard skins over their shoulders to denote their status. Leopard and tiger skins are still worn today by bass drummers in army bands: they were worn originally to protect their uniforms from the rubbing of the heavy instrument but have become traditional.

A leopard is a symbol of power in **dreams and visions**, and how you interact with it will give the relevance of this power to you. If the leopard is friendly and accompanies you, it speaks of power becoming yours, or of acquiring powerful friends. If you kill or chase away the animal, that means you will overcome a hostile power that has beset you. A black panther has additional meanings, some of which may come from its most famous literary representative, Bagheera in Kipling's *The Jungle Book*. In this case, the animal speaks of a mentor, someone who will help you understand yourself and your circumstances.

As a **totem animal**, it gives power, courage, confidence and strength, as will any big cat as totem.

Leopard Cat
(*Prionailurus bengalensis*)
Element: fire.
Deities: none specifically identified, but all cat and leopard deities.
This pretty Asian cat, the only wild cat native to Japan and the Philippines, is the ancestor of our domestic Bengal, a pet cat breed produced by crossing the leopard cat with the domestic cat. The leopard cat gave its beautiful coat

to the offspring: a confection of spots and stripes in golds, browns, greys and black. Their coats vary remarkably and it is said that no two cats look alike. Sadly, the cat is hunted for its beautiful fur and also because it may attack domestic poultry, but it is not considered endangered – although its numbers have declined.

In **dreams and visions**, this cat has many of the meanings of a leopard and of a domestic cat.

As a **totem animal or power animal**, it is also very similar, but brings mischief and playfulness as well.

Lion

(*Panthera leo*)
Element: fire.
Deities: Cybele, Durga, Herakles, Lakshmi, Parvati, Rereti, Sekhmet, Tanit.
Was there ever a more iconic animal? Without the lion, so many company logos and heraldic devices would be blank. Its beauty, size and ferocity have made this big cat a symbol of royalty, power and even divinity across the globe.

Lions are the second largest of the cat family, after the tiger. Handsome, powerful animals with golden fur and in the males regal manes around their heads and necks, they live in family groups appropriately called *prides*, and are native to Africa, though a subspecies, the Asiatic lion, survives in the Gir National Park and in some areas around it, in the Indian state of Gujarat. The Asiatic lion, once found across Asia and the Middle East, is a little smaller, with a smaller mane which shows the male's ears, and its colours vary from the tawny-gold of African lions to greyish and darker brown hues. Lion cubs have spots, particularly on their lower bodies, which may help camouflage them when they are small and vulnerable.

Despite its noble appearance, the lion's behaviour is not always admirable. Male lions joining a pride (perhaps because they have driven away the original pride leader) will kill the cubs of the pride, because their mothers will not come into heat while they have them. Lions eat larger prey, such as antelopes, wildebeest and zebra, hunting in groups with some lions driving the prey towards an ambushing lion, but the greater part of the animal's diet is now believed to be carrion, and lions are known to steal kills from hyenas and other predators.

The lion has been a symbol of kingship in many cultures, particularly in Britain, where it is common on heraldic shields and appears several times on the nation's coat of arms, as a device (the Scottish lion and the "leopards" of Anjou – actually lions, as a lion *passant regardant* is known as a leopard in heraldic terminology) and as a supporter opposite the unicorn. It is also well represented in literature and art, and embodies the astrological sign of Leo, which speaks of majesty, power, courage, generosity and ability.

Such a prestigious animal is bound to have a great deal of meaning in **dreams and visions** – and so it does. Dreaming of a lion speaks of glory, triumph, power, courage and confidence, or it could signify coming up against someone fierce and relentless if you dream of being chased or attacked by lions. It can also warn of the danger of anger and harbouring hatred for your enemies.

As a **totem animal**, it confers all these qualities, with some gifts associated with the classical god Apollo: of art, music, inspiration, beauty, dignity and even healing.

Lizard
(*Squamata spp*)
Elements: earth and fire.
Deities: Abas, Adnoartina, Atum, Gauri/Parvati.
Lizards are an enormous group that includes big animals like the marine iguanas, monitors and the Komodo dragon, but most people will think of the small gecko-like lizards to be found sunning themselves on stone walls on a warm day, long-tailed, flexible and often green. Actually, they come in many shapes and sizes and in a range of colours, some very beautiful and multi-coloured (the chameleon is a lizard), some large, some small and some with adaptations such as having no legs (the slow worm, although technically all snakes are legless lizards), scaly crests or even the ability to fly or glide, like the "dragons" of the genus *Draco*. Some lizards employ poison to keep away predators, others can lose their tails to effect an escape, and then regrow them. Although they are roughly the same shape as newts, lizards are not related, nor are they slimy: typically they have dry scaly skins.

In **dreams and visions**, lizards are another creature that speaks of transformation and moving on because, like many reptiles, they shed their skins as they grow. Yet dreaming of a lizard can also speak of approaching danger, so the transition may not be easy or comfortable. Dreaming of a flying lizard signifies a change in location, or a change in basic beliefs and spiritual goals.

As a **totem animal**, lizards bring the ability to react and adapt quickly to new situations, to move on and reinvent themselves if changes come, whether these are good or bad.

Llama
(*Lama glama*)
Element: earth.
Deities: Apu Illapu, Pachamama, Urcuchillay.
This woolly member of the camel family has been used as a pack animal and also kept for its meat, wool and hides since the Palaeolithic times in South America, and is now becoming popular in Europe and is commonly to be found being farmed or kept as a pet in the UK. Though it is a camelid, the llama looks more like a sheep with a long neck, and it gets on very well with sheep. Llama lovers report that a llama will happily join the sheep and behave like one of the herd – but will show its fiercer nature if the sheep are threatened, perhaps by a dog, and it has been used as a guard animal in the US to keep coyotes and other predators away from the flock.

Also popular is the alpaca (*Lama pacos*), a mini llama that is closely related and can interbreed with llamas. Their appearance and behaviour is very similar to that of their near cousins.

Llamas and alpacas are friendly, sociable animals, and although they have the camel's trick of spitting, this is rarely used against humans. In recent years, they have even been used as therapy animals in hospitals and hospices, in the same way that dogs and cats are.

The pack-horse of the Americas, the llama speaks of a journey of some length when it appears in **dreams and visions**, of committing to change and to travel, though this might be spiritual progress rather than actual movement across the Earth. It speaks of hope and faith in your future, and of the strength to continue. The alpaca shares much of these meanings and also signifies gentleness.

As **totem animals,** both these creatures bring good fortune and a natural ability to fit in within a community and to work at one's best level for that community. Some South American peoples see black or white llamas as bad luck (they come in a range of colours), but generally speaking the llama and the alpaca speak of good fortune.

Lobster

(*Homaridae spp*)
Element: water.
Deities: the Ikhthyokentauroi, Kiwa, Oceanus, Pontus, Triton.
This large and handsome crustacean is associated with fine dining in many people's minds, yet there is a great deal of mythology and folk belief associated with it. It has connections to the zodiac signs Cancer and Scorpio.

Lobsters are generally caught in lobster pots: large woven baskets that have their entrances constructed so that it is easy for the animal to enter but much harder to get out. The methods used for cooking a lobster often involve plunging the live animal into boiling water, although this is illegal in some countries. Some chefs will bring the live animal slowly to the boil in the belief that the creature will "go to sleep" before it dies, and some will put it in a freezer for a short while by way of anaesthetising it, but it remains an ethical problem. The lobster is initially a blue-green colour but, like prawns and shrimps, turns reddish pink when cooked. Their rich flavour is due to their omnivorous diet.

Lobsters were associated with many sea deities and were believed to live forever (they are in fact very long-lived, achieving up to 50 years, going by size and other factors). Mediaeval sailors believed in lobster monsters that would seize seamen in their giant claws and drag them down into the depths to be eaten.

A lobster showing up in **dreams and visions** speaks of strength, and especially of showing strength in a difficult and threatening situation. Lobsters can regrow lost body parts such as claws and legs, so they also speak of regeneration. A lobster seen in a negative dream may speak of bad emotions surfacing.

As a **totem animal**, it gives strength and self-belief, and the tendency to grip onto things it wants and never let go. Lobster people can be remote and implacable – unless you find a way to tap into their warmer emotional side.

Locust: see **Grasshopper.**

Lungfish
(*Dipnoi spp*)
Elements: air and water.
Deities: Amphitrite, Eri, Yemaya.
These living fossils mark the first attempts by animals to move from the seas and onto dry land; their ancestors were the first fish to do this, and the six remaining species alive today in South America, Africa and Australia still have the ability to move on land and breathe air. The modern lungfish is confined to freshwater, and some of them can survive the drying out of their environment by burrowing into the mud to stay safe and damp until the water returns. They eat small fish, amphibians and invertebrates, with any fruit that might drop into their environment as dessert. A four-foot (1.2 metre) specimen living in a tank at the California Academy of Sciences is known to be 90 years old!

In **dreams and visions**, lungfish are about ancient abilities and strengths that have been passed down in your family, in your DNA, when you perhaps had no idea you possessed these qualities.

As a **totem animal**, it gives the ability to move between worlds, whether this means fitting in well with different social or cultural classes or adapting to different ways of life.

Lynx
(*Lynx spp*)
Element: fire.
Deities: Dionysys, Freyja, Lleu Llaw Gyffes/Lugh, Mafdet, Mishipeshu.
Four species of this beautiful cat are alive today in North America, Asia and Europe – and in the sky, where it is represented by the constellation Lynx. The types are the Canada lynx, the Eurasian, the Iberian and the bobcat. They are easily recognised by their short tails (which look as though the cat has lost half the appendage in an accident) and their tufted ears. They also have ruffs around their necks which, in some cases, can form a distinct beard. They are long-legged, with large-padded paws and thick fur which, in the case of the Canadian lynx, is very thick and shaggy indeed to cope with hard winters in Canada and Alaska. Lynx are extinct in the UK, but there are suggestions they should be repopulated here, as they have been in Croatia, Germany, Slovenia and Switzerland.

The lynx speaks of feminine power, and its appearance in **dreams and visions** may refer to a woman you know who is an authority figure, or powerful in some way. The lynx in dreams is said to speak of secrets and the need for secrecy, but its connection with Sun deities like Lugh and Mafdet seems to signify that secrets would be uncovered and exposed to the light of day.

As a **totem animal**, it gives power, protection, confidence and self-reliance, especially to women.

Lyrebird
(*Menura spp*)
Element: air.
Deities: Angus, Apollo, Bragi, Bride, Canens, Hat-Hor, the Muses (especially Euterpe), Oshun, Saraswati.

The two species of lyrebird are ground-dwelling Australian birds with striking tail feathers and a gift for music. The Albert's lyrebird is smaller and does not have such a striking tail as the superb lyrebird, but both have an impressive range of songs and sounds like clicks, whistles and tweets, and can mimic natural sounds from their environment as well as artificial sounds such as telephone ringtones, machinery and even music and human speech. They are even alleged to be able to reproduce computer game sounds! The bird's appearance is quite well-known due to its appearance on coins, stamps and as company logos.

A lyrebird in **dreams and visions** is about the voice, whether that is your own struggle to find your voice and speak your truth, or that of another who needs to be coaxed into expressing themselves, or a reminder to you to listen when others speak. Speak truly, says the bird, speak from the heart but bear in mind that others have truths to speak, and theirs may differ from your own.

As a **totem animal**, the lyrebird is still connected with speech and music, giving inspiration and the gift of peace-making and of enabling others to speak together without resorting to quarrels or shouting.

Macaque
(*Macaca spp*)
Element: air.
Deities: Hanuman, Sarugami, Sun-Wukong.

The macaques are a huge family of monkeys which have managed to be both a curse and a blessing to the human race. They carry diseases which are dangerous to humans, including the Herpes B virus, and have become an invasive nuisance in some areas, even in towns, where they steal food and have been known to attack humans. On the other hand, they are valued as pets and their genus includes the rhesus monkey, which has been used in the laboratory to help develop vaccines for polio, rabies and the HIV virus – and also in the space programme.

There are around nine species of macaques across Asia and North Africa, including the spectacular lion-tailed macaque and the famous Barbary apes of the Rock of Gibraltar (the macaque is actually a monkey, not an ape).

In **dreams and visions**, macaques share a lot of meaning in common with other monkeys: they are about fun and mischief and friends and family, about playing and teasing, though not in a nasty way, and about your social life generally. Seeing the Barbary apes of the Rock of Gibraltar might have the meaning of travel for you, or a holiday, depending on what you associate with this place.

As **totem animals**, they bring sunshine into your life, with fun and frivolity: macaque people are party animals and love to socialise and have fun, go on holidays and help friends celebrate special occasions.

Macaw: see **Parrot.**

Magpie
(*Pica pica*)
Element: air.
Deities: Bacchus/Dionysus, Skadi.
Magpies have been the subject of folklore and superstitions the world over for centuries, perhaps because their plumage marks them out as special – not many birds are black and white. The Eurasian magpie, which is found in the UK, is black and white with blue flashes on the wings, but other species in the order may be all black, scarlet, blue or green, or a combination of colours, and other unrelated species are also called magpies. My thought is, if you call it a magpie, then it is, for the purpose of your vision or work.

Highly intelligent members of the crow family, they are known for being able to mimic human speech and other sounds, and for thieving. Magpies cannot resist bright shiny objects, and many a rural woman has come to grief by leaving a piece of jewellery on a windowsill with the window open. Its Latin name, *pica*, suggests it may eat the things it steals, but it was long believed that they used the bling to attract a mate. Recent research suggests they are not attracted to shiny objects, and may even be afraid of them! What they eat is a lot less glamorous: carrion, especially roadkill (they are a common sight on the side of roads picking at a crushed rabbit or mouse), small birds and mammals and insects.

They are considered good luck in many countries, but sometimes the luck is dependent on other factors, especially how many magpies you see: *"One for sorrow, two for joy..."* goes the old English rhyme. The bird has also been associated with death (perhaps because of its carrion-eating lifestyle) and with witchcraft and the Devil.

The meaning of seeing one in **dreams and visions** is quite dependent on how you see the bird. If the old rhyme quoted above (Google it for the full version) means anything to you, count the number of birds you see. To some people, especially pagans, the magpie is a messenger, alerting you to some news to come from the gods: I always look for a rune or other sign if I see one while I am out. Others believe dreaming of them means a scandal is brewing in your community, or some problem such as a serious quarrel in your family.

As a **totem animal**, the magpie brings wisdom, intelligence, intuition and resourcefulness. Magpie people are sociable, gregarious and not afraid of taking risks – but they usually seem to come out on top.

Manatee: see **Sea Cow.**

Mandrill
(*Mandrillus sphinx*)
Element: earth.
Deities: Babi, Haapi, Hanuman, Sun Wukong, Thoth.
Peacocks are not the only creatures to attract mates with colourful displays. The African mandrill is a monkey (in fact, the largest monkey of all) but still one of the most colourful animals on Earth. The male has blue and red plates on his face, areas of blue, purple, pink and red on his rump and brightly coloured genitals, all of which he uses to impress the female, who is attracted to the most brightly coloured male. Although the female is smaller and drabber, she is most certainly in charge: mandrill hordes are led by females and if the males misbehave, they will be shown the highway!

In **dreams and visions**, mandrills speak of your behaviour in the community, particularly self-control and being careful not to offend others or step beyond the bounds of what is acceptable in disputes. Mandrill males do not fight, as their long canine teeth could cause serious injury; they confine themselves to face-pulling and threatening noises.

As a **totem animal**, they bring restraint and the ability to fit into a community without disruption or strife, and self-understanding.

Marlin
(*Istiophoridae spp*)
Element: water.
Deities: all sea deities.
These magnificent fish are among the largest of the bony fishes, and both the blue and the black marlin can reach five metres in length. Although they look very much like the swordfish, they are not related. Unless they are sea fishers, most people might know of this animal primarily through stories like Hemingway's *The Old Man and the Sea*.

Fish generally have to do with the emotions when they appear in **dreams and visions**, but a large fish can signify a gain, either of assets or monetary, or at least a piece of very good luck. Keep the feeling of the dream in mind as you assess its content: if the fish appears to bring happiness then this may well be what it signifies. If it evokes other feelings, keep these in mind as you look for its meaning.

As a **totem animal**, it gives power, confidence, skill and the ability to be alone without feeling alone.

Markhor: see **Goat.**

Marmoset: see **Monkey.**

Marmot
(*Marmota spp*)
Element: earth.
Deities: Yuki-Onna. All deities of early spring.
The marmots are a large family of rodents which includes woodchucks, groundhogs and other ground squirrels across the world. Generally stubby and short-legged, they live in burrows and do not much resemble tree squirrels. Highly social animals, they live exclusively on vegetable matter and communicate with one another through whistles. They are champion hibernators, spending over half their lives curled up underground waiting for the spring. In the US and Canada, a folk custom revolves around watching the first groundhog emerge from hibernation at the beginning of February. If the animal sees its own shadow, it is said it will retire back to its burrow and spring will be postponed for another six weeks. Since the 1993 film, *Groundhog Day*, starring Bill Murray, the term has also come to refer to the nightmare of living the same day over and over again.

Seeing a marmot in **dreams and visions** can refer to the family estate, as in money being kept in trust for a relative not yet of age to inherit, or the protection of a young relative who has perhaps been orphaned or needs help in some other way. Some sources state that the marmot speaks of honey-traps: of being lured into danger by an attractive person who is actually an enemy. Seeing a groundhog may hint that you have been sweeping a problem under the carpet, but that it is now time to face it and its consequences.

As a **totem animal**, the marmot brings the ability to use one's strength and energy wisely, to know when it is time to act and when it is time to rest and do nothing.

Martin: see **Swallow.**

Mayfly
(*Ephemeroptera spp*)
Element: air.
Deities: Aion, Chronos, Janus, Myiagros.
This creature is the embodiment of ephemerality, famously living for only a day or so after emerging from its larval stage. These creatures may all emerge on the same day, in huge numbers, mate, lay their eggs and then die. Fishermen have used this lifecycle to their advantage, making artificial flies that mimic the appearance of the mayflies, which are then flicked across the surface of the river in *casts*, with the aim of luring to the hook fish that mistake the artificial flies for the real thing.

But while the fly may live only for a day – or in some cases for minutes – the creature has already enjoyed a much longer life in the water as a *nymph*, a life cycle stage that can last for months or even years.

It seems pretty obvious that if you **dream** of a mayfly, your subconscious is telling you to *carpe diem*, seize the day, for life or time is short. Yet the mayfly, in common with other insects including butterflies, speaks also of transformation and new beginnings. Have you been a child too long? Is it time you stepped into your power and took responsibility for things you have long left to others?

This is the meaning that comes through in the fly as a **totem animal**, bringing the ability to transform, to *grow up* and become the person you were truly meant to be.

Mealybug: see **Aphid**, which has the same meaning.

Meerkat

(*Suricata suricatta*)
Element: air.
Deities: Atum, Horus, Ikaggen, Mafdet, Ninkilim, Ra, Thoth, Wadjet.
These little animals, members of the mongoose family, have been well known to everyone in the UK since the *comparethemarket* advertising campaign used CGI meerkats with Russian accents, wearing silk dressing gowns and paisley scarfs. In real life, they are engaging beasts with bright, intelligent eyes who often adopt an upright pose to check for danger. In the African wild and in parks, meerkat families use "sentries" who take turns to stand upright, watching for danger while the others feed and play. Like most of the mongoose family, they are gregarious and live in large groups of up to 40 animals.

Seeing a meerkat in **dreams and visions** means needing the support of your family circle, because someone or something is about to attack you, whether that is a person who dislikes you or a piece of bad luck or an illness.

As a **totem animal**, the meerkat brings loyalty, sociability, family values and intelligence, with intuition and forward-thinking. See **Mongoose** for further meanings.

Millipede

(*Diplopoda spp*)
Element: earth.
Deities: Sepa-Osiris.
I seem to remember calling the centipede "the prince of creepy-crawlies", but the millipede goes one better. Not only can it be bigger, but it has two legs on every segment, where a centipede has only one. Yet its habits are much gentler: where the centipede feeds on insects it has poisoned with its venom, the millipede is one of Nature's cleaners, hoovering up rotting vegetation, nor is it venomous (although some species can emit unpleasant fluids in self-defence). There are 62 species in the UK alone, though these are quite small, but in warmer climates some species can be well over 35cms long. Its name means "thousand feet", and some of the larger specimens can have many more than this number.

Seen in **dreams and visions**, millipedes seem to indicate annoyance, at a situation or a person who has been bothering you, but the important thing is that the annoyance is hidden. You do not share your feelings. Like the centipede, it can speak of an obstacle, one that you are afraid or unable to overcome, or of secret fears, doubts or guilt you just cannot share with anyone.

As a **totem animal**, it brings a great ability to adapt and survive, just as the creature itself can survive in difficult conditions.

Mink

(*Neogale* and *Mustela spp*)
Element: air.
Deities: Galinthias and Hecate, Zhaangweshi (totem of a clan).
Best known for its contributions to the fur trade, this animal is a ferocious little predator that, amongst other things, has decimated the UK population of water voles, attacks chicken runs and will swim in your garden pond and eat your fish. Its beauty is undeniable: soft, richly coloured, glossy fur has caused it to be the most popular choice for fur coats, stoles and collars, though it has fallen from favour since the very successful anti-fur campaign mounted by animal rights activists from the 1970s. In 2021, Israel put a total ban on the sale of real fur – the first country in the world to do so. However, mink are still farmed for the fur trade, and it is farm escapes which have led to the mink becoming somewhat of a pest in the UK.

Seen in **dreams and visions**, this animal, because of its historical association with the fashion industry, can symbolise vanity and ostentation, but it could also signify that you feel afraid that you will not be wanted for your true self, but for the glamour and signs of wealth that you have about you.

As a **totem animal**, it brings a strange mixture of predatory fierceness and fun: these are the kind of people who will get you into trouble on a night out, persuading you to knock a copper's helmet off, or worse.

Mole

(*Talpidae spp*)
Element: earth.
Deities: none identified.
"The little gentleman in the black velvet waistcoat" was once the subject of a popular toast by supporters of James II, due to the mole having caused the death of William III, whose horse threw him after stumbling on a molehill. William had taken the English throne from his uncle and father-in-law, James II, whom he deposed. His statue in St James Square, London, shows him mounted, the molehill at his horse's feet.

For such an invisible creature, the mole certainly makes its presence felt. How many gardeners have not fumed after finding the characteristic row of heaps of freshly-turned soil in their pristine lawn or among newly planted vegetables? The mole is classified as a pest in many countries because of the damage it does to crops and gardens, although it also improves soil and eats pests, such as slugs. Perfectly adapted for its lifestyle, it has huge spade-like front paws and fur that will lie in any direction to avoid friction with tunnel walls.

The best-known example in literature is Mole in *The Wind in the Willows*, but the natural animal is very different from Kenneth Graham's shy, good-natured bachelor. Moles avoid one another, and when they do meet they will fight savagely. There is an urban myth that if two moles are left in a bucket overnight, only one will remain in the morning, having completely destroyed and eaten the other.

In **dreams and visions**, the mole has rather unfortunate meanings. It speaks of someone betraying you, of a secret enemy undermining you, of people not trusting you.

People with the mole as **totem animal** lead rich, solitary lives and value their privacy above all else, but they do not do well in social situations.

Mole Cricket
(*Gryllotalpidae spp*)
Element: air.
Deities: Apollo, Saki Yama Hime, Tithonus.
At close quarters this insect looks terrifying, like a cross between a grasshopper and a bulldozer, but they are just large crickets that love to burrow, and they produce an extra loud chirping song. Like their mammalian namesakes, they are anathema to gardeners, because their burrowing activities can disturb newly planted seeds and seedlings and even your lawn, but they are otherwise harmless.

Like ordinary crickets, they are a fortunate creature to see in **dreams and visions**, and they signify solutions to problems, either because you will find a solution yourself where others have failed, or because powerful help is on its way to you.

As a **totem animal**, the mole cricket gives perseverance and the ability to stand your ground and speak your truth.

Mongoose
(*Herpestidae spp*)
Element: air.
Deities: Atum, Horus, Ikaggen, Mafdet, Ninkilim, Ra, Thoth, Wadjet.
The most famous mongoose in literature is the valiant Rikki-Tikki-Tavy in Kipling's children's story, who defeats the evil-meaning cobra pair, Nag and Nagaina, and saves the life of a young boy who has befriended him. There often seems to be something magical, indeed superhero-y about the mongoose. How can a small animal prevail against large and fast-moving venomous snakes? Why doesn't it get bitten and die like almost every other animal that takes on a poisonous serpent? Part of the answer lies in the superfast reflexes and agile body of this relative of the stoat and weasel, and in its very thick fur, but the secret Kipling did not know was that mongooses

(no, the plural is not *mongeese*!) have a natural antivenin in their central nervous systems which gives some protection from the effects of snakebites.

Once called the ichneumon, the mongoose preys on snakes, birds, small animals, insects and invertebrates, and on eggs and carrion. It will kill any snake that comes near its nest (for snakes will eat baby mongooses as well) but it will also kill them for food.

In **dreams and visions**, the mongoose is a very fortunate sign, signifying that your fears and worries are about to be chased away by someone powerful who will have all the answers to your problems, and will even take on people who are bullying you or trying to harm you.

As a **totem animal**, the mongoose gives great power, energy, courage and invulnerability against people who are bent on harming them.

Monitor: see Lizard.

Monkey
(*Simiiformes spp*)
Element: air.
Deities: Babi, Hanuman, Sun Wukong.
These humanlike animals have brought us so much colour and fun over our shared history, including a wealth of verbal expressions like "monkeying around". They are always a popular attraction in zoos and animal parks, and have been kept as pets for much of human history. Sadly, they are also killed and eaten in some parts of the world as "bushmeat". The word "monkey" refers to two large families of animals known as "old world monkeys" and "new world monkeys". Both types belong to the *Simiiformes* but have some differences, including having claws or fingernails, having tails or no tails and the shapes of their noses. New world monkeys, as their name suggests, are found in the Americas.

Monkeys range in size from the tiny marmoset (as small as 3.5oz) to the 37kg male mandrill, and come in a huge array of shapes and sizes. Some have brightly coloured fur and coloured fleshy patches, or manes; some have long prehensile tails while some have none. They have been seen as evil, as spawn of the Devil, possibly due to the Christian preoccupation with sex as sin and the often conspicuous genitals and unselfconscious sexual behaviour of monkeys. The Chinese see them as sharp, clever, naughty and funny, the personality ascribed in the Chinese zodiac to people born in the Year of the Monkey.

Monkeys are a huge family with many different manifestations, and each species will bring its own flavour to the basic meaning monkeys have in **dreams and visions**. Usually they signify fun and jollity, often to do with your friends and family, but if the dream has a darker feel to it then they may signify trouble, trouble-makers and thieves.

As **totem animals**, they give great intelligence, a mercurial personality and a sense of fun and playfulness, but monkey people can also be untrustworthy and disloyal.

Moorhen: see **Coot.**

Moose
(*Alces alces*)
Element: earth.
Deities: Artemis/Diana, Cernunnos, Onhdagwija, Pamola.
This stately animal (known as an elk in Eurasia) is the largest member of the deer family, standing around two metres tall at the shoulder and weighing in at up to a ground-thumping 700kg. Its impressive antlers, which grow only on the male of the species, can be two metres in width.

The sheer size of this animal has inspired the nickname "Moose" for the wrestler and US football player, Quinn Ojinaka (and doubtless others who rely on their physical size and strength in their chosen field), as well as being a cruel epithet for a plain or ungainly woman.

In **dreams and visions**, the moose has a variety of meanings to do with travel, but physical travel is the least of these. The animal speaks of travel in the emotional and spiritual sense, of knowledge and progression and development, and also of learning to learn: learning to listen to others instead of imagining that you know best, particularly to those who are older and wiser. It can mean progression within your career and may indicate a one-off triumph within your professional field.

As a **totem animal**, it brings good fortune and strength, including strength of character, and determination, with ambition and ability in your chosen path.

Mosquito
(*Culicidae spp*)
Element: air.
Deities: Sagawehn, Tithonus.
This huge group of biting insects includes the common gnat, but also insects that can carry deadly diseases like malaria, Dengue and yellow fever. Even when they do not carry a disease, their blood-sucking bite may cause an allergic reaction to the chemicals in their saliva which keep the blood from clotting while they feed. However, not all mosquitoes feed on blood: some are adapted for sucking plant juices or the nectar from aphids and other insects. Their life cycle includes larval stages in water, typically stagnant, and some species in colder countries may actually survive being frozen solid at some times of the year, reviving when the weather warms up in the spring.

A **dream or vision** of a mosquito is telling you what you already suspect, that someone in your life is being a huge nuisance and sapping your strength, wasting your time and annoying you, taking advantage of your kind and easy-going nature. It also reminds you that everything changes and nothing is forever.

As a **totem animal**, the insect gives adaptability and an ease with making your own way in the world.

Moth

(*Lepidoptera spp*)

Element: air.

Deities: Morpheus, Psyche, all deities associated with sleep, dreams, death and rebirth.

There are far more species of moth than butterfly, but as they are generally nocturnal they are only seen when they flit in through the window and crash into a lamp, as they are famously wont to do. Most people are more familiar with their caterpillars, which are found all round the clock right next to those of the butterflies.

Moths make up the larger part of the order *Lepidoptera*, with butterflies being the other part. The easiest way to tell them apart is that almost all butterflies have long, thin antennae with a small knob or ball at the end, while moths have fernlike antennae. Many moths are small, pale, dusty creatures; others can give the butterflies a run for their money in terms of their beauty and size, and their larvae are also frequently impressive far beyond the eventual form of the imago. The hawk moths, which are themselves large and beautifully patterned, have caterpillars up to 10cms in length which often feature a sharp horn on the rear end. The elephant hawk moth caterpillar in particular can give you a start, as it seems to have a large head with staring eyes on one end.

In **dreams and visions**, moths speak of impermanence, of things that "pass in the night" and then vanish, and they can be a warning to keep clear of a situation which is drawing you in but that may be dangerous. Like butterflies, they and their larvae speak of transformation and rebirth. Finally, a moth in a dream may speak of things lying unused, when they should be enjoyed, as in fine clothes that have been put away and are later found to be moth-eaten.

As a **totem animal**, the moth gives beauty and grace and, like the butterfly, the ability to effect changes within oneself and to instinctively understand situations others do not. Moth people are positive and cheerful, but are vulnerable in bad relationships.

Mountain Lion: see Cougar.

Mouse

(*Rodentia spp*, especially *Mus musculus*)

Element: earth.

Deities: Apollo, Cernunnos, Horus, Karni Mata, Ninkilim, Ratatoskr.

Mouse: the very word brings all sorts of images to the modern mind … characters from Beatrix Potter's books, women standing on chairs screaming, cartoon cats sitting by a mousehole, cheese and traps. Yet, thanks to modern building standards, the twenty-first century person has little to do with these little animals compared to his forebears, who would have lived with them in the home. The house mouse (*Mus musculus*) found it easy to enter the house of the past, which had no concrete raft and was often constructed of materials like cob or lath and plaster, which could be easily burrowed or gnawed through. Once they had moved in, mice could be hard to eradicate – in fact, the domestic cat first became accepted by humans mainly for its ability to sort out mouse infestations in food stores.

"Mouse" is a very broad term for a range of small rodents which share characteristics such as small round ears, a long hairless tail and particularly a small size: they are distinguished from the closely related rats chiefly by their size. Their relationship with humans has moved on from historical times, and they are now exploited by us, being used as laboratory subjects, as food for pets, such as snakes, and as pets themselves. They form part of the human diet in some Eastern countries, and have been eaten in Britain as recently as during rationing in World War II. Fried mice were once given as "medicine" to children who wet the bed.

Seeing mice in **dreams and visions** signifies secrecy and secrets, of people performing tasks in secrecy because of danger or for other reasons (if the dream is positive in feel, this may be a surprise party for someone's birthday, for example). But most typically, mice speak of secrets kept for other reasons, of fear, shame and guilt. A mouse caught in a trap may indicate your secret is in danger of being exposed.

As a **totem animal**, the mouse brings an increased awareness of what is around you, and mouse people may often be very shy but have an ability to leave a situation long before it becomes dangerous.

Mudpuppy: see **Salamander.**

Mule: A mule is a cross between a donkey and a horse, and shares most of the former's meanings. See **Donkey** for meanings.

Musk Ox (sometimes **Muskox**)
(*Ovibos moschatus*)
Element: earth.
Deities: Agni, Artemis/Diane, Baphomet, Dionysus, Faunus, Hera/Juno, Marduk, Pan, Wi.

This impressive Arctic bovine gets its name from the strong musky odour given off by the bulls during the mating season: they splash it around like cheap aftershave to attract the cows. The musk ox's most noticeable feature is its heavy dark brown or dark grey coat of long wool, which can reach to its hocks and fetches premium prices as yarn for clothing. It is also killed for its meat. Its legs are relatively short-haired and usually whitish, and both sexes have heavy curled horns springing from a heavy horny base which protects the skull.

A musk ox turning up in your **dreams and visions** is telling you that better times are on the horizon and that you will soon overcome your problems, whether or not the problem is another person, and turn the whole thing to your own advantage.

As a **totem animal**, it brings the powers of endurance that can help you last until your problems are solved.

Muskrat

(*Ondatra zibethicus*)

Element: water.

Deities: none identified but the muskrat was important in Algonquin and other Native Americans' beliefs.

This North American water rat has been introduced into Europe (where it is classified as a pest) and Asia, and has even infiltrated the UK in the past, though it was eradicated. It has a lot in common with its distant cousin, the beaver: they are both large, plump-bodied rodents, both are aquatic and live on aquatic plant material and construct *lodges* with an underwater entrance to foil predators – though the muskrat does not fell trees for this purpose as the beaver does. It gets its name from the characteristic smell of the males in the mating season.

In **dreams and visions**, seeing a muskrat speaks of success in your career and of youth and health.

As a **totem animal**, it brings the ability to co-operate fully with others and use resources wisely to achieve the best results.

Mynah (or Myna) Bird

(*Sturnidae spp*)

Element: air.

Deities: Isis, Parvati, Ram Deo.

The term "mynah" is applied to any Asian member of the starling family, but most people will be more familiar with the common hill mynah (*Gracula religiosa*) – a black bird with blue and green tints, decorated with orange and yellow wattles and skin patches. This bird is often kept as a pet and valued for its ability to mimic human voices and to learn words and phrases.

In **dreams and visions**, the mynah speaks of hope and opportunities, as well as achievement and promising messages.

As a **totem animal**, it brings happiness and freedom.

Naked Mole Rat

(*Heterocephalus glaber*)

Element: earth.

Deities: none identified.

This little beast looks like something from a 1980s horror movie with its bleached, deeply wrinkled, hairless skin, almost blind eyes and enormous incisors. It isn't a mole, but an African rodent (sometimes called a sand puppy) and its physical characteristics are due to its subterranean lifestyle, feeding on roots and tubers.

Let's all get digging, for the naked mole rat has cracked the health and longevity conundrum! It is insensitive to pain, has an immune system like a nuclear reactor and is the longest-lived rodent, living up to 30-plus years. It is being investigated by medical science because of its seeming immunity to cancer. This unusual animal does not regulate its body temperature like most mammals, though it will huddle with others if things get too chilly.

Seeing one of these unique little beasts in **dreams and visions** speaks of wealth, but more likely the sort of wealth expressed in the old song: *"Money have I none. But I have silver in the stars and gold in the morning Sun."* This animal is monarch of all it surveys, it is rich, for it has enough of everything and does not need to work over hard to eat and enjoy everything it owns.

This meaning feeds through into the mole rat as **totem animal**; those with this animal totem are content with what they have – happy, peaceful people who envy no one.

Narwhal (sometimes Narwhale)

(*Monodon monoceros*)
Element: water.
Deities: Atuqtuqarnaq, Ceto, Sedna and all sea deities.
This unicorn of the sea is a toothed whale and closely related to the beluga whale but, unlike any other cetacean, the male sports an enormous tusk up to three metres long which projects forward from its jaws. This spiral-shaped tooth (actually the enlarged left-hand canine tooth of the animal) may have helped to inspire traveller's tales of unicorns. In some cases, males grow two tusks, and around 15 per cent of females also have tusks. The purpose of the tusk was long a source of mystery, with scientists speculating that it was used in fights over females or to break up ice in the Arctic seas in which it lives. It is now believed that it serves the same purpose as an antenna or whisker, helping the animal "feel" currents and movement in the water.

In **dreams and visions**, the narwhal speaks of an important message, but it can also speak of magical things, of spiritual journeys and dreams coming true, of predestined meetings and of a long lost love returning.

As a **totem animal**, it can bring magical powers, but certainly brings empathy, healing ability and a sense of resolve on your spiritual journey.

Newt

(*Pleurodelinae spp*)
Elements: water and fire.
Deities: none identified.
No gods seem to be associated with newts, yet they have been deeply associated with mystery, magic and witchcraft for thousands of years. "Eye of newt" is an ingredient of a witch's potion in many a clichéd text, inspired by Shakespeare's "eye of newt and toe of frog" from the three witches' cauldron in Macbeth. Like many amphibians, newts can be poisonous, secreting toxins through their skin to protect them from predation, and at least one US species, *Taricha granulosa*, produces enough to kill an adult human. Whilst many people's reaction to these slimy water animals might

be, "Ugh!", they can be surprisingly beautiful, brightly coloured and with crests and long tails.

Newts are salamanders, and so have an association with fire: legend had it they could put out a fire by crawling through the flames, and many newts have bright red, orange and yellow markings.

Seeing one in **dreams and visions** speaks of finding your own solution to danger, of being your own saviour and finding your way through a dark time to the light beyond. They are also symbols of transformation and regeneration.

As a **totem animal**, the newt gives a calm, practical cast of mind, an ability to avoid danger or to resolve it without recourse to violence.

Nightingale
(*Luscinia megarhynchos*)
Element: air.
Deities: Philomela and deities of music.
"While thou art pouring forth thy soul abroad, in such an ecstasy." As Keats' famous words suggest, the song of this bird is almost unreal in its beauty, including a large repertoire of different sounds, often culminating in a stunning crescendo of whistles and liquid notes. Its name means "night singer", though only males seeking to attract a mate sing at night. It has long been a symbol of beauty, music and love throughout Europe, Asia and North Africa. In contrast to its music, arguably the most beautiful of all birdsong, the nightingale itself is a drab little brown bird.

The bird is a bringer of good omens when seen in **dreams and visions**, speaking of a pleasant change in circumstances, of riches and maybe of an addition to your family. Always bear in mind the cultural significance to you of the animal seen in the dream, so the nightingale may also speak of the medical profession – not necessarily as a sign that you may need a doctor, but perhaps as a change of career, or as a reference to someone you know who is unusually compassionate and self-sacrificing.

As a **totem animal**, it brings protection (especially of the family) and artistic ability (especially in music).

Nilgai/Nilghai: see **Antelope.**

Numbat
(*Myrmecobius fasciatus fasciatus*)
Element: earth.
Deities: none identified.
This is a small striped Australian marsupial, sometimes called a walpurti, and it is distantly related to the Tasmanian devil and the quoll. It eats insects and from being very widespread in the past is now considered very endangered, a subspecies having gone extinct in the 1960s.

Seeing one in a **dream or vision** can be a warning of danger to you or to someone you care about, and it can also speak of dissatisfaction with your life and a wish for change, perhaps from a stressful or unsatisfying career. Do not let things distract you from what you truly want, says the numbat.

As a **totem animal**, it brings an ability to focus on goals despite distractions.

Ocelot

(*Leopardus pardalis*)
Element: fire.
Deity: Tezcatlipoca.

This stunningly beautiful cat is found in the Americas and increasingly in people's homes, for although it is endangered in some areas, it has become a popular household pet. The artist, Salvador Dali, had a pet ocelot. Sadly, the capture of young ocelots for the pet trade usually involves killing the mother, and although the trade in ocelot and other wild cat skins has been outlawed in many countries, it still goes on. Nevertheless, the ocelot is listed as of least concern, largely because of its large population across the many countries in which it is found.

Seeing an ocelot in **dreams and visions** is a sign that you should get in touch with your wild side and care less about what people may be thinking of you. Be yourself, says this animal, relax and do your own thing and free yourself from care.

As a **totem animal**, it brings the ability to relax in any situation, and is also the bringer of good relationships and good fortune generally.

Octopus

(*Octopoda spp*)
Element: water.
Deities: Kanaloa, Na Kika.

What a very strange animal is the octopus! It has eight strong, rubbery arms or tentacles, with which it can walk or swim or latch on to prey (and which can regrow if severed), it is poisonous and one species can kill humans, it can change colour like a chameleon, its blood is green and it is also highly intelligent. No wonder that some people have put forward the theory that octopuses came from an alien planet!

This animal is a member of the mollusc order, which also includes snails and shellfish, and its blood is green (like Mr Spock's) because it is based on copper, instead of iron like ours. Ranging from tiny creatures a few centimetres across to giants with a tentacle-tip to tentacle-tip spread of nine metres, it is found in all oceans – though never in fresh water. Despite folk myths like the Kraken and its habit of attacking ships, these creatures are shy and prefer to avoid humans who enter their world. Their intelligence – equal to that of many mammals – has caused several countries to outlaw their use as laboratory animals without anaesthesia.

In **dreams and visions**, octopuses generally convey a warning of some kind. It may symbolise a powerful being or group which is exerting influence in your environment, and which you may resent or even act against. If it is one person then the dream warns you to be on your guard, that this person has many connections they can use against you.

As a **power or totem animal**, the octopus gives great flexibility, powers of concentration and an ability to fit in with everyone and everything. Octopus people do indeed seem to have eight arms, for they can work on many problems at once.

Okapi

(*Okapia johnstoni*)
Element: air.
Deity: Set.
This elegant long-necked ungulate is the giraffe's country cousin; where the giraffe lives on the plains, the okapi prefers to hide away in the forest, and its hide is dark brown, with less markings than the giraffe, in order to provide camouflage. This worked so well that the okapi was unknown to Western science until the twentieth century!

There is very little information on what the Okapi means in **dreams and visions**, perhaps because of this animal's relatively recent discovery by the Western world. Some think it is an omen that a death is about to occur. Myself, I feel it is about secrecy and mystery: the deep mysteries of life that we encounter from time to time, from seeing a ghost to having a deep and very meaningful spiritual experience.

As a **totem animal**, it brings a need for privacy and concealment: people with this totem are less than forthcoming about their emotions, although they may not actually tell lies.

Opossum: see Possum.

Orang-utan

(*Pongo: three species*)
Element: air.
Deities: Gekhre, Ngi, Pan.
The most famous orang-utan in literature is probably the Librarian of the Unseen University in Terry Pratchett's *Discworld* books. *"A magical accident had once turned the university's librarian into an orang-utan, a state which he enjoyed sufficiently to threaten, with simple and graphic gestures, anyone who suggested turning him back."* Ook.

This animal, slightly comical in its body language (to human eyes at least) has an expression of deep and thoughtful wisdom: it is easy to imagine it has read extensively and spends its days pondering what it has absorbed. Unlike the other great apes, orang-utans spend almost all their life in trees, where they travel by swinging and climbing. They are easily identified by their orange hair, which grows long and abundant to form, in extreme cases, long capes. The males have a different facial appearance to the females, with wide cheeks.

While seeing one in **dreams or visions** speaks of some unwelcome drama in your life, the animal also signifies that you will be well on top of the situation and will deal with it, using your own strength of mind.

As a **totem animal**, the orang-utan brings the sociability generally associated with the great apes, as well as your own way of doing things, which generally works out better than the method you have been told about.

Orca

(*Orcinus orca*)
Element: water.
Deities: Rep-un-Kamui, Sedna, all sea deities.
The so-called killer whale is actually a large dolphin, with all the intelligence and social behaviour of these friendly creatures, and they have never been recorded deliberately killing human beings in the wild. When confined in a theme park and deprived of their freedom and families, they may well become vicious, and attacks are common. One orca, the infamous Tilikum, killed three trainers during his 33 years of captivity.

These striking black and white animals live in groups called pods, and work together to capture and kill prey, often large whales. They have also been known to cooperate with human whalers, taking some of the flesh of the dead animals in exchange for their work.

In **dreams and visions**, orcas, like many social creatures, may speak of family matters, or things within your wider social circle. Look at the behaviour of the orca to see what it is pointing out: orcas swimming together in a friendly way means all is well; if they are fighting, perhaps things are not going so well. A commonly accepted meaning for the orca is also a challenge, one that you are afraid to take up, yet the animal is telling you it is well within your ability.

As a **totem animal**, it brings strength, intelligence, playfulness and a free spirit.

Ostrich

(*Struthio camelus*)
Element: air.
Deities: Ma'at, Shu, Thoth.
The biggest bird, the biggest egg…the biggest feet and the most beautiful eyes. Soft feathers…and muscles that could put you in the hospital, if not the morgue. The ostrich is celebrated for its qualities and for the stories it attracts: you can ride an ostrich, it is the fastest living bird, it hides its head in the sand when it is anxious, it has three stomachs, its egg is hard enough to stand on. Most of these are true, but not the one about the bird hiding its head in the sand, although this is probably its most famous, if mythical, attribute.

The ostrich is tall, as high as two to three metres, with lush feathers, particularly on the wings: the black and white plumes of the male were a favourite adornment for hats in the past. Its large muscular legs are naked and end in powerful, two-toed feet. The long neck is also bare of feathers, but the small beak is not nearly so threatening. Its cry is a warbling trill reminiscent of an Australian wobble-board.

The story about the head-burying has sunk into our collective unconscious, and therefore seeing the bird in **dreams and visions** is said to signify that you are afraid of reality and taking refuge in a fantasy world to escape from your fears. It speaks of feeling overwhelmed by life, of wanting to dive under the duvet and stay there until all is well. Yet it also says: you are strong enough for this, or for anything, if you can just summon the courage.

As a **totem animal**, it brings power and strength and, strangely, the ability to deal with just about anything life throws at you. Ostrich people are more likely to run towards danger than away; they are fierce and strong.

Otter

(*Lutra spp*)
Element: water.
Deities: Ahura Mazda, Ceridwen, Hnoss, Manannan, Otr, Semi, Wadjet.
Seldom has any animal been so graceful in both water and on land. The otter, of which there several species across the world, including two-metre giant otters in the Amazon basin and sea otters, has a balletic beauty underwater as it swims, its pelt garlanded with silvery bubbles. On land, it has the speed and litheness of all the *Mustelidae*, with handsome shining fur and an intelligent face.

Sadly, otters have been hunted for their fur, and in the UK just for "sport", and their numbers declined sharply before they were given protection in 1981. Although still rare, their numbers have rallied.

Otters are about play and fun, and seeing one in **dreams and visions** may be telling you not to take life so seriously, to enjoy life while you can and relax, instead of worrying about every little thing. Their association with water and their joy at being in it may suggest a watery holiday as an antidote to stress; or the otter may be telling you that your health is better than you thought.

As a **totem animal**, the otter brings wisdom, intelligence, adaptability and a relaxed, playful attitude to life.

Owl

(*Strigidae spp*)
Element: air.
Deities: Athena/Minerva, Blodeuwedd, Frigga, Horus, Hypnos, Idun, Lakshmi, Lilith, Ragana.
The owl has been a symbol of wisdom for many centuries, and often appears in children's books and films, holding a book and wearing spectacles. But it can also be associated with stupidity and foolishness, perhaps because of its surprised, blinking appearance when disturbed in daylight. It is deeply woven into folklore and belief in magic, particularly beliefs around death and graveyards. Certainly, it can produce some ghostly sounds, and the barn

owl has a ghostly appearance as well, with its whitish plumage and silent flight.

Found all over the world, even within the Arctic circle, owls are predators, living on small animals or sometimes fish. They regurgitate the indigestible parts of their food, the bones and other hard parts, as pellets.

Seeing an owl in **dreams and visions** may draw heavily on cultural associations: you may subconsciously be conjuring wise old owls from childhood stories, but they generally do speak of wisdom, knowledge and intelligence, particularly of book-learning, and also spiritual and academic development. The bird is strongly connected with hidden wisdom of the kind that needs to be searched for and found, perhaps only by the deserving. It can also speak of transformation, and if you have Hinduism in your background then also wealth and prosperity.

As a **totem animal**, it brings great intuition and an ability to find out secrets and knowledge that is concealed from most people.

Ox: see Cattle.

Oyster

(*Ostreidae spp*)
Element: water.
Deities: Aphrodite/Venus.

The name of this edible shellfish often appears in the same sentence with "champagne" as a costly luxury, but in the past it was the food of the metropolitan poor. Overfishing of the oyster beds reduced numbers to transform the animal into a rare delicacy. Oysters are now commonly farmed around the world, and their other gift to mankind – pearls – are cultured. The pearl is formed when a piece of grit gets into an oyster's shell, and the shellfish slowly covers the irritant in nacreous coating to make it more comfortable.

These poor creatures are eaten live – they should flinch when lemon juice is sprinkled on them – possibly to reduce the danger of food poisoning from eating dead ones, which decay very quickly. The eating of oysters "only when there is an R in the month" is also due to this danger. They are extremely nutritious and believed to be an aphrodisiac.

Seeing oysters in **dreams and visions** speaks of wealth and wellbeing, whether it is the ability to enter a very expensive restaurant and order them to eat or owning the pearls they may be found to contain. They speak of bodily health and good living. There is sex mixed in with this, as they are associated with romance and sexual potency, so they could be telling you of a very successful date!

As a **totem animal**, they have quite a different meaning, and oyster people can be solitary and jealously guard their privacy, especially their financial affairs. It will take a lot to break through their barriers and get to know them.

Pangolin
(*Pholidota spp*)
Element: earth.
Deity: Waghjai.
Looking like a cross between a crocodile and a pinecone, this amazing animal is actually a mammal, though not really related to any others on Earth. Found throughout Asia and sub-Saharan Africa, it is sometimes called the scaly anteater, and is now seriously threatened, being the most trafficked animal in the world for its meat, skin and scales; the latter being used in traditional Asian medicine. Ironically, this trade was at one time believed to have been one of the main sources of the spread of Covid-19, though this was disproved.

Seeing a pangolin in **dreams and visions** brings hope of all kinds, but is most often associated with the hope of having children. It could still happen, says the pangolin.

As a **totem animal**, it brings the need for a solitary lifestyle, and pangolin people always work better if left to their own devices.

Panther
This is not really a species, but a term applied to several species of big cat, including cougars, black leopards and jaguars. See under each animal's listing for the meaning.

Parakeet: see Parrot.

Parrot
(*Psittaciformes spp*)
Element: air.
Deities: Kama and Rati.
This huge family of colourful and often vocal birds includes some of the most intelligent birds. Parrots and parakeets have long been popular pets, providing company and entertainment to many who live alone. They come from tropical and warm climates no further north than India, and are also rumoured to live to great ages.

Because of their amazing ability to mimic human voices, the word *parrot* has become an expression meaning to mindlessly repeat words and phrases to which one has been exposed, i.e. to exhibit signs of having been brainwashed. Yet parrot owners will tell you that these clever birds often seem to know exactly what they are saying and will tailor their speech to the situation, often reserving their worst language for when the vicar or a maiden aunt comes to visit!

In **dreams and visions**, parrots speak of long life and of long marriages, faithful partners and happiness. They also (strangely for a bird best known as anchored to a perch or shut in a cage) speak of freedom and adventure. In some cultures, the sight of a parrot on the roof means protection – so happiness and security in the home is another meaning.

As a **totem animal**, the parrot and parakeet are very far removed from the brainless, chattering image they may have in some minds: these birds bring great intelligence and strength of mind, along with loquacity which can change minds and always help them get their own way.

Peacock

(*Pavonini spp*)

Element: air.

Deities: Argus, Buddha, Hera, Kartikeya, Kaumari, Mayura, Santoshi.

The species Pava and Afropava are actually *peafowl*, yet who recognises the rather drab peahen when they see her? The word peacock instantly conjures up this most exotic and gorgeous of all birds, with its enormous blue-green, eye-studded tail feathers, its crowned head, its iridescent wings and neck, and its strident call of "*No!*". Its name has become a byword for male display, ostentation and vanity, while the peahen, apart from having the coronet on her head, is dull and grey.

From time immemorial, humans have envied the peacock its beauty and stolen its tail feathers for ornaments, clothing and hats – despite the fact that they are said to be unlucky if kept in the home. Equating beauty with power, the Moguls referred to their seat of power as the Peacock Throne. Peacocks were eaten at very special mediaeval banquets, and brought to table with their tail feathers attached: *the peacock in its pride*.

Under Christianity, peacocks have come to symbolise pride in a pejorative sense, that of vanity and senseless ego.

Seeing a peacock in **dreams and visions** can speak of abundance, riches and prosperity, but may also be a warning to take a long look at your behaviour; and it particularly relates to vanity, pride and snobbery: go by the "feel" of the dream for which meaning to take. Vanity – in the sense of pride in one's appearance, so that one spends time and money on improving one's looks, buying expensive clothes, jewels and cosmetics – is also included in this.

As a **totem animal**, the peacock brings a sense of self-worth and pride in one's appearance, as well as great creativity and artistic ability. Peacock people are resourceful and self-reliant, but are prone to ignoring criticism, even if it is constructive.

Pelican

(*Pelecanus spp*)

Elements: air and water.

Deities: Christ, Henet.

With many animals there is a mythical and heraldic side to be considered, and the pelican is one of these. In ancient belief, the bird was believed to feed its young on its own blood, pecking its breast to let the blood flow so the chicks could drink when no other food was available. This appears as a heraldic device, "the pelican in her piety," which is also associated with the sacrifice of Christ, and the colleges of Corpus Christi at both Oxford and Cambridge feature the device on their arms.

In reality, the pelican is a large water bird which feeds on fish and has an enlarged pouch as part of its beak to enable it to carry away fish it has not time to swallow or wishes to take back to its young. Most people will immediately think of the white American pelican, but the various species can be brown, grey or black, sometimes with patches or stripes of another colour.

In **dreams and visions**, a dichotomy arises, for many people see the bird as a symbol of greed, gobbling down huge amounts of food and selfishly carrying away what it cannot stuff into its stomach. Yet the heraldic pelican in her piety is still in there somewhere and the meaning can include self-sacrifice, service and selflessness. Again, take the "feel" of the dream to decide which meaning is relevant.

As a **totem animal**, the pelican again brings a sense of selflessness, of a desire to work within a community for the good of all. It also brings freedom and courage.

Penguin
(*Spheniscidae spp*)
Element: water.
Deitiy: Tawaki.
The little gentleman with the black tie and tails has attracted a good press over the centuries, so it is surprising that it was chosen as the image for one of TV's (and comic books before that) best-loved villains, the Penguin in the Batman franchise. These birds do not fly, but swim like fish, and spend about half their lives in water. I was delighted to discover that a collection of penguins on dry land is called a *waddle*, while in the sea the collective term is a *raft*!

Cartoon imagery often shows penguins consorting with polar bears, but they literally inhabit opposite ends of the planet: the bears live around the Arctic circle, while penguins live around Antarctica and the southernmost reaches of continents like South America and Australia. Penguins range in size from the majestic emperor penguin (at 130cms tall) to the little blue (barely more than 30cms).

A penguin in **dreams and visions** is telling you about stability and staying where you are most comfortable, perhaps when you are tempted to uproot and change your life completely – yet it can also convey the meaning that if you have to change your circumstances, you will adapt and prosper.

As a **totem animal**, it brings a strong grounding in the community and your own circle of friends, with an ease in adapting to situations.

Pheasant
(*Phasianidae spp*)
Elements: earth and air.
Deity: Amaterasu.

These gorgeous birds are almost as ornamental as a peacock; with the common pheasant surely being the most colourful bird in the UK (it is also found almost worldwide). As with many bird species, it is the cock bird which has the glamorous looks: the hen is much duller and mainly brown, and lacks the long, eye-catching tail feathers and the bright red wattles of the male. Sadly, the pheasant is best-known as a game bird, reared for shoots on the land of the wealthy, and afterwards destined for the dinner table. They are unfortunately a very common sight as roadkill, as they seem to lack a fear of vehicles and will run straight into the road, or run along in front of a car instead of getting off the road.

Like the peacock, the pheasant enjoys a mixture of meanings when it appears in **dreams and visions**. It may be a sign of good fortune or it can mean inequality and jealousy in a marriage, and a situation arising where the marriage is threatened by relationships outside, not necessarily amorous ones, but unsuitable friendships.

As a **totem animal**, it brings adaptability and great ability with problem-solving, but it may also bring vanity and an inability to work at relationships.

Pig

(*Sus scrofa* and *S. domesticus*)
Elements: earth and air.
Deities: Arduinna, Cerridwen, Diana, Eubuleus, Freyr and Freyja, Isis, Moccus, Varahi.
Few animals have had such a close relationship with humans as pigs, yet the benefits are all one-sided. Pigs give us meat and leather and sometimes their friendship as pets, but in return they receive cruel treatment, opprobrious names and death. *Pig* is used as a term of abuse, implying filth, obesity, greed, stupidity and generally unacceptable behaviour, and some religions forbid contact with them or the eating of their meat, classifying them as "unclean". Yet pigs are of high intelligence – higher than dogs, for example – and prefer to keep clean if they are kept in conditions in which they can achieve this.

Domesticated at least 11,400 years ago, the pig is the subject of the oldest piece of cave art yet discovered: *the Sulawesi Pig*. The pig is common to nearly all cultures, and in England it was once stated that "you can use every part of a pig – except the squeal!" From Alison Uttley and Beatrix Potter to later creations like Porky Pig, Wilbur and Peppa, the pig has been a firm childhood favourite and was historically kept by almost every household in a sty, often very close to the home, where it was fed on kitchen scraps, weeds and meal. In medical science, pigs have been used for research and for organ transplants (e.g. of the heart) as their tissues are close to those of humans. Sailors see them as unlucky, and in some cultures it is forbidden to name a pig while on board a vessel, or before it sets to sea.

In **dreams and visions**, pigs speak of fertility and prosperity, of marriage and money, and of love. If the tone of the dream is less positive, the animal may be warning you of your inability to control your appetites, and of the health implications of greed and overeating, or the dangers of sexual promiscuity.

As a **totem animal**, the pig brings good health, good luck and a sense of honour and commitment within one's society.

Pigeon

(*Columbidae spp*)

Element: air.

Deities: Aphrodite/Venus, Asherah, Ceres/Demeter, Hachiman, Hera/Juno, Inanna, Irene, Ishtar, Jesus, Utnapishtim.

This is one of the best-known birds on Earth, partly due to its colonisation of city habitats and its own popularity as an introduction to parks and gardens, especially as its white form (generally referred to as *doves*), and kept in purpose-built dove-houses. Its cooing song soothes the human mind and it has long been considered a symbol of peace and amity. Yet they have also begun to be despised as "flying rats" – vermin which carry a number of diseases dangerous to humans, and which can be transmitted just through the dust of their droppings. The word "pigeon" has also become a derogatory term meaning a fool or simpleton, one who is easily used by others.

Pigeons and doves have been domesticated for centuries, for their meat, for their ornamental and musical qualities and as sacrifices in religious temples. The ability of these birds to "home" back to their original location has also caused them to be used to carry messages, especially in wartime situations.

In **dreams and visions**, pigeons speak of a yearning to return home, not just to one's geographical home and family, but perhaps to a time in the past when one was very happy in one's domestic or professional life.

Doves speak of peace and tranquillity, acceptance, purity and the importance of maintaining good relationships.

As a **totem animal**, the pigeon and dove bring gentleness and a great attachment to home and family, with an ability to get on well with everyone and bring tranquillity, peace and ease into relationships and situations.

Pika

(*Ochotona spp*)

Element: earth.

Deities: Andraste, Aphrodite/Venus, Artemis/Diana, Eostre, Eros, Osiris, Weneu and Wenenut.

A rabbit that barks and makes its own hay! The pika, despite its appearance, is not a rodent, but a lagomorph – the order that includes rabbits and hares. Small and very rabbity in appearance, with rounded ears, the pika behaves much like a rabbit, digging burrows and preferring to be active at dawn and dusk. However, where rabbits are usually silent, the pika has a distinctive call, which is used to warn of danger or to attract a mate. In some species, it is a simple "*eep*" sound, but the sound varies across species, and the North American pika can bark almost like a dog.

Instead of hibernating, pikas collect grass and green stuff in a safe place to live on through the winter.

In **dreams and visions**, pikas signify calmness, home comforts and a harmonious, friendly social circle.

People with the pika as their **totem animal** are natural peacemakers and avoid any disharmony. They are also good at integrating all aspects of their own lives.

Pine marten
(*Martes martes*)
Element: air.
Deities: Magni and Modi, Maeve.

I was privileged to see one of these beautiful but rare beasts running along the road towards the Isle of Skye: I recognised it at once by its intense, chocolate-brown fur and primrose "bib". A member of the stoat family, it is found across Europe in wooded regions. Until recently in the UK, it was found only in Scotland, but there is now evidence that it is returning to some northern areas of England.

The best-known pine marten in popular culture is probably Pantalaimon, Lyra's daemon in Philip Pullman's *His Dark Materials*.

Seeing a marten in **dreams and visions** speaks of courage and luck, both essential qualities in any new venture or adventure.

People with a marten as **totem animal** have a natural grace and agility, are faithful and loyal, and never hold a grudge.

Piranha
(*Serrasalmidae spp*)
Element: fire.
Deity: Itzamna.

The stuff of horror films, the piranha is a devil fish with a mouthful of razor-sharp teeth that make it look like a cartoon bulldog. Tales of piranha shoals stripping a cow to the bones in minutes may be exaggerated, but not entirely false. The red-bellied piranha in particular, is extremely aggressive and has the most powerful bite for its size of any fish. However, piranhas, which live in freshwater around Central America, are omnivorous and include plant material in their diet.

Seeing a piranha or piranhas in **dreams and visions** means, unsurprisingly, that a terrible danger is approaching, one that you should make every effort to avoid as it will cause catastrophic damage to you, your family and your lifestyle. A single fish may also mean inconsistency, as in a strange mixture of things affecting you that do not seem to be related.

As a **totem animal**, the fish brings ruthlessness, self-confidence, but also an inability to trust others. Typically, a wall is put up against strangers or people who do not invoke total trust.

Platypus (Duck-Billed)

(*Ornithorhynchus anatinus*)
Element: water.
Deity: Yhi.

This beast is like a chimera, apparently made up from parts of several different animals, with its duck-beak snout, its beaver tail, its otter-like shape and fur, its egg-laying and its venomous claws. In fact, when a specimen was first brought to the West, people suspected it was a trick made up by a skilled taxidermist, like the fish-and-monkey "mermaid". It is a monotreme – the third order of warm-blooded animals after mammals and marsupials – and is found throughout Australia in freshwater streams.

Seeing a platypus in **dreams and visions** signifies a lack of confidence in a social situation, or being worried about your appearance and your place in society.

As a **totem animal**, it naturally brings great adaptability, but also a desire for privacy and one's own home and occupations, rather than being out in the world.

Polecat

(*Mustela putorius,* though the name is applied to other *mustelid* species)
Element: air.
Deity: Hecate.

Found throughout Eurasia and North Africa, this animal is related to stoats and weasels and famous for being smelly: its musky ammoniac scent can be discharged at an attacking enemy, very much like the distantly related skunk. Very closely related to the domestic ferret (to whom it is certainly an ancestor), the polecat carries many of the same meanings, though its appearance in **dreams and visions** may indicate something stinks! This might not be you, but something about a situation that is unfair or just downright wrong.

As a **totem animal**, the polecat brings self-sufficiency, courage and an ability to defend oneself.

Porcupine

(*Hystricognathi spp*)
Element: fire.
Deities: Ganesh, Kaggen.

What are these magnificent beasts? Are they hedgehogs or armadillos, or something in between? Porcupines comprise two families of animals: the New World porcupines and the Old World porcupines which, though they are both rodents, are not closely related. However, both families share the sharp quills which are their trademark defence against enemies. When threatened they will erect these sharp horny quills and vibrate them, sometimes emitting an unpleasant smell as well. In situations of serious threat they may run into their attacker, deliberately sticking their quills into it. Porcupines "firing" their quills at an enemy, however, is a myth – though the quills may cause a serious injury when they are rammed into another creature's body.

In **dreams and visions**, a porcupine can mean you are well able to defend yourself, or it could mean you are being injured by gossip – look at the "feel" of the dream for the relevant meaning. It can also be a warning about being too "prickly" and jumping to the defensive when no one has meant you any harm.

As a **totem animal**, it brings coolness: these are people who do not really get on with others and are over-sensitive to remarks made about them, fearing gossip and emotional hurt. In some cultures, they are seen as symbols of purity and innocence.

Porpoise
(*Phocaenidae spp*)
Element: water.
Deities: Aphrodite/Venus, Amphitrite/Salacia, Apollo, Ganga, Melicertes, Neptune, Poseidon, Triton.

Porpoises are so similar to dolphins that most people could not tell them apart, and in terms of divination and vision they are the same: see **Dolphin** for meanings.

Possum
(*Phalangeriformes spp*)
Element: fire.
Deities: none identified.

Possums and opossums are not rodents, as they appear, but members of the marsupial order, which includes kangaroos – though opossums are found in America and possums in Australia. They are related, but not the same species. To make matters more confusing, in North America they are frequently referred to as 'possums, with an apostrophe to mark the dropped letter, which of course is not discernible in speech!

Omnivorous, small and pointy-snouted, they are often described as creepy because of their rat-like appearance (though they are not remotely related to rats) and are known for their trick of playing dead when attacked or frightened (playing possum), a behaviour similar to fainting in which they defecate, and also emit an unpleasant odour which can cause a predator to take them for decayed carrion and turn away in disgust.

Seeing one in **dreams and visions** speaks of the need to conceal yourself, avoid danger and keep your head below the parapet: if you manage this then the danger you are facing might go away.

As **totem animals**, they bring resourcefulness and the ability to cope with many hazards without ever approaching them head-on or putting themselves at risk.

Prairie Dog

(*Cynomys spp*)

Element: earth.

Deities: none identified, but all earth gods.

These little ground squirrels are found across the Americas, from Mexico to the north, in areas high above sea level, and are famous for constructing burrows in which they can keep warm in the winter and cool in the summer. These complex structures include nurseries, bedrooms, living rooms and communal areas, and many hundreds may exist within a "town" of burrows that can cover many hundreds of acres. Their behaviour seems very human: family members kiss one another, though they do not kiss animals outside their family. Male dogs may have several "wives", but these females do not make friends with one another. They also "bark" during the mating season.

Seeing prairie dogs in **dreams and visions** speaks of the complexities of community, the various interwoven relationships, loves, hates and friendships we all construct in our lives, and how important these are to us.

As a **totem animal**, the prairie dog brings – as you might expect – a strong sense of community and a desire to be part of that community and work within it for the benefit of others.

Prawn

(*Decapods spp*)

Element: water.

Deities: Aphrodite/Venus, Bride.

These common crustaceans, many of which are edible, are probably best-known to most people as part of a prawn or shrimp cocktail or a paella. In the UK, shrimps are smaller species of decapods and prawns are larger, whilst in the US the term "shrimp" is generally applied to both.

When looking at the meaning of these crustaceans in **dreams and visions**, it is important to remember what your own associations with them are. Do you think of happy times, perhaps a celebration at a posh restaurant? Or do you loathe them because you once had food poisoning after eating some? In China, the word for "shrimp" sounds like the word for laughter, so the fish has become associated with happiness, family get-togethers and playing children. They are also a symbol of longevity. In the West, we might also associate them with parties, barbecues, meals out at restaurants for a special occasion, but always go by the "feel" of the dream to be sure.

As a **totem animal**, they bring good luck and more good luck, constantly renewed, and an ability to enjoy life to the full, concentrating on real pleasures rather than dreams of "what might have been."

Praying Mantis

(*Mantodea spp*)

Element: earth.

Deities: IKaggen, Isis, Oshun, Shiva.

This elegant and striking creature is best known for its "praying" posture and for the female's habit of biting off her partner's head after – or during – mating. Distantly related to cockroaches, it grows to a large size in some climates and has been the subject of horror films and comics, honoured as a spirit guide in some cultures, has inspired martial arts manoeuvres and is sometimes kept as an unusual pet. In African belief, the insect brought good fortune, while to the Ancient Egyptians it was one of the guides that helped the dead find their way to the Afterlife.

Seeing a mantis in **dreams and visions** can speak of hypocrisy in someone near you, as in the person who wears a virtuous demeanour, yet is underhand or malicious behind your back. It can speak of a femme fatale, a woman or other possible sexual partner who is bound to betray you. Yet the colour of the insect can alter this slightly: a green or blue mantis also carries the message of forgiveness and reconciliation, perhaps through this person's determination to change their nature, while a red one may mean hatred and revenge.

As a **totem animal**, the mantis gives many strengths, including patience, a strong belief in oneself, focus, insight, intuition and wisdom, but it can also bring selfishness and a less than pure set of ethics.

Puffin

(*Fratercula antlantica*)
Elements: air and water.
Deities: Aphrodite/Venus, Njörd.

These endearing birds, with their clumsy flight and painted beaks, have become a symbol of the vulnerability of our seabirds, their numbers having declined significantly in recent years, despite their wide range. It has been impacted by many manmade factors over the years, particularly oil spills and other pollution. On the island of Lundy (the name of which may derive from the Norse word for puffin), one of the bird's important breeding sites in the UK, the population had declined to 10 pairs, although it has recovered slightly after the population of rats (which had been feeding on their eggs) was removed.

Puffins are popular symbols on stamps and flags, and well known to British children through the Puffin children's book range introduced by Penguin Paperbacks in 1939.

Seeing a puffin in **dreams and visions** speaks of fun and parties: the appearance of the bird, with its white face, strangely shaped eyes and multicoloured beak, suggests clowns, fancy dress, Mardi Gras and merriment. It speaks of relationships, long lasting ones, perhaps for life, but also implies this will be the ride of your life, always fun. It speaks of your soulmate.

As a **totem animal,** the puffin brings the ability to form long lasting relationships and happy families, and to work hard for these. This may imply being an absent parent, as providing is important and working away may be part of the equation.

Puma: see **Cougar.**

Quail
(Galliformes spp)
Element: earth.
Deities: Artemis/Diana, Asteria, Bel, Hephaestos/Vulcan, spring goddesses.
The term "quail" covers a large number of species of game birds found across the world, yet the overall description of the bird is readily recognised: quails are small, with often patterned brown plumage and a squat, "cobby" shape. They are not strong flyers, spending most of their lives on the ground, although they can take off and fly for a short distance when threatened. Quail are eaten as a delicacy, as are their eggs, which are now commonly available in supermarkets.

Seeing a quail in **dreams and visions** can imply the onset of fear, via a pun on the word "quail", or it can mean the difficulty of getting one's project off the ground. Either way, it can be a warning that things may not be going your way.

As a **totem animal**, this bird brings an ability to sense danger, to see through the intentions of others and to be aware always of their ulterior motives.

Quoll
(Dasyurus spp)
Element: fire.
Deities: none identified.
Six species of this pretty marsupial predator are found in Australia and New Guinea, where they sleep in their dens all day and emerge to hunt at night. All quolls have smooth fur patterned with white spots, a long tail and a long snout. They are solitary animals – although they like to use a "public lavatory"! Quolls often have a communal area in which to defecate, which may also serve as a "noticeboard", letting other quolls know who is around, and whether females are ready to mate. The main threat to these attractive animals is human behaviour: when they helped reduce the numbers of introduced rabbits (now a major plague in Australia) they were shot and trapped; now in some areas they are threatened by the introduced cane toad, which poisons any animal that eats it.

In **dreams and visions**, seeing a quoll speaks of the vulnerability of a person who does not see this, perhaps sees themselves as invincible, which means a shock is on the way.

As a **totem animal**, the quoll brings a sense of self-worth and a confidence in one's plans and projects.

Rabbit

(*Leporidae spp*)

Element: earth.

Deities: Andraste, Aphrodite/Venus, Artemis/Diana, Eostre, Eros, Nanabozho, Osiris, Weneu and Wenenut, all moon Gods and Goddesses.

"My people are the strongest in the world!" boasts the mythic character El-Ahrairah in Richard Adams's classic novel, *Watership Down,* and at the time it was written, he had a point. Rabbits were introduced into the UK from Europe for meat in the mediaeval era, where they soon escaped from their warrens and overran the countryside – as they did in Australia in the twentieth century. Not even myxomatosis could make much of a dent in their populations, although this lab-bred, germ warfare virus is still out there today. However, another disease, transferred to wild rabbits without deliberate intent, has made huge inroads on the species in the last 10 years: viral haemorrhagic disease. This comes from pet rabbits that, whether they escape or live in outdoor hutches, often have contact with wild ones. Where the pet rabbits are generally vaccinated, the wild ones are not, and the disease has a 90% mortality rate.

How do you tell a rabbit from a hare? Generally, the hare is larger, has longer ears and longer legs and a different lifestyle. In the UK, a cluster of grey-brown animals at the corner of a field will be rabbits, while a single ginger-brown animal in the centre of the field will be a hare.

They are hugely popular with children and adults, well represented in folklore and fairy tales, literature, movies and as soft toys, and even in the porn industry: the bunny ears and the bunny-girl are both recognised emblems of the Playboy Club.

In many cultures, they are seen as lucky and a rabbit's foot may be worn as a good luck charm, typically as a brooch. Like hares, they are associated with the Moon, as the shape of the lagomorph made up by the various lunar seas could be seen as a rabbit or a hare. It is customary to say, "white rabbits", and to turn over the change in one's pockets, when the new moon is spotted.

Because of their strange mix of sexuality and fertility with doe-eyed innocence and playfulness, rabbits in **dreams and visions** can speak of relationships between young people, first love, first sexual experiences, and of course the frequent results: babies and a growing family. Or they can just speak of physical attraction and sex between mature people. They can also indicate fertility in other ways: wealth, crops, good luck, bonuses and pay rises.

As a **totem animal**, the rabbit pretty well lives up to El-Ahrairah's boast: bringing self-sufficiency, the ability to survive and overcome all problems and to emerge on the field of battle as a victor, having outnumbered and outfaced all its enemies (this meaning may change with time as the VHD epidemic continues to take its toll on the rabbit populations).

Raccoon

(*Procyon lotor*)

Element: air.

Deities: Azeban, Fulla, Tezcatlipoca.

This intelligent, curious animal, with his highwayman's mask, bushy ringtail and long-fingered hands, is seen as a pest in the US, much as the fox is in the UK. Like the fox, raccoons have moved into towns and urban areas, attracted by the rich pickings around homes, food outlets and garbage bins. Despite these dirty habits, they are known for washing or rinsing food in a stream or other water (where available) before eating it or feeding it to their young. Their cunning, agility and their habit of clanging dustbin lids around while humans are trying to sleep has earned them a reputation for mischief and trickery. However, they should be treated with respect: not only can they deliver a painful bite, but they are known to carry rabies as well as a host of parasites.

Seeing a raccoon in **dreams and visions** may call your attention to a member of your family, perhaps a younger person, who has such a sense of mischief that he or she is always getting into trouble. It can also speak of the possibility of being the victim of an actual crime, so be careful to lock up your house and your car if you see this creature!

As a **totem animal**, the 'coon gives great intelligence, problem-solving ability and endurance. Raccoon people are the ones who will be living off the fat of the land after WWIII!

Rat

(*Rattus spp*)

Element: earth.

Deities: Arimanius, Cernunnos, Ganesh, Karni Mata, Ninkilim.

If ever a species were universally loathed, it is the rat. Their naked tails, their habit of feasting on garbage and even faeces, their invasions of human homes, their stealing of eggs and stored grain, all have contributed to a mythology of disgust that has been woven around them. Their very name is used as a term of abuse. The Black Death and bubonic plague, both believed to have been brought by rats, have not helped the situation; while horror writers from Poe to Stephen King and James Herbert have exploited their reputation, as have movie makers. Yet they are intelligent, seldom aggressive, useful in many ways (including as meat in some cultures, as "sniffer dogs", for medical detection and also as laboratory animals), and make delightful pets.

Seeing rats in **dreams and visions** does speak of ill luck, which can manifest in a number of ways. It speaks of ingratitude shown by someone you have been kind to, of being taken for granted, perhaps abused, stolen from or slandered unfairly. It can mean illness and disease, or financial difficulties, even total bankruptcy. Yet seeing a white rat, or other "fancy" rat of the type favoured as pets, can have a very different meaning and refer to family, to children and to home.

As a **totem animal**, the rat has a very different meaning, bringing success and mastery of your environment. These are clever people who can manipulate events and people to get their own way.

Raven: see Crow.

Ray
(*Batoidea spp*)
Element: water.
Deities: Dagon, Punga, Tlaloc.
Though related to sharks, these animals are not usually harmful: one species lives entirely on plankton, and most eat shellfish or other small fish on the ocean floor. However, the stingrays (*Myliobatoidea spp*) may cause injuries if a human comes into contact with their venomous spines – the popular TV wildlife presenter, Steve Irwin, was killed when a stingray "stabbed" him in the chest. These fish range in size, from the tiny teacup stingray to the 7-metre wide manta ray, which is believed to be the most intelligent of all fish.

In **dreams and visions**, the grace and beauty of these creatures manifest in good omens and gentle advice: go with the flow, says the ray, float through life without making waves – or enemies.

As a **totem animal**, it brings a gentle elegance and languidness…but no one provokes or injures it and gets away unscathed!

Reindeer: see Caribou.

Rhinoceros
(*Rhinocerotidae spp*)
Elements: earth and fire.
Deities: Agni, Dhavdi.
These impressive megabeasts are now desperately endangered, their ongoing extermination being fuelled by killing for trophies and for Asian medicine, which sees the fibrous horn as an important resource. Four species remain, of which some are down to four figures in terms of animals remaining. Because of its size and potential for aggression, the rhino has no natural predators other than man. In native African belief, the animal is seen as a fire-fighter which is able to stamp out forest fires with its large feet.

Seeing a rhino in **dreams and visions** may speak of money, as the term "rhino" has been a popular slang term for currency for many centuries. Their meaning may also be that of stability and resilience, of someone who is secure in their place and has no desire to move, but they may also signify an intense experience involving emotion, perhaps love or grief.

As a **totem animal**, the rhino brings strength and tenacity and an ability to overcome all obstacles – in fact, rhino people may gain a name for plunging on recklessly in the face of all odds, though they also usually win through.

Robin

(*Erithacus rubecula*)

Element: air.

Deities: Hephaestus, Jesus, all sacrificed gods.

The European robin, often fondly called robin redbreast, has strong associations with pagan mythology and the legends of the fertility god who dies at harvest to feed the people. It was sacred to the Norse God Thor and associated with the Celtic Oak God of Summer, and killing one has always been held to be unlucky. The poet, William Blake, wrote: "*A robin redbreast in a cage/Puts all heaven in a rage.*" With the advent of Christianity, it was annexed by the Church, who reinvented it as a symbol of Christ's passion (the bird was now supposed to have gained its red breast by trying to succour the bleeding Jesus on the cross) and has since become strongly associated with Christmas. It is known for its apparent liking and lack of fear of humans, and gardeners will often find it coming close to their feet as they dig, looking for unearthed worms, or even perching on their spade handle if they pause. They will even seek out manmade items, such as old kettles or broken pots, in which to nest, in preference to trees.

It has long been seen as a symbol of good luck and happiness, yet it can also be associated with death and sorrow. Despite its pretty song and appearance, it is one of the more aggressive songbirds and males will attack not only other robins that enter their territory but often other small bird species. In the 1960s, it became the unofficial national bird of the UK.

In **dreams and visions**, the robin speaks of hope and promises, of spring, new beginnings and rebirth after misfortune or death.

As a **totem or power animal**, it brings a love of truth and straight dealings, a dislike of anything underhanded or dishonourable.

Sable

(*Martes zibellina*)

Element: air. Deities: subterranean and death deities.

This pretty creature shares much meaning with the marten and mink, to which it is closely related. It speaks of a selfish person bent on amassing wealth at any cost, and not caring who they walk on in the process, a person who will never share, nor care about the community in which they live. It can also, confusingly, speak of glamour, as the animal's fur has been popular in the fur trade, and its black colour can also mean bereavement and mourning. In **dreams and visions** its appearance can also be a warning against extravagance, while the **totem animal** has an almost opposite meaning, bringing an ability to manage on very little and cut one's coat (ha!) according to one's cloth.

Salamander

(*Urodela spp*)

Elements: water and fire.

Deities: Hephaestos/Vulcan, Xolotl.

The salamander is an amphibian, with a slimy, froggy skin and a lifestyle closely connected to water … yet this often beautiful, jewel-like creature has traditionally been associated with fire. The animal looks very much like a newt, to which it is closely related, but it has a smoother skin and is often brilliantly patterned with stripes and spots of gold, red and yellow, particularly in the breeding season. Some species have toxins in their skin for protection against predators; some have no limbs and resemble eels. The giant salamander, native to Asia, can grow to almost two metres long.

Our ancient ancestors believed the salamander had such a wet, cold skin that it could put out a fire. The Aztecs identified their fire god as an axolotl – a species of salamander which is often white with large, leathery red gills. In Western mystery traditions, the salamander is the spirit of the element fire, as gnomes are of earth and mermaids (or undines) are of water.

You can walk through the fire, says this creature when it makes an appearance in your **dreams and visions**; nothing, not shame, imprisonment, social rejection nor any other situation can deter you from reaching your goal.

The salamander – which can grow back limbs when it loses them – also speaks of rebirth and second starts and, as a **totem animal**, it brings the ability to constantly reinvent oneself, after disappointments, after mistakes, after quarrels and bad feelings and misfortune.

Salmon

(*Salmonidae spp*)

Elements: water and air.

Deities: Eqatlejoq, Loki, all water deities.

Salmon are well known as a luxury foodstuff, but also for their ability to return from the sea to the same river in which they themselves hatched, to lay their eggs. In an amazing display of strength and determination, these large silvery fish leap up high waterfalls, trying again and again tirelessly when they fail. Their deep pink flesh is extremely high in omega-3 and potassium (which are beneficial to the heart), as well as protein and calcium.

The fish was extremely important in Celtic mythology as the Salmon of Knowledge (or Wisdom), which gained its knowledge from eating nuts from a sacred hazel tree that fell into its pool. The seer and poet, Finn Eces, catches the fish and instructs his pupil, Fionn Mac Cumhaill, to cook it – knowing he will absorb its wisdom with its flesh. However, young Fionn burns his hand on the fish, puts his hand in his mouth, and the magical knowledge comes to him instead.

In **dreams and visions**, the salmon usually appears as a symbol of wealth and wellbeing, but it also speaks of knowledge and wisdom, perhaps gained over some time, perhaps through a study course or an apprenticeship. It may also indicate some kind of regeneration, such as a new job or a new relationship.

As a **totem animal**, it brings determination and the ability to keep trying, never being discouraged, until one achieves one's goal.

Sambar or Sambhar: see **Deer.**

Sardine
(*Clupeidae spp*)
Element: water.
Deities: all sea and fish deities.
These small silvery fish need no introduction to most people, as they are a confirmed favourite at teatime, served on toast or in sandwiches or, more adventurously, on the barbecue. Few households have been without a tin or two of sardines or pilchards, and their harvests in fishing communities have been a cause for celebration.

In **dreams and visions**, they may speak of good luck, of a financial bonanza, of the ability to store wealth against hard times, as is the case in communities that rely on them. Today though, they may conjure childhood memories for people whose only experience of the sea is with a bucket and spade. Look carefully at the "feel" of the dream to see what the fish are signifying, whether your past memories (good or bad) are being evoked.

As a **totem animal**, it brings good fortune, a sociable nature and an ability to do well on very little.

Sawfish
(*Pristidae spp*)
Element: water.
Deities: none specifically identified, but they are central to many mythologies.
These astonishing fish bear a double-edged "saw" (complete with rows of teeth) on the end of their snouts, which has given them their alternative name of "carpenter fish". The saw is used to dig out the crustaceans on which they feed. Members of the ray and shark family, they are much endangered, but have been extremely important in the mythology and religious practices of many cultures.

In **dreams and visions**, the sawfish speaks of an impressive person, one who is held in esteem and carries weight and authority with everyone they meet.

This meaning also feeds through to the fish as **totem animal**, giving sawfish people influence wherever they go.

Scorpion
(*Scorpiones spp*)
Elements: water and fire.
Deities: Chelamma, Hedetet, Ishkara, Malinalxochitl, Scorpius, Selket, Ta-Bitjet, Xochiquetzal.
This eight-legged beast carries its tail – with the murderous sting – in a threatening posture over its body, pointing at any enemy that approaches. It is closely related to spiders, and strikes fear into most people – yet it is a popular aquarium pet.

Found all across the world, except Antarctica, it includes species of many colours and sizes, including the yellow-tailed scorpion, which is found in the UK at Sheerness.

Scorpions have a wide range of meanings in **dreams and visions**, but their primary symbolism is that of sex, particularly sex that is slightly off the "beaten track", fetishism and alternative sexualities, as well as so-called normal sex. They also speak of death and rebirth and healing, but may also indicate the approach of an enemy.

As a **totem animal**, the scorpion brings great power, the power to make others fear one, as well as respect. The personality traits associated with the birth sign Scorpio are also relevant: jealousy, secretiveness and resentment but also courage, loyalty and honesty.

Sea Anemone

(*Actiniaria spp*)

Element: water.

Deities: Aphrodite/Venus.

It looks like a flower, rooted to a rock and waving colourful "petals", yet a closer look reveals a hungry mouth and a set of tentacles that look like something from HP Lovecraft. This is an animal and a successful predator (it can move when it wants to) – and it has friends! Anemones are fond of attaching themselves to shellfish, such as crabs, to take advantage of the scraps dropped by their hosts, and they also permit some fish (such as the "*Finding Nemo*" clownfish) to live safely among their stinging tentacles as camouflage or bait.

In **dreams and visions**, these animals signify changes after a long period, perhaps of moving from a house you have lived in for many years, due to unforeseen circumstances.

As a **totem animal**, it brings the ability to take advantage of any situation and the will to take the best that life has to offer.

Sea Cow

(*Sirenia spp*)

Element: water.

Deities: Aphrodite/Venus, Neptune/Poseidon.

Sea cow is a general term given to dugongs and manatees – similar animals which share a common ancestor with the elephant and are not related to seals, dolphins or whales. Large gentle plant-eating animals, they lack hind limbs but have a massive tail with a whale-like fluke. Their heavy, fat-storing bodies are normally around 2-4 metres long. Their classification *sirenia* stems from the Greek word for mermaids, as these animals are believed to have been one origin of the legends. When surfacing briefly, perhaps suckling a baby at their breast, they may have been mistaken for these legendary fishy ladies. Sea cows are found in the oceans and in fresh water in Africa, Asia and South America.

Seeing a sea cow in **dreams and visions** speaks of gentle, passive behaviour coupled with great wisdom: those who know the Kipling story, *The White Seal*, will remember the silent guru-like sea cow who leads Kotick to the promised haven where his people will be safe from seal hunters.

As a **totem animal**, it brings these qualities to the personality and behaviour, along with good fortune and health.

Sea Lion or Sealion

(*Otariidae otariinae*)

Element: water.

Deities: Proteus, Psamathe, all sea deities.

Although related to seals (and walruses), sea lions have quite a few differences, the most visible being the way they bounce along on dry land using their flippers as legs, whereas seals tend to heave themselves about sprawling on their bellies. Sea lions are well known for their loud barking cry and for having prominent ears, which most seal species lack. They can be aggressive towards humans and, as they migrate quite far onto dry land to breed, they are often impacted by human activity and may be run over by vehicles or killed because they have invaded gardens or farmland. *Sealioning* is a modern slang term for a type of internet trolling in which a person is relentlessly questioned to their own detriment, with the intention of showing them as unreasonable.

In **dreams and visions**, sea lions speaks of friendly help, particularly in business – though the internet term mentioned above needs to be borne in mind if you are familiar with it. They can also speak of transformation, life enhancing change and enjoyment.

People with a sea lion **totem animal** are friendly, playful and artistic.

Sea Slug

(*Gastropod spp*)

Element: water.

Deities: Doris and Nereus.

The word slug conjures the grey slimy pests that munch on our garden vegetables and leave a trail of goo behind them as they crawl, but sea slugs can be awesomely beautiful, and also delicious: although some species are venomous, the Chinese are very fond of dried sea slug skins. They are also popular aquarium pets. There is a huge diversity of species, from the sea lettuce (which has green frills) and the sea hare to neon-bright blue and pink species.

Seeing them in **dreams and visions** speaks of being out of control in some way, usually through emotion, but they also speak of a surprise – usually a pleasant one.

As a **totem animal**, they bring gifts such as clairvoyance and clairaudience, and are symbols of transformation.

Sea Urchin

(*Echinoidea spp*)

Elements: water and fire.

Deities: Hebe and Hercules.

The sea urchin gets its name from the old rural term for a hedgehog, because they are small, round and covered in sharp spines: in fact, an unwary foot can suffer a nasty injury from them, although they are not poisonous. The ancients believed them to be petrified thunderbolts and wore their shells as amulets. Popular as food in Asia, they are also kept in aquaria.

In **dreams and visions**, urchins have many meanings, including a quarrel with a loved one, spiritual progress and development and a windfall of some kind – check the "feel" of the dream for the right one.

As a **totem animal**, it brings protection but also some isolation and loneliness.

Seagull

(*Laridae spp*)

Elements: air and water.

Deities: Aphrodite/Venus, Danu, Leocothea.

The term "gull" is applied to many seabirds, but every person who has ever been on a seaside holiday will recognise what it means to them: large noisy white birds with yellow bills, fierce eyes and attitude! They are found all along coastal areas and are particularly drawn to fishing ports, as they are natural scavengers. In fact, they also spend a lot of time inland, visiting garbage tips and following the farmer's plough for worms. Due to holidaymakers feeding them, many have become very aggressive and have been known to snatch ice-creams from children's hands or steal sandwiches or even fish suppers! I have personally encountered a young gull which had grown so fat on this diet that it could no longer fly.

Seeing them in **dreams and visions** speaks of a struggle towards improvement, whether in the work environment or the spiritual life: remember the journey of Richard Bach's *Jonathan Livingston Seagull*? However earthbound (in the spiritual and intellectual sense) the gull may seem, it symbolises the desire for freedom and advancement.

As a **totem animal**, it brings self-sufficiency, independence and freedom – these are people that are very happy with their own company, though they may also have a rich social life.

Seahorse

(*Hippocampus spp*)

Element: water.

Deities: Makara, Neptune/Poseidon.

These creatures have an undoubted resemblance to a horse, yet are tiny: typically less than 30cms long, and they are related to pipefish not ponies. Cartoons and books have long portrayed them whimsically as beasts of burden for sea people. Their other famous characteristic is that the male seahorse brings up the family. The female lays her eggs in his belly pouch, and he tends them until they hatch and sometimes beyond.

In Chinese medicine they are used for bedwetting and initiating labour.

In **dreams and visions**, seahorses speak of the need to show your true colours, to break free of the enforced environment in which you find yourself and seek your real place in the world.

As **totem or power animals**, they bring peace, freedom and adaptability.

Seal
(*Pinnipedia: otariidae* and *phocidae spp*)
Element: water.
Deities: Proteus, Psamathe, all sea deities.
These creatures have a definite split personality: in the sea they swim gracefully and swiftly, masters of their watery domain, whilst on land they shuffle their huge fat bodies along, apparently with immense effort, clearly not at home on dry land. In the water their huge brown eyes glisten; on land they appear sore and watery. Intelligent and for the most part friendly, they have played a large part in mythologies, particularly the legends of the selkie, a seal creature that may come ashore and shed its skin to become apparently human. Selkies were believed to sometimes marry humans – especially if the bridegroom had taken the precaution of hiding the sealskin – and even to have children with them, returning to the sea if they ever found their skin.

In **dreams and visions**, seals symbolise buried emotions and secrets, particularly family secrets revolving around paternity or hidden family wealth. They also speak of feeling at one with one's world and not wishing to leave it for another (in which, one would not be as comfortable).

As a **totem animal**, the seal brings a playful spirit, and a friendly disposition which will always help the person as they go through life, making friends and allies wherever they go.

Serval
(*Leptailurus serval*)
Element: fire.
Deities: Bast, Mafdet, Pakhet, Sekhmet.
This African wild cat has the longest legs of any cat, including the cheetah (which it resembles), relative to its body size, which it uses to leap right up into the air, descending on some luckless rodent or lizard that it has earmarked for dinner. It has recently been interbred with the domestic cat to produce a hybrid pet that combines its striking looks with the tameness of an ordinary moggie.

In **dreams and visions,** the serval speaks of self-awareness and self-sufficiency, of being your own person and holding to your own opinions and objectives whoever you are with.

As a **totem animal**, it brings these same qualities into the personality, with a certain fierce pride and individuality that does not make compromises to please others.

Shark
(*Selachimorpha spp*)
Element: water.
Deities: Dakuwaqa, Kamohoali'I, Ketea, Lamia, Sebek.

Sharks have been an object of terror to people since the first humans took to the water to swim or boat after fish, and the classic movie *Jaws* (1975) did nothing to ease this fear. Yet hardly any shark species are dangerous: only four types have been associated with unprovoked attacks on humans in any number. Research has tended to demonstrate that sharks are only dangerous if they somehow mistake a swimmer for the prey they are currently feeding on – so that a man in a black wetsuit, for example, might be attacked in an area where sharks are predating on seals.

These most ancient of fish have some interesting symbolic meanings attached to them when they appear in **dreams and visions**, and not all about swimmers getting eaten. While a shark in a dream does speak of danger, it is also about strength and power, and the injunction to never give up, but to stay focused on one's goals no matter what.

As a **totem animal**, it gives strength and grace, creativity and renewal: sharks grow their teeth throughout their lives – as teeth are lost at the front, another row is always developing behind to replace them – thus they symbolise endlessly renewed power.

Sheep
(*Ovis aries*)
Element: fire.
Deities: Amun, Andjety, Ares/Mars, Baal, Banebdjedet, Bride, Dummuzi, Duttur, Ea, Ishtar, Khnum, Pales, Pan, Psyche, Thor.

Sheep have been a blessing to mankind for millennia, bringing milk, meat and wool for clothing – yet they are not esteemed in return. "Sheep" has become a byword for a stupid, easily led person with no thoughts of their own, "sheepish" is an adjective meaning foolish and lacking in confidence. Yet recent research has shown that they have high intelligence and social structures and recognise up to 50 sheep faces, even for years.

Sheep formed the matrix of the English economy long before industry, and the Speaker in the House of Lords sits on the Woolsack (a huge cushion stuffed with wool) in recognition of this. Sheep were a favoured choice for sacrifice to the gods in ancient times, and Jesus Christ is often likened to a lamb – as a symbol of innocence and sacrifice, or as a shepherd – and sheep imagery has been used in many ways in Christianity. They are an important source of meat worldwide, but particularly in cultures where other meats are taboo.

While sheep and lambs are seen as timid and helpless, rams are made of sterner stuff and are seen as aggressive and determined. The name "ram" has been given to mechanical and other devices created for battering, pumping and pushing, and the personality traits assigned to the zodiac sign of Aries include confidence, determination and impulsiveness.

Found in many folk tales, poems, books and cartoons, they have also been important in science (for example: Dolly, the first cloned sheep), in heraldry and even as a resource for the sleepless, who might count imaginary sheep as an aid to falling asleep.

In **dreams and visions**, sheep may symbolise wealth and comfort, or they may speak of stupidity and stupid people, perhaps people who are failing to heed warnings and are rushing headlong into trouble. Or it could be a warning against being pressured into making the wrong decision against your better judgement. Check the "feel" of the dream to see which meaning is relevant. A ram may speak of perseverance, or the need for this, or it may be a warning that you are wasting your time on something you can never change. A lamb is a symbol of innocence and harmlessness.

As **totem animals**, sheep bring a strong sense of community and a willingness to make sacrifices for the greater good, as well as an innate innocence.

Shellfish

(*Mollusca spp*)
Element: water.
Deities: Aphrodite/Venus, Kiwa, Nerites.
The term shellfish includes animals like crabs and sea urchins but this section is about shelled molluscs, such as winkles, limpets and whelks, which are related to land snails. These are the shellfish that leave their hard, calcareous shells on the beach when they die, to be collected by children. Holding a shell to one's ear is said to enable you to hear the sea, even when you are nowhere near it (actually what you hear is the blood circulating in your ear). These shellfish range from tiny micromollusks to the metre-long Australian trumpet. Some have had cultural significance: the beautiful conch shell has been used in religious practice as a wind instrument, while the cowrie shell has been used as money and for jewellery. Some shellfish produce pearls by coating an irritating piece of grit that has got into their shell with nacre; these and the inner surface of the shell ("mother-of-pearl") are used in jewellery and other luxury products.

In **dreams and visions**, shellfish, like crustaceans, are often about the need for protection, or the feeling that you need privacy, to be alone for a while. Large, colourful or tropical shellfish may speak of the need for magic and excitement in your life. They can be about sex: many shellfish have structures that suggest female genitals. Or they can be about spirituality and the life beyond death.

As **totem animals**, shellfish bring shyness and a desire for one's own company, but also an unwillingness to cause any harm to others and the need to live peacefully with one's neighbours.

Shoebill

(*Balaeniceps rex*)

Element: water.

Deities: none identified.

This seriously endangered bird may be a stork or a pelican: it has been called the whale-headed stork because of its large head and massive bill. At up to five feet tall (150cms), it is one of the largest wading birds. Although it can fly, it does not achieve any great speed, make long flights nor rise high in the air.

In **dreams and visions**, it symbolises clumsiness.

As a **totem animal**, it brings good fortune and an ability to be content with what you have, envying no one.

Shrew

(*Soricidae spp*)

Element: fire.

Deity: Horus.

The term "shrew" has been used as an opprobrious term for a sharp-tongued woman, as in Shakespeare's *The Taming of the Shrew*, perhaps because the common shrew found in the UK is one of several species of shrew that is venomous – the only mammal to have such a trait. All true shrews are tiny, including the Etruscan shrew, which is the smallest mammal at less than 2g. The shrew's metabolism is so fast that it must eat several times its own weight in food every day.

Although it looks like a mouse, the shrew is not a rodent, but more closely related to moles and hedgehogs, and it has small needle-sharp teeth instead of the rodents' large incisors. There are a huge number of species, and some animals which are not related also bear the name "shrew".

In **dreams and visions**, shrews speak of problems in the community, of jealousy, envy, gossip and spite, particularly among women. Their appearance may warn against this, or against taking part in it.

As a **totem animal**, the shrew brings an intensely restless spirit, with great energy – although this may happen in bursts.

Shrimp: see Prawn.

Skunk

(*Mephitidae spp*)

Element: air.

Deities: Artemis/Diana, Cernunnos, Mephitis.

With an odour that can knock you off your feet, leaving you blinded and vomiting, and the likelihood that it carries rabies, the skunk does not seem likely to make many friends. Yet it has become a fairly popular pet in the US (with its scent glands removed) and has been depicted in many animated films and programmes as cute and cuddly.

The skunk we have all come to know (from *Bambi*, the immortal Warner Bros character, Pepé le Pew, and Sonic the Hedgehog) is black with white stripes down its back and tail. Yet, although all skunk species have the stripes, some species may be brown or ginger.

Its appearance in **dreams and visions** is telling you that, whatever you may come up against, you have your own defences, against which few will prevail. It says that you can assert yourself, walk calmly through the danger zone and need only fear things which will not be affected by your own abilities. It may also tell of gossip, rumour and a bad reputation…in other words: something which *stinks*. Skunks can also be speaking of the danger of putting people off through your behaviour, when you would want them as friends.

As a **totem animal**, it brings calm confidence, fearlessness and assertiveness without aggression.

Sloth

(*Folivora spp*)
Element: water.
Deities: Aergia, Ignavia.
Is any animal more suggestive of the art of chillaxing? The sloth moves so slowly that algae grows in its fur, and moths make their home there! Even its face suggests it is in a sublime place of relaxation. Although its name is linked with one of the seven deadly sins, it is a charming, attractive and gentle beast.

Although they do descend to the ground about once a week to relieve themselves, sloths are pretty helpless on the forest floor, their feet with their gigantic claws being adapted entirely for climbing and hanging from branches. However, they can swim well. As its Latin classification suggests, it lives on leaves, although the three-toed sloth may also eat insects and even carrion.

In **dreams and visions**, the sloth calls to mind all the more negative qualities (or are they?) that twenty-first century people have been taught to despise: shyness, lack of ambition, contentment with little, languorousness, dreaminess and passivity. Look at the other components of the dream to see whether you are being warned away from these traits or drawn towards having more of them in your life (your own lifestyle should tell you this in any case).

Nobody is more relaxed than someone with the sloth as their **totem animal**; life is a holiday, as they never feel the need to challenge others or strive towards goals that others care about.

Slow-worm

(*Anguis fragilis*)
Element: earth.
Deity: Bride.
The slow-worm, also called the blind worm, is not a snake but a legless

lizard, as can be seen by examining its eyes. Unlike a snake, the slow-worm has eyelids. Small and usually silvery-pink or brown (though it may have faint spots and stripes), it looks for all the world like a large earthworm and, like worms, it likes to burrow underground. It is completely harmless.

In **dreams and visions**, the animal speaks of discoveries, perhaps rediscoveries of things long lost and forgotten, or of events you have tried to forget or have buried in your subconscious, of family secrets and personal bad memories.

As a **totem animal**, it brings transformation and healing: its ability to regrow its tail links it to recovery and repair.

Slug
(*Gastropoda spp*)
Element: water.
Deities: none identified.
Basically, a shell-less snail, this animal does not seem the most attractive invertebrate, with its squishy body and the slime that coats it and forms a trail behind it as it creeps along. Yet it is vital to the ecosystem, eating and recycling decaying plant matter (and sadly often living plants as well, usually your prized lettuces!). Slugs have none of the charm of snails, however closely related they may be, no pretty patterned shell, just a leathery area on its back called the mantle.

In **dreams and visions**, slugs conjure disgust, which may be aimed at a person in your life, perhaps someone who has tried to initiate a relationship with you or someone close to you. They also speak of a fear of change and of social situations, or situations in which confrontations with others are likely. Like the snail, it speaks of patience, slow progress and endurance.

As a **totem animal**, it brings patience and the ability to aim for a goal and keep going, however slow the progress, knowing you will get there in the end.

Snail
(*Gastropoda spp*)
Element: water.
Deities: Amun, Hermes, Nerites, Quetzalcoatl, Tecciztecatl.
The despair of gardeners everywhere (and basically just a slug with a shell), the snail still manages to be a lot cuter than its shell-less cousins. Unlike the slug, you will see snails as ornaments, pictures, designs on cushions, pottery and textiles, and even as children's toys and characters in children's books. We won't mention the slime. No one would dream of eating a slug, yet snails are considered a delicacy (the Roman snail, *Helix pomata*) and are served in posh restaurants.

The shell makes all the difference, and it can be beautiful, even the brown shell of the common garden snail, *Cornu aspersum, is* a striking mosaic of browns and black. Some of the smaller species found in the UK and in other countries have vivid and colourful shells in peach, pink, lime-green, lemon-yellow and silver, sometimes with black stripes. The snails we see in the UK tend to be around a maximum of 3.5cms in diameter (shell size), yet land snails may be much larger in warmer countries – up to the 30cms giant African snail (*Achatina achatina*).

In **dreams and visions**, the snail speaks of travel and adventures, yet also of staying close to shelter (no one is closer to his home than a snail!). Whether this means a weekend of glamping or a luxury ocean cruise, it will be something to be experienced and enjoyed. However, it may also suggest danger and the need for protection, or the need to be a little less outspoken, to retire "into your shell" a little. It could also suggest that you are being over sensitive on some matter and need to come out and face the music.

As a **totem animal**, the snail brings patience and thoroughness, the pace is slow and yet the goal will be achieved in due time.

Snake

(*Serpentes spp*)

Element: earth.

Deities: Apepi, Asclepius, Buto/Wadjet, Hecate, Hermes/Mercury, Jörmungandr, Manasa, Meretserger, Nehebkau, Ouroboros, Quetzalcoatl, the Rainbow Serpent, Renenut.

Found on all continents except Antarctica, snakes are often beautiful, colourful creatures, sinuous and lithe, also dry: they are not slimy, as many *ophidiophobes* assume, but have smooth scales which give them the feel of beadwork. Venomous snakes often have vivid colours designed to warn off would-be predators. Snakes range in size from the tiny (10cms) Barbados thread snake to the leviathans of the snake world: the anaconda, the python and the boa constrictor, and the King Cobra, largest of the poisonous snakes. In the UK, we rejoice in the grass snake (a harmless beauty which can grow up to 150cms in length), the adder or viper (our only poisonous snake) and the smooth snake (also harmless but bearing a faint resemblance to the adder).

Perhaps more than any other real animal on Earth, the snake has become the subject of fears, superstitions, folk tales and legends. It has always been strongly linked with dragons and with other mythical beasts like the cockatrice, the basilisk and the hydra. While many faiths see it as sacred, Christianity has cast it in the role of pure evil – as the Devil. Despite often having a venomous bite, it has also been associated with medicine and healing, and appears on the caduceus: the serpent-twined staff which has been used as a symbol of the medical profession (though it has two snakes instead of the one shown on the staff of Asclepius). In fact, snake venom is now being used in a wide range of ways, from pain relief to cancer therapy. So many deities are associated with snakes that I have had to list just a selection.

Due to their habit of living in – or disappearing into – narrow holes and crevices, these reptiles have long been associated with the Otherworld and the Underworld, with magic and mystery. Because they shed their skins as they grow, they are associated with regeneration and rebirth, and their ability to swallow their prey whole has led to them being linked to myths about the creation of the world and its end, eclipses and the daily cycle of night and day. They have been symbols of wisdom throughout time, and as symbols themselves they appear in many places, from the staff of Asclepius to the modern Alfa Romeo logo. The spiral shape formed by a coiled snake, or the circle formed by one biting its own tail, have symbolised eternity or immortality or the Mother Goddess, and the phallic shape of the snake also links it with sex and fertility.

In **dreams and visions**, snakes may appear as a symbol of fear – this is particularly true of those with a real phobia – or may often speak of sex and sexual needs, the furtive and "dirty" colour that has clung to sex since Christianity's spread is emphasized here. Otherwise, the animal may be telling you that healing is needed, that you need to get that funny mole checked, or those odd pains you have been getting. But the snake is also a fortunate creature, and the additional message it carries is that you will be all right – as long as you act. For mystics, witches and other magical practitioners snakes may conjure their own personal deity (see list above, though it is far from complete), indicating a more spiritual message offered through other elements of the dream. Seeing sea snakes (or snakes of any kind in water) is a message from your subconscious mind, perhaps a warning about your health or about some threat to your wellbeing.

As a **totem animal**, the snake brings great power, self-awareness, wisdom, energy, the ability to constantly reinvent and refresh yourself, with charm, confidence and innate knowledge. People with the sea snake as totem animal particularly have the ability to adapt themselves to all circumstances.

Snow Leopard or Ounce

(*Panthera uncia*)
Elements: water and fire.
Deities: Dionysus, Durga.
More closely related to the tiger than the leopard, this gorgeous snowy-coloured cat is found in mountainous areas throughout Asia and into Siberia, and is well-adapted for living in very cold conditions; having a thick coat, broad paws to stop it sinking into snow, a fat-storing tail and small, neat ears to minimise heat loss. It is listed as threatened with extinction, as there are believed to be less than 10,000 specimens left in the wild.

Seeing one in **dreams and visions** can suggest that a friend has been undermining you, passing gossip around, or does not have your best interests at heart.

As a **totem animal**, the snow leopard is all about intuition and messages from spirit, which you will receive – if you can recognise them when you do. It also gives adaptability and self-reliance.

Sparrow
(*Passer domesticus*)
Element: air.
Deities: Aphrodite/Venus, Apollo, Demeter.
Although sparrows comprise a fairly large family of birds, they are all quite similar to the house sparrow, which is the one with which everyone in the West is familiar, largely because it is drawn to human habitations and loves to nest in eaves and visit gardens. It was once a great deal more common in towns and villages than it is now, and Londoners were fond of the term "Cockney sparrow" – meaning a chirpy, friendly person who was London born and bred.

It has been seen as the embodiment of "commonness" and vulgarity, of fertility and sex (because its numbers were once so high) and also as a symbol of humbleness and humility (God sees the meanest sparrow fall, unnoticed in the street), and of smallness. Its numbers are estimated to have fallen in the UK by almost 70% since the 1970s. It is a drab little bird, its feathers grey and brown with only the male having the dark brown cap-and-bib markings. It is known for its sociable habits and chattering.

Seeing a sparrow in **dreams and visions** speaks of smaller things growing larger – whether this is about finances or problems. It can also speak of families, and of more children arriving. Generally, it is a good-omened bird associated with friends, chat, parties, gatherings and communities, but if the dream has a darker tinge to it then the bird may be signalling nasty gossip.

As a **totem animal**, the sparrow brings good luck, a cheerful and sociable disposition and the potential for a happy marriage.

Sparrowhawk: see **Hawk.**

Spider
(*Araneae spp*)
Element: water.
Deities: Anansi, Arachne, Athene, Uttu.
Now, before the arachnophobes (me included) start getting on chairs and screaming, let me say that spiders do have a bad press. According to Wikipedia, only 100 deaths were proven to be due to spider bites in the whole world in the whole of the twentieth century. Does that make you feel better? Probably not, for there are good genetic reasons why people fear spiders, and why far more women than men (something like five to one) fear them. We are hard-wired to be afraid of anything that looks even remotely like something that could harm us – and women more so, as they have children to protect. That is why horror films like *Arachnophobia* (1990) produce the result they do.

Spiders are actually amazing and beneficial creatures on the whole (we won't mention the horrors like the black widow and the James Bond tarantula ... gahhh!), which dispose of pests like flies and spin those beautiful webs on bushes and on the grass which we admire in the autumn when they are bejewelled with dew. The silk has some uses in industry, and in some countries spiders form part of the human diet. In African culture, the spider Anansi (the cultural ancestor of the Brer Rabbit stories) is a likeable trickster who always comes out on top.

Spiders vary enormously in appearance and size. The large-bodied, colourful "autumn spiders" that hang in the bushes in late September do not worry an arachnophobe nearly as much as the black "hairy" varieties, such as *Tegenaria domestica*, which are far more likely to come into the house. And the very tiny "money spiders" are even welcomed, with the customary, "You're going to come into some money!"

Dreams and visions of spiders are about fear, perhaps a fear that you have not acknowledged, or a fear that is about to manifest, and the best way to deal with it is to face it head-on (with a rolled-up newspaper?). It may be about long-buried things in your past (maybe your childhood) that you have refused to come to terms with but must now deal with as they are having repercussions in your life. It may be to do with fears about sex and (again) this may stem from your childhood experiences.

As **totem or power animals**, they bring great creativity (remember the story of Arachne, who challenged Athene Herself to a weaving contest?) with the patience and the methodical nature to carry it through. Spider people are gentle and always prefer to avoid conflict but, if pressed, are well able to take care of themselves.

Sponge

(*Porifera spp*)
Element: water.
Deities: Hygieia and all sea gods.
You probably first became aware of this animal at bath-time, for before artificial polymer sponges became the norm, the skeletal remains of real sponges were used to wash. They can still be bought, as some people prefer them, and they are also used for arts and crafts – for example, "sponging" a wall to produce a textured effect. If you mention the word "sponge" to a modern child you will probably get a delighted cry of "Spongebob Squarepants!" (who must be the only representative of his kind in the world of animation). In real life, sponges are multi-shaped, multi-coloured and mobile, living off food particles filtered from seawater.

The quality most people think of in connection with sponges is their ability (when dead and processed as bath accessories) to absorb in huge amounts, and it is this quality that they signify when they appear in **dreams and visions**, whether this is knowledge, money, drink or some other substance.

People with sponge as their **totem animal** carry on this idea – being receptive, absorbing information and ideas, and being always open to suggestions from others.

Springbok: see Antelope.

Squid

(*Decapodiformes*)
Element: water.
Deities: Kanaloa, Na Kika, the Kraken.
Closely related to the octopus, squid share many features in common, including their high intelligence: squid have even been observed hunting co-operatively. They differ from octopuses in that they have ten tentacles instead of eight, two being longer and equipped with a suckered pad or *manus*. Squid comprise a huge range of species, from the 2cm pygmy squid to the giant and colossal squid, which are of mythic size and the subject of many folktales. Ancient woodcuts showing monstrous squid attacking galleons may be fanciful, but the giant squid (*Architeuthis dux*) is known to grow to around 40 feet, and may grow even larger in the depths of the ocean. The colossal squid (*Mesonychoteuthis hamiltoni)* does not achieve this length, but its huge 700kg body qualifies it for the title of most massive invertebrate. Squid are a popular food, especially in Asia.

In **dreams and visions**, squid speak of problems which can reach into other areas of your life, perhaps come from guilty secrets of the past which have come home to roost. Face your fears, says the squid: it is time to lay them to rest.

As a **totem animal**, the squid brings intelligence, flexibility, resourcefulness and the drive and ability to achieve your aims.

Squirrel

(*Sciuridae spp*)
Element: air.
Deities: Rama, Ratatosk.
In the UK, we have two species of squirrel: the pretty, cherished red (which looks as though it stepped straight from the pages of a Beatrix Potter book) and the grey (which is generally despised as a pest, an interloper and a "tree rat", though it is almost as pretty and graceful as the red). Much bolder than the red, which is now confined to pine forests in the north and odd pockets elsewhere, the grey will cheekily invade gardens and steal food from bird tables.

Squirrels are found all over Europe, Asia, Africa and the Americas, and have been introduced into Australia, where one species is now considered a bio-hazard. They are best-known for their agility in the trees (there are even "flying squirrels" which have a furry membrane between their fore and hind legs and can glide for some distance) and for their habit of storing ("squirrelling away") nuts and other food over the winter. Unlike many other rodents, squirrels do not hibernate; they are "winter snoozers" who will wake up at regular intervals, and so rely on the food they have secreted to survive the cold season.

In **dreams and visions**, a squirrel is telling you of the need for careful conservation of your resources, to set aside something "for a rainy day."

As a **totem animal**, it brings a great sense of fun and enjoyment of life, but also a careful mind and an ability with housekeeping of all kinds.

Starfish

(*Asteroidea spp* and *Ophiura ophiura*)
Element: fire.
Deities: Isis and Mary.
Innocent as they seem, these cute little star-shaped invertebrates are actually fierce predators which roam the ocean floor looking for smaller creatures to gobble. Some have the charming habit of emptying their stomachs over their prey, to give the gastric juices a head start (however inefficient this may seem underwater). One species, the crown-of-thorns (*Acanthaster planci*), has wrought havoc on the Great Barrier Reef, as it eats coral polyps. Starfish are also toxic – though they are eaten in some countries – and can grow back arms if they are lost.

In contrast to their ferocious lifestyles, starfish have good, reassuring meanings when they crop up in **dreams and visions**, signifying good luck, new beginnings, healing and regeneration (or they may speak of the need for healing and time out), as well as success in current ventures. Their association with the Goddesses Isis and Mary, who both carry the title Stella Maris (Star of the Sea), makes them very protective.

As a **totem animal**, it brings the ability to continually reinvent oneself to face all challenges and to come back from illness, disgrace or other misfortune – every time.

Stick Insect

(*Phasmatodea spp*)
Element: earth.
Deity: Tane.
A master of disguise, this insect looks exactly like a twig (other species may look like leaves) and is only given away when it starts to move. I kept a stick insect when I was a kid. It grew to over a foot long and produced hundreds of eggs, which hatched: stick insects are parthenogenetic and do not need males to reproduce. Stick insects, which represent the longest insects on Earth, generally do not fly and many species are wingless. The Maoris regarded them as sacred and believed a stick insect landing on a woman was a sign that she was pregnant.

In **dreams and visions**, the stick insect speaks of good luck, perhaps disguised as something else, but ultimately revealing itself. It can also speak of nature, of the need to go somewhere green and relax, away from noise and stress.

As a **totem animal,** it brings a certain cleverness and an ability to blend in with any community or situation.

Stoat
(*Mustela erminea*)
Element: fire.
Deities: none identified, although the stoat has been important in many mythologies.

The stoat is one more animal that people may have two views about: on the one hand, it is a smelly, sneaky little predator which will steal eggs and kill your chickens; on the other, its fur is simply the most luxurious of all, fit only for monarchs and nobles … ermine.

Stoats are easily distinguished from weasels by their black-tipped tail (which is quite bushy at the end), by their brown colour (weasels are more gingery) and their considerably larger size. They prey on small rodents and rabbits – creatures much larger than themselves (which they are reputed to hypnotise by sinuous movements), also birds, eggs and nestlings.

Very common in the UK and Europe, this animal can turn pure white in the winter if it is sufficiently cold, only the black tip of its tail remaining unchanged: the tails form the black spots on ermine, which has been used to line and edge ceremonial robes from early times.

In **dreams and visions**, stoats speak of friendship, and while a white stoat may signify a real friend, the brown version may speak of a false friend, one you should not trust.

As a **totem animal**, it brings ingenuity, intelligence, the ability to trick and bluff others, but also a predisposition for learning.

Stork
(*Ciconiidae spp*)
Element: air.
Deities: all gods and goddesses of healing.

These tall, elegant birds have been important in the myths of many cultures; today they are probably best-known in the West for the story told to young children to explain the appearance of a new brother or sister: "the stork brought him/her." At the other end of the spectrum, the Slavs saw the stork as a psychopomp, carrying the souls of those recently dead to the next world. In the ancient world, the stork was believed to be able to heal itself with herbs.

Storks have always been believed to be monogamous (until modern tagging and tracking methods proved that this is not necessarily so) and in Norse mythology they represented family values and marital faithfulness.

In **dreams and visions**, storks speak of new beginnings and happy ones, too, particularly in the context of family. Whether this is a simple family holiday or a reconciliation between an estranged couple depends on what is happening in the life of the dreamer, but of course a major meaning of the stork is the suggestion that a new baby may be on the way.

As a **totem animal**, the bird brings elegance and beauty, kindness and an ability to know oneself – to connect with one's inner knowledge and emotions.

Sturgeon
(*Acipenseridae spp*)
Element: water.
Deities: Goddesses of wisdom and fertility, Jesus.

These ancient fish, with their bony back plates and their long crocodilian snouts can frighten anyone who sees one nearby: one suggested explanation for the Loch Ness Monster sightings is a large sturgeon living in the loch. Certainly they thrive in fresh and brackish water, as well as seawater and, salmon-like, they return to the river in which they were spawned to lay their eggs. Long-lived and often very large (up to 5 metres long), they are found all over the Northern Hemisphere.

Unfortunately, the demand for their roe – caviar – has resulted in overfishing, and sturgeon numbers are on the decline.

Generally, dreams about fish are to do with emotions, but seeing a sturgeon in **dreams and visions** can be about wealth and luxury, as its caviar suggests. Enjoy the fine things in life while you can, says this fish, which also speaks of the beauty and mystery of nature, particularly water.

As a **totem animal**, it brings strength, endurance and prosperity.

Sugar Glider
(*Petaurus breviceps*)
Element: air.
Deities: none identified.

Basically a flying possum, this Australian marsupial lives for its sugar hits! It is omnivorous, but a large (and preferred) part of its diet is sweet plant sap, nectar and honeydew exuded from insects or crystallised plant juices. They "fly", or rather glide, by the use of furry membranes between their fore and hind legs, and can cross some 50 metres of air space between branches.

Seeing one in **dreams and visions** is telling you, "life is sweet … and it will get even better." It says: go with the flow and trust in your own good fortune, for right now you are in clover.

As a **totem animal**, it brings the gift of enjoyment of whatever life brings, and the good fortune to ensure this is usually nice things.

Swallow and Swift
(*Hirundinidae spp*)
Elements: air and water.
Deities: Aphrodite, Nephthys, Isis.

These iconic birds conjure the feel of autumn with the very mention of their names, as most people notice them most when they are arrayed along telephone wires, preparing to migrate to warmer climes. No one really sees them arriving, but they are also a symbol of summer (*one swallow does not a summer make*). Swallows, swifts and martins are all closely related and have similar behaviours, and most people would find it difficult to tell them apart on the wing. These birds are generally black, dark grey or dark blue on the upper side, with white, pink or red on their breasts, with long tails. They are particularly enjoyed by bird lovers for their habit of building nests made from mud, under the eaves of houses: while this can be messy and noisy for the inhabitants, it is thrilling to see the eggs hatch and the nestlings grow and finally fly.

Hirundines can have a number of meanings when they show up in **dreams and visions**, including a happy marriage and fidelity to a partner, love of home and of family. Most birds speak of news and messages in divination, but if these birds are seen gathered on branches and cables, as they prepare to leave for southern latitudes, then they can speak of journeys, farewells, partings and endings, even death.

As **power or totem animals**, they bring not (as you would expect) a free spirit and a love of adventure, but a preference for routine, for habit and for much loved and well-trodden ways. Yet they love their lives and are not in the least drawn to change for its own sake.

Swan

(*Cygnus cygnus*)
Element: water.
Deities: Aphrodite/Venus, Artemis/Diana, Bride, Laima, Sarasvati, Sif, the Valkyries.
From earliest times, the swan has been seen as a symbol of purity, serenity and beauty, and it is easy to see why. This graceful creature with its pure white plumage and delicately arched neck floats, unhurriedly and seemingly without effort, on the water – a vision of beauty and grace. Swans also pair for life, so have been linked with love and fidelity: when interacting, they can even form a heart shape with their two necks as they canoodle!

Popular in art and heraldry, swans also appear in many myths and stories, including The Children of Lir, the Greek Tale of Leda and The Wooing of Etain.

The other side of their personality is aggression. Although the urban myth about their being able to break your arm with their wings is nonsense, they certainly will attack any human that ventures near their nest, and can inflict nasty injuries with their beaks. Four species of white swan are known, plus a species in Australia that is black, and a black-necked species.

A white swan seen in **dreams and visions** speaks of harmony, grace, beauty, joy and hope, especially relating to romantic issues. The human mind being what it is, however, one should bear in mind the twenty-first century adage of the swan as representing calm, grace and competence on the surface, accompanied by panic and turbulence beneath! A black swan symbolises something totally unexpected coming into your life: this meaning comes from the Roman poet Juvenal's snide remark about a virtuous woman being as rare as a black swan (i.e. something that does not exist), before the black swan became known, as a result of the discovery of Australia.

As a **totem animal**, the swan brings all the virtues one would expect, those of grace, serene calm, beauty and inner beauty, plus happiness in romantic partnerships.

Tamarin: see **Monkey.**

Tapeworm
(*Cestoda spp*)
Element: earth.
Deities: Fames/Limos.
Not a nice subject, but did you know that fashionable ladies in Edwardian times were supposedly wont to deliberately acquire these parasites in order to keep their trim figures? Actually, it probably did not help, as having worms famously gives the victim a big appetite, and worm infestations can also give their host a pot belly. Many tapeworms target particular kinds of host, for example your dog will have a completely different species of tapeworm to that which you yourself might acquire from eating, say, undercooked pork. There are a lot of very nasty stories out there concerning tapeworms, but in fact the host may be quite unaware that they are infected, as symptoms may be minimal.

Oddly enough, tapeworms do not have a horrible meaning when they occur in **dreams and visions**: they speak of unneeded materials passing away from you, especially if you dream of them actually coming out of your body. They can mean healing is needed and, if the dream indicates a person in your life, it can signify a person who is draining you, feeding off you in some way, that you need to cast off.

As **totem animals**, they have much in common with earthworms, giving a grounding influence.

Tapir
(*Tapiridae spp*)
Element: earth.
Deities: Baku, Iriria, Tlaloc.
Found in the Americas and Malaysia, this animal looks like a large pig with an elongated snout or short trunk. It comes from the ungulate family, and is distantly related to the rhinoceros, yet its lifestyle is closer to that of the hippopotamus. Tapirs love water and spend a large proportion of their lives in it, feeding, cooling off and even mating underwater. Their size makes them fairly invulnerable to predators, and they are well able to defend themselves with their teeth and their bulky bodies. Most tapirs are brown, the mountain tapir also with thick wool to protect it from the cold in its native Andes, but the handsome Malayan tapir is black and white, in a similar pattern to the giant panda.

Seeing a tapir in **dreams and visions** may speak of the need for healing and specifically the use of the healing properties of water. It speaks of long life, but also the need to ensure this with the care of the body.

As a **totem animal**, the tapir brings toughness and endurance, and an ability to work hard and enjoy work for its own sake, which leads to success and prosperity. Yet it can also bring shyness and a disinclination for any social life.

Tarantula: see **Spider.**

Tasmanian Devil
(*Sarcophilus harrisii*)
Element: fire.
Deities: none identified, but the devil has been important in cultures outside Australia. Christians have associated it with their Devil.

This animal was immortalised by the Looney Toons character Taz, created in 1954 and voiced by Mel Blanc (though his speech consists largely of gibberish, raspberries and buzz-saw effects). The real animal on which he is based is a small marsupial predator – which is now quite endangered – and it does share some characteristics with Taz, including its ferocity, its loud and terrifying screeching cry and its incredibly powerful bite – the most powerful of any living warm-blooded predator. It also has a strong and unpleasant smell. The size of a terrier dog, it is jet black, apart from a white stripe across the chest and white marks on the rump (although many devils do not have these markings). Like its distant relative, the now extinct Tasmanian tiger, it has suffered from the depredations of man, being hunted extensively in the early days of European settlement of Tasmania because it was believed to attack sheep (it is capable of killing sheep and small kangaroos, but prefers carrion). Climate change and Devil Facial Tumour Disease have continued to lower populations, but conservationists have been working on reintroducing devils to mainland Australia, where it has been extinct for 3,000 years. The devil has a very short lifespan: around five years.

Seeing a Tasmanian devil in **dreams and visions** speaks of madness, fury and utter aggressiveness, perhaps even being out of control altogether. Although it is also a symbol of personal power, its message is clear: calm down or stand to lose everything. Find another way of dealing with a situation, as the course you are on leads to all sorts of harm.

As a **totem animal**, the devil does bring power, but this can often be quite destructive. However, the animal is also connected with healing.

Termite
(*Termitidae spp*)
Element: earth.
Deities: Amma, Bramari.

Although related to ants, termites have some important differences, including their social structure, which stems from a mated pair, a king and queen, who pair for life. They commonly build large mounds from soil to house the colony, showing instinctive awareness of how to place and shape the mound so that it benefits from the heat of the Sun or avoids the hottest rays, depending on the climate. Some termites nest underground and some in trees. They have become greatly feared by homeowners in countries where homes are largely built from wood, as they will gnaw at the structure and are often not detected until it is in danger of collapse. Termites are used in African folk medicine.

Seeing them in **dreams and visions** speaks of unease and anxiety, of fears that your life, your whole world, may be about to collapse due to a problem which has been going on for some time but which you have been powerless to change.

As a **totem animal,** the termite brings strength, co-operation and a predilection for hard work, especially work that involves others and is carried out as a community activity.

Thrush
(*Turdidae spp*)
Element: air.
Deities: Apollo, the Morrigan, Wahineomo.
This most familiar garden bird is easily recognised by its speckled breast, its pretty song (it is also referred to as the song thrush) and its habit of bashing snails on a convenient stone to get at the meat – a rare example of birds purposefully using tools. Like many garden birds, it has been eaten by humans in the past.

Thrushes in **dreams and visions** are all about romance and sweetness, friendship and happiness. The bird may be telling you that a new friend who has entered your life may become more than a friend, or it may just be an expression of happiness and contentment.

As a **totem animal**, the bird brings good fortune, a positive attitude to life and a security in relationships.

Tick
(*Ixodida spp*)
Element: water.
Deity: Tara.
Not a pleasant subject, this parasite is familiar to anyone who walks their dog in wet meadows: it looks like a pearl, usually attached to the chest or neck of the animal, but closer inspection shows tiny legs or tentacles at the base. It lives on the blood of the creature to which it has attached itself, and may become quite bloated with blood. For its size, it is straight out of *Alien* (1979). In case it needed to be any nastier, it is an arachnid, closely related to spiders and it may carry various diseases with which it infects its host, including Lyme disease and meningoencephalitis.

Astonishingly, ticks have been seen as harbingers of good fortune in many cultures, and in **dreams and visions** they speak of patience and endurance – qualities they also bring as **totem animal**.

Tiger
(*Panthera tigris*)
Element: fire.
Deities: Dawon, Dingu-Aneni, Dionysus, Durga/Kali, Waghoba.

Tyger, tyger, burning bright
In the forests of the night.
What immortal hand or eye
Could frame thy fearful symmetry?

This largest and arguably most beautiful of all cats has had a profound effect on man, who has worshipped it, feared it and hunted it from earliest times. Sadly, the hunting – or rather poaching – goes on, and tiger numbers are still being depleted for Asian medicines, despite the work of international conservation bodies.

From the ebullient Tigger in *Winnie the Pooh* to the sinister Shere Khan in Kipling's *The Jungle Book* and the friendlier but still dangerous animal in Tea Obreht's *The Tiger's Wife*, the tiger has invaded literature and also movies: most famously the CGI Richard Parker in *The Life of Pi* (2012). In the UK, most of us grew up with Tony the Tiger on our breakfast cereal packets. In Asian belief, there are "were-tigers", people who can turn into tigers, and the Chinese zodiac has a tiger year, and a white tiger represents the West in their astrology. White tigers are not common, but there are numerous specimens in zoos – and very beautiful and mysterious they look. There are also tales of Maltese tigers – with blue-grey fur and black stripes – but they have never been proven to exist.

A tiger in **dreams and visions** is the ultimate symbol of power: look at the dream content to decide whether this is something that belongs to you or whether it represents a threat to you. It speaks of huge willpower, courage and motivation, together with the energy to fulfil any desires.

As a **totem animal**, the tiger brings a wild nature that is not easily subdued, but also the great patience and serenity of one who knows they need fear nothing and no one.

Tit

(*Paridae spp*)
Element: air.
Deities: Hermes/Mercury.
The variety of these small passerine birds is truly surprising: there seems to be one for every mood! From the monochrome coal tit to the great tit, they gather on your bird feeder, chattering and bustling and pushing one another aside. All tits and chickadees are small and have short beaks to cope with their seed and nut diet, but usually have some other common characteristics, typically the "cap and bib" markings and often a brightly coloured breast.

See **Finch** for meanings.

Toad

(*Bufo bufo*)
Element: earth.
Deities: Hecate, Heket, Tlaltecuhti.
The toad is one of those animals that no one has a good word for...apart

from witches. Ugly, slimy, warty and creepy are some of the words commonly applied to this animal. Yet it is not slimy at all, but dry and warm and, whatever you think of its looks, it has the most beautiful eyes, like orange jewels. It is also prized by gardeners, for it does good work in the vegetable bed, devouring slugs and snails.

Toads generally are warty, dry-skinned frogs, and tend to be brown rather than green, also preferring to creep rather than hop. They are also known for having toxins in their skins to protect them from predators: which has given rise to the relatively new drug craze called toad-licking. Those seeking a high, however, usually find nausea, chest pains and other unpleasant symptoms instead.

The most famous toad in culture is the owner of Toad Hall in Kenneth Graham's classic children's story, *The Wind in the Willows*, and no story about witches would be complete without a toad squatting in the corner of one of the illustrations. In past times, the toad was associated with the Christian Devil and with evil sorcery, whilst in Ancient Egypt toad amulets were worn for protection. Toads were once believed to have a magical jewel inside their heads (which must have caused many of these poor animals to be killed and dismembered) which could protect from poison if worn on the person.

Modern attitudes are more enlightened, and there are even "help a toad across the road" schemes, involving volunteers holding up traffic when toads are travelling to their breeding ponds (like frogs, they need water in which to lay their spawn).

In **dreams and visions**, toads take on a much more positive tone, symbolising wisdom (especially ancient wisdom), magic and healing, and also hidden treasure. Their connection with poison continues, and they may speak of illness approaching, but also of its healing. They may also indicate some negative emotions: repugnance and fear, or jealousy.

As a **totem animal**, the toad brings wisdom, love of secrecy and the ability to transform oneself through self-improvement.

Tortoise

(*Testudinidae spp*)
Element: earth.
Deities: Hermes, Kurma.
Slow and steady wins the race … One thing the tortoise is famous for is its leisurely pace, yet in the Aesop fable it managed to best the fleet hare in a race, simply by continuing to walk at its own steady pace without pausing, while the over-confident hare took a nap. Its slow pace seems to pay other dividends, for the animal is the longest-living creature on Earth, with a recorded lifespan of up to 150 years. In China it is, unsurprisingly, a symbol of longevity.

Tortoises are members of the turtle family, but the term is generally applied only to land-dwelling specimens, which have a shape adapted to dry land, with longer legs rather than paddles, and a harder shell. The polished shell has been used for many kinds of decorative objects throughout history.

Sizes vary from the speckled tortoise to the Egyptian (that's the little chap you might buy your children) to the mighty Galapagos giant tortoise, big enough to ride on.

Always a symbol of good fortune, prosperity and health, the tortoise continues to bring a smile when it turns up in **dreams and visions**, where it speaks of steady progress towards your goal and big rewards at the end.

As a **totem animal**, it brings the ability to work steadily without pause or rest until the object is achieved, impassive and determined, and not to be turned aside by anyone or anything.

Toucan
(*Ramphastidae spp*)
Element: air.
Deities: none identified, but the bird was sacred to many South American cultures.
This eye-catching bird has a beak that is almost as big as itself, a dazzling colour scheme and a repertoire of sound effects that could put a stage performer to shame. No wonder it has always been such a favourite with people, often used as a logo on zoos and animal conservation organisations. When I was a child, many years ago, the Guinness clocks were still to be seen on urban roundabouts and other prominent sites, and featured a toucan as one of the iconic animals on there – all toting and guzzling the advertised beverage.

Native to the Americas, from southern Mexico down to Argentina, toucans can be a variety of vivid colours, the most familiar Ramphastos toucan being black, white and yellow, but their brightest hues are on their oversized beaks. The beak is not very useful for many things, but it can produce a huge variety of calls, from growling, barking, braying like a donkey and croaking like a frog to percussive clattering.

Nature's clowns, toucans symbolise fun, magic and happiness when they enter **dreams and visions** – and also romance and glamour.

As **totem animals**, they bring a unique quality of positivity, enjoyment, mischief and fun.

Trout
(*Salmoninae spp*)
Element: water.
Deities: Aphrodite/Venus, Ea, Dagon, all fish and water gods.
These handsome fish – many with multicoloured patterns of spots and dapples – are not only an important and healthy food for people and animals, but are important in mythology as well. If it were not for the magical salmon (to which trout are closely related), they might well occupy the top spot when it comes to folklore and magical belief. Their fish stories include the mythical furry trout supposedly found in Arctic regions, the white trout of Irish folklore and the giant trout, whose back became the base of the world in Ainu legend. In Asian belief, they are considered extremely lucky and may even have the ability to grant wishes.

Trout are very similar to salmon and also migrate to breed, although (unlike the salmon) they are confined to fresh waters. They are highly prized by fishermen, who use fishing flies to catch them in a similar manner to salmon fishing. Populations of wild trout are declining as climate change affects the water temperatures (they are cold water fish), but trout farming is now well established as a source of food.

In **dreams and visions**, trout (like many edible fish) speak of success and prosperity; even a windfall, and if the fish is a rainbow trout, with its beautiful multicoloured patterning, the good luck is amplified. The fish may also denote spiritual progress, an increase of wisdom and abundance of health.

As a **totem animal**, it brings hope, change for the better, courage, wisdom and determination.

Tuatara
(*Sphenodon punctatus*)
Element: fire.
Deities: Sacred to the Maoris and to Whiro.
These living fossils are the only remaining species of an order that was once larger than that of lizards, but which became virtually extinct towards the end of the Cretaceous Period. The tuatara looks like an iguana, but is not a lizard and is found only in New Zealand – where it has its own exclusive species of tick!

In **dreams and visions**, the tuatara is about hidden gifts, perhaps abilities you did not realise you had, that you must come to appreciate and use to the full.

As a **totem animal**, it brings the ability and the desire to explore one's own gifts and use them, with a particular emphasis on working with and appreciating nature.

Tuna
(*Thunnini spp*)
Element: water.
Deities: Hina, Kohara.
This distinctive fish, with its bullet-shaped body, polished silver skin and narrow tail, is one of the most important seafood sources, though many ethical issues surround its capture, including the danger to dolphins and porpoises from tuna nets. Large, meaty fish, they are sold canned, fresh and frozen. There has long been anxiety about the levels of mercury found in their flesh. Once called "tunny fish" it makes a guest appearance as a character in the children's book, *Pinocchio*.

Seeing one in **dreams and visions** signifies strength and agility, as in the speed of this limber fish as it weaves and flies through the water. Like many edible fish, it speaks of good fortune and prosperity, but this may come at a cost in other ways.

As a **totem animal**, it brings endurance, patience, energy and wisdom.

Turkey
(*Meleagris gallapavo* and *M. ocellata*)
Element: air.
Deity: Chalchihuihtotolin.
Once sacred to the Mayans, these magnificent birds are now linked in most Western minds with Christmas dinner (and Thanksgiving in the US). The famed Norfolk turkey can be black or bronze, but is increasingly likely to be white (as shoppers prefer the clean-looking pink skin of this variant) and has been bred over the centuries to produce ever larger birds with ever plumper breasts. Turkeys originated in the Americas, but soon travelled to Europe, and were imported to the UK in the eighteenth century – the origins of the Norfolk turkey.

The bird has engendered many common expressions in English, including *cold turkey*: the process of coming off drugs or alcohol without medical help, *turkey shoot*: meaning a situation in which the defenceless victims are attacked with many assorted weapons, *talking turkey*: meaning to get down to serious discussion, and the simple use of the word *turkey* to mean a flawed, stupid or useless person or item.

In **dreams and visions**, the given meaning for a turkey is a bad situation in your future. Yet these birds are typically associated with plenty and prosperity, good living and celebrations, with something to look forward to, family reunions and pleasure. In the US, it might also be connected with gratitude and celebration of your way of life. The former, ill-omened, meaning would only be applicable if the dream had a very bad feeling to it, perhaps with other components that spoke of misfortune.

As a **totem animal**, this bird brings the ability to care for oneself, to know what one needs and not to be afraid to go for it, where others might deny themselves through fear or modesty.

Turkey Vulture: see **Buzzard.**

Turtle
(*Testudinidae spp*)
Element: water.
Deities: Akupara, Aphrodite/Venus, Apollo, Artemis/Diana, Asha, Enki, Fjorgyn, Hermes, Kim Qui, Kurma.
The difference between turtles and tortoises is simply that the latter dwell on land (and have more domed shells), while turtles and terrapins live in the water and have a flatter shape. In the US, there is a tendency to call all testudines *turtles*. The family includes the leatherback turtle (the largest turtle of all and the fourth largest reptile) and, at the other end of the scale, tiny reptiles like the 7cm North American bog turtle.

The turtle has always been important in culture, appearing as a cosmic entity supporting the world in more than one mythology (also in Terry Pratchett's *Discworld* series of humorous fantasy books) and in literature and movies, from the Mock Turtle in *Alice in Wonderland* to the modern Gamera (a variant on the Godzilla theme in Japanese films) to the Teenage Mutant Ninja Turtles.

Turtles carry on the theme of supporting the Earth when they appear in **dreams and visions**; symbolising harmony with nature, peace on Earth, contentment and love for one's environment. They are also symbols of strength and endurance, physical ability and wisdom – qualities which the turtle brings as a **totem or power animal**.

Vicuna

(*Lama vicugna*)
Element: earth.
Deities: Apu Illapu, Pachamama, Urcuchillay.
With the closely related guanaco, the vicuna is the ancestor of the llama and alpaca – both of which have been domesticated for generations. The vicuna, which has a more slender, deer-like appearance, is valued for its wool (which was once kept exclusively for royal use) but was never kept as a domesticated animal. By the 1970s, the animal was endangered but populations have since recovered. They are especially valued by the locals in the southern Andes, who still use them as the focus for spiritual practices for prosperity and fertility.

Appearing in **dreams and visions**, the animal speaks of your spiritual path and that of your ancestors, your place on the Earth and your goals as a spiritual being. More than the llama, it speaks of your beliefs and your closeness to nature and to nature spirits.

Those with the vicuna as a **totem animal** may have a deep reverence for Nature and a desire to be at one with Her – to have respect for all life and to use nature as a path towards spiritual enlightenment.

Vulture

(Old World vultures: *Accipitridae*; New World vultures: *Cathartidae*)
Element: earth.
Deities: Ares/Mars, Isis, Mallku (condor), Nekhbet, Prometheus, Zeus.
These magnificent and useful birds are under threat today because of excessive tidying up! In developing countries, it is not seen as desirable to have carrion lying around, so the vultures are deprived of their main food source and populations have declined. In India, agricultural drug therapies have been banned, as their use was affecting the birds that fed on farmed animals after they had died. Other practices that benefited vultures, such as sky burials (exposing corpses on high platforms), have also died out.

To most eyes, they are not attractive creatures: many have bald heads and necks, large sharp beaks, and of course their diet is repugnant to most people. Yet, Nature's refuse collectors; they play an important part in the natural cycle. The bald skin on vultures' heads and necks is necessary, as they may burrow their whole heads into a dead animal carcase, and feathers would become filthy and perhaps breed infection. Their digestive system is specially adapted to deal with decaying meat and fruit, producing high strength acids which kill bacteria and neutralise toxins.

Since they were worshipped as gods by the Ancient Egyptians, vultures have had a poor press: they are scavengers, they callously wait for animals to die and they feed on filth. Yet the other side of this coin includes the aforementioned clearing up of rotting meat and their helpfulness to game wardens, who follow the birds' movements in their pursuit of poachers of conserved animals.

However, in **dreams and visions**, vultures are probably going to be associated with the traditional view of them, and they will signify a morally bankrupt person, someone who enjoys the suffering of others and benefits from their misfortunes. They can also bring the warning that you need to clean up your life and get rid of bad habits and unnecessary baggage, but also friends who are a bad influence or who impact on you in other negative ways.

As a **totem animal**, these birds bring endless patience and are symbols of rebirth, as well as endings. The South American condor is associated with the Sun, so also with justice, honour and hope.

Wallaby

Wallaby is a non-specific name for smaller members of the kangaroo family, and they have the same meaning in **dreams and visions**. See under **Kangaroo**.

Walrus

(*Odobenus rosmarus*)
Element: water.
Deities: A'akuluujjusi, Hoenir/Ve, Sedna.
Immediately recognisable by its huge blubbery body and its pair of long white tusks (which both males and females have and which can reach a metre in length), the walrus is a creature of cold seas, more numerous in the Arctic region than further south. It is a valuable creature to the Inuit and other northern peoples, who hunt it for its meat and fat, its sinews and its hide, even using the bones and teeth as tools. The historic Isle of Lewis chessmen, which date from the twelfth century, are mainly of walrus ivory.

Seeing a walrus in **dreams and visions** speaks of your own personal power and your ability to take the lead in any situation. It may also speak of travel, in the sense of migration – perhaps not only of yourself, but your family and even your community.

As a **totem animal**, it brings great wisdom and strength, and natural leadership abilities, with many other gifts, such as the facility for reconciling quarrelling people and bringing others round to your way of thinking.

Warthog

(*Phacochoerus africanus* and *aethiopicus*)
Element: earth.
Deities: Freyr and Freyja, Moccus, Vahara.
An opprobrious name for an intelligent and sociable creature which does not

actually have warts: the four protrusions on its face are hide-covered tusks. This medium-sized pig has been hunted for its ivory: both males and females have large sharp tusks, though those of the female tend to be smaller. They are razor-sharp, grow throughout the animal's life and are used in self-defence and fighting. Unlike other pigs, the warthog has no subcutaneous fat. It lives on vegetable matter and occasionally meat.

In **dreams and visions**, a warthog signifies someone not very pleasant, who has targeted you for spiteful behaviour such as gossip-mongering or even more practical tricks like poison-pen letters or keying your car. Typically, this person is driven by jealousy; perhaps they are not very physically attractive and feel you outshine them, perhaps with a person to whom they are attracted.

As a **totem animal**, the warthog brings strength, confidence and a rather driven, goal-oriented nature.

Wasp

(*Apocrita spp*)
Element: fire.
Deities: Brahmari, Set.

This insect's name immediately brings to mind the little yellow-and-black striped horrors that circle the jam pot, build nests in your loft and sting you in summer, but there is much more to wasps than the nuisance and painful sting of the common *Vespula vulgaris*. Some are very beautiful, with ruby-red or green bodies and metallic wings; some are very useful and are even sold as remedies for horticultural pest infestations. They are particularly known for their tiny "waists", and the Victorian fashion for a small waist – created by corsetry – was referred to as a wasp waist. Their sting – which can be potentially fatal by bringing on anaphylactic shock – has caused many battle ships and other machines of war to be named after it.

Though most wasps are solitary, common wasps are social and live in a nest like bees, though the nest is made of "paper" scraped from nearby timbers by the workers, rather than wax. They play no part in pollinating flowers, but are drawn to any sweet substances, such as rotting fruit, and also to carrion.

Wasps in **dreams and visions**, especially if they sting you, are about painful obstacles and difficulties in your life, perhaps unpleasant duties that have to be performed, however reluctant you may be. It may also signify a spiteful person known to you, who has decided to make your life difficult.

As a **totem animal**, the wasp brings an independent outlook, and an attitude that anyone who tries to harm you had better look out!

Water Vole

(*Arvicola amphibius*)
Element: water.
Deities: none identified, but all riparian gods.

The "Ratty" of the children's classic, *Wind in the Willows*, the water vole has had a hard time of it in recent decades, and is seriously endangered. There are many reasons for this, including loss of habitat, but chiefly the introduction to the UK of the mink, which escaped (sometimes with the help of anti-fur trade protesters) from farms and is now widespread. Despite Kenneth Graham's name for his character, the water vole is not a rat, and has a furry tail to prove it. The animal lives on vegetation in or beside the water.

In **dreams and visions**, water voles speak of feelings, perhaps being overcome by these, or being someone who likes to live in a continual state of drama over them.

This carries over into the effects of the water vole as **totem animal**, though here it also brings persistence and self-belief.

Weasel

(*Mustela spp*)
Element: fire.
Deities: Aphrodite, Galinthias.
The tiniest mammalian predator in the UK, the common weasel (*M. nivalis*) is rumoured to be able to creep through a wedding ring. For its small size, it is more savage than a leopard! Closely related to the stoat but smaller and lacking the tufty black tail tip, the weasel is around 25cms long (including its tail) and spends its life hunting, as it must devour a third of its body weight every day. The weasel is not found in Ireland, but is very common in the rest of the British Isles. Other species referred to as weasels are generally smaller members of the *Mustelidae* and are found in many regions, including the Arctic where their fur may be pure white.

The term "weasel" is not complimentary, implying someone who is sneaky, cowardly and less than honest, and it also operates as a verb, meaning to sneak in somewhere one is not wanted, or doing something one should not do.

Thus, in **dreams and visions**, the appearance of a weasel indicates someone you should not trust, someone you should certainly keep an eye on, as they will try to do something you do not like, or will not do what they have been asked.

As a **totem animal**, the weasel brings great self-sufficiency. Weasel people prefer their own company, not from shyness but because they are complete unto themselves. Yet they can emerge as leaders or saviours, should the occasion arise.

Weaver Bird

(*Ploceidae spp*)
Elements: air and earth.
Deities: none identified, perhaps Arachne.
These species of finch-like birds create their own homes; not humble nests such as most birds are content with, but amazing complex structures with walls and a roof to protect their young – often great colonies of nests are woven together in the treetops, the entrances hidden underneath. These

African birds may also be very beautiful themselves, often with brightly coloured plumage. They build their nests close to water.

In **dreams and visions**, weaver birds speak of construction and problem-solving, of building your life as you want it, using your own special skills, or acquiring those you need.

As a **totem animal**, the bird brings this problem-solving ability, with a sociable nature and a kindness and compassion for those in your community, and a readiness to be there with a listening ear or more practical help if needed.

Wild Dog or African Wild Dog

(*Lycaon pictus*)

Element: fire.

Deities: all dog and wolf deities, particularly African ones.

This handsome animal is sometimes called a painted dog because of its richly patterned fur. Found across sub-Saharan Africa, it is closely related to jackals and lives on hoofed game, which it hunts down by sight, pursuing until the animal is so exhausted that the pack can overtake and kill it. Unlike other canids, its packs are permanent family groups from which males do not leave when they reach puberty.

In **dreams and visions**, these animals represent strength and family closeness.

As a **totem or power animal**, the dog brings a sense of territory, strong commitment to family and confidence within a community.

Wildebeest: see Antelope.

Wolf

(*Canis lupus*)

Element: fire.

Deities: Apollo, Apuat, Ares/Mars, Artemis/Diana, Fenrir, Forseti, Leto, Loki, Luna/ Selene, Moona, the Morrigan, Odin, Zeus.

Perhaps the most feared of all land predators is this largest of the canids, for as well as its supposed ferocity, it has become entangled in a web of superstitious beliefs and stories. With its powerful jaws, long legs and its habit of hunting as a pack, it is certainly a fearsome animal, though attacks on humans are rare. However, natural human fears and the wolf's own behaviours (including forest-dwelling and howling at the Moon) have often led it to be considered a supernatural creature, giving rise to stories such as that of the werewolf – a monster which occurs in some form in many cultures. In Norse belief especially, the wolf is a terrifying and evil creature, with one supernatural wolf scheduled to eat the Sun at the end of the world, plunging the Earth into darkness. These wolf tales have come down through the generations to appear, in watered-down form, even in children's stories such as *Red Riding Hood* and the *Three Little Pigs*; and the musical tale, *Peter and the Wolf*: "the big, bad wolf." The whole subject of wolves and werewolves was explored fully in the 1984 movie, *The Company of Wolves*, and a jungle wolf pack is the setting for Kipling's immortal *The Jungle Book*.

Wolves have given many expressions to the English language, including "a wolf in sheep's clothing" – meaning someone who is more dangerous than they appear, "to cry wolf", "a lone wolf", "keep the wolf from the door", "hungry like a wolf" and the verb *wolf*, meaning to eat quickly and greedily. The term *wolf whistle* implies the predatory behaviour of some men towards women.

Wolves seen in **dreams and visions** are generally about deep-seated fears: perhaps there is a situation in your life that frightens you so much that you are having difficulty in facing up to it, typically a situation that might leave you impoverished or alone. It could even imply actual hunger, or even homelessness. Perhaps it is a person who frightens you; perhaps someone who has physically threatened you or that you feel might do so. If you dream of more than one wolf, this could relate to being bullied at school, in the workplace or by people within your community.

As a **totem animal**, however, the wolf is very positive, bringing strength, courage, and a strong sense of family and community.

Wolverine
(*Gulo gulo*)
Element: fire.
Deities: Kuekuatsheu, Vidarr.
All right, forget Hugh Jackman and his titanium claws – this is a real animal, a member of the stoat and weasel family found across the Arctic regions of the Americas, Europe and Russia. A medium-sized predator with powerful jaws and claws, it is popularly held to be aggressive and vicious far beyond its size, and to be able to bring down prey much larger than its size would suggest. In mediaeval belief, the "gulo" was a symbol of gluttony, and there is a disgusting little story about it using two close-growing tree trunks to squeeze its constipated body through, in order to discharge faeces!

As the *X-Men* character has impacted on our view of the wolverine, this must be taken into consideration when it appears in **dreams and visions**: the animal is telling you that you have strengths and abilities you did not know, that you can face any situation (no clash with Hugh so far), but also that you should watch your diet and perhaps reduce your food intake.

As a **totem animal**, it brings great strength and determination, a total lack of fear and an ability to survive wherever you find yourself and whatever life throws at you.

Wombat
(*Vombatidae spp*)
Element: earth.
Deities: none identified.
This endearing marsupial looks rather like a very large guinea pig, though they are not related. A stocky, short-legged, slow-moving creature, it has a

blunt face, small ears and is found in wooded and scrubby areas of Australia and Tasmania. Despite their resemblance to guinea pigs, they can be quite dangerous, as they will charge when alarmed, and have very sharp claws and teeth. Although it is now protected, the animal was once hunted for its meat, and wombat stew was considered one of the first truly traditional Australian dishes. They are known for leaving dice-shaped droppings!

In **dreams and visions**, a wombat speaks of being underestimated or undervalued by those around you, and of being able to surprise them with your wisdom and ideas.

As a **totem animal**, it brings a deep happiness with your own company and your own home, but also an ability to fit in with a community and see and respect others' points of view.

Woodchuck: see **Marmot.**

Woodlouse
(*Isopoda spp*)
Element: water.
Deities: none identified.

These little beasties – actually crustaceans, not insects – were a much commoner sight in the past, when all doors and windows were made of wood, rather than uPVC or metal. For, as their name implies, they love wood, particularly damp wood that is starting to rot, though they will also eat fruit. They love damp places anyway, and an old log with flaky bark and lots of rot is their idea of paradise. They have been known by many names, including the common cheesy bug or slater (because they look a little like a tiny, tiled roof), and pill bug: some species can roll up into a ball, others cannot. They are generally grey in colour, but some species may be pale orange or even whitish. When they are breeding, the female carries a mass of yellow eggs on her underside. They were once popped like antacid tablets….not as silly as it sounds, as their exoskeleton contains calcium carbonate, which could neutralise stomach acids.

Seeing woodlice in **dreams and visions** is about insecurity and fear, but also the home, protection and safety: these little animals carry their home on their back and love to scuttle into dark and inaccessible places – and they can move quite fast when they need to.

As a **totem animal**, the woodlouse brings emotional maturity, contentment with your lot – no matter how humble – and also love of home.

Woodpecker
(*Picidae spp*)
Element: air.
Deities: Ares/Mars, Picus, Thor.

The most amazing thing about these often colourful and noisy birds is the way they spend hours bashing their delicate head against a tree trunk – without causing the slightest harm! In search of the insects on which it lives, the bird pecks hard against tree bark until it uncovers what it seeks, and it is easy to imagine its brain must be shaken up like a milkshake. Not so, the bird has a well-designed skull and other refinements to ensure its brain is protected from shocks and G-force.

These birds, found almost everywhere on Earth, are often brightly coloured. In the UK, we have the green woodpecker, which is…green, and the greater and lesser spotted woodpeckers, which are both black-and-white. All three species sport red caps.

The laughing cry, often rendered as "yaffle", gave the Universal Pictures mascot Woody Woodpecker his call, but other species have a variety of cries, including trills, whistles, rattles and screeches.

In **dreams and visions**, a woodpecker may speak of opportunities, but also indicate that you are not ready, that you are still carrying baggage from a previous situation, or that you are "beating your head" against an obstacle of your own making.

However, as a **totem animal**, the woodpecker brings determination and resilience, making you more likely to benefit from the opportunities life offers, despite any obstacles.

Wren

(*Troglodytes troglodytes*)
Element: air and earth. Deities: Arianrhod, Chliodhna, Lleu/Lugh, Taranis.
This tiny brown bird, with its characteristic high-cocked tail, is the subject of many a story and folk custom. It will be best known to older people through its appearance on the reverse side of the old farthing (quarter-penny) coin abolished on decimalisation in 1971. Its Latin classification troglodytes (cave-dweller) probably refers to its ground-loving habits and fondness for creeping under low bushes. They are found more or less across the world.

In mythology the wren was referred to as the "king of the birds", a position it gained through tricking the eagle, and traditionally in the UK harming or bothering a wren was sure to bring bad luck. The exception to this rule was St Stephen's Day (Boxing Day), when wrens were hunted, sometimes killed and carried on poles by Wrenboys. The custom may go back many centuries, as in Celtic belief the wren is associated with Samhain (Halloween) and the year that has passed.

The Celtic Sun God Lleu (or Lugh) was connected with wrens, as He won His name by shooting one. His mother Arianrhod, having refused to name Him because of the shame of His birth, commented on seeing the shot, "the young lion has a steady hand", giving Him His name Lleu Llaw Gyffes.

Seeing a wren in **dreams and visions** speaks of good fortune, of being able to stand up for oneself, despite being apparently small and unimportant, through the use of one's superior wits. While the wren represents the year that is past, it also speaks of the year to come, with high hopes and good omens. As a **totem animal** it brings a bright spirit, a sharp intellect and an ability to deal with most situations with wit and trickery.

Yak

(Bos mutus and grunniens)
Element: earth.
Deities: Vajrabhairava. Yaks are sacred in Tibet.
The wild yak, *B. mutus*, one of the largest members of the cow family, is found in the Himalayas, where their thick shaggy coats protect them from the cold. They are the ancestors of *B. grunniens*, the domestic yak, a highly valued animal in Tibet, where it fulfils the function of the cow in other countries. The yak is kept for its rich milk, its meat, its hair and leather, and even its droppings are collected and dried for use as fuel. It may also be used in sports, such as yak racing. It is now found in North America, Canada, Northern Europe and New Zealand.

In **dreams and visions**, the yak has many of the same meanings as the cow (see **Cattle**), plus the additional meaning of stability and balance, which the creature personifies in its ability to traverse mountainous territory. It may also indicate travel.

As a **power or totem animal**, it brings dependability, gentleness, adventurousness and a nurturing nature.

Zebra

(Equus hippotigris spp)
Element: air.
Deities: Padma, Poseidon/Neptune.
A favourite with every child that visits the zoo, this wild horse in pyjamas has featured in games at the Coliseum, been driven in harness to Buckingham Palace and been painted by the horse artist, George Stubbs. Three species exist – one now endangered – and all have the dazzling black-and-white striped hide that makes them immediately recognisable. The stripes are completely different in every zebra – like fingerprints on humans – and vary considerably in design, and may include blobs and spots. Naturalists are still not sure what value the stripes have – they seem unlikely camouflage, but may deter biting insects. Rudyard Kipling puts forward a theory in his short story, *How the Leopard got his Spots*.

Zebras appearing in **dreams and visions** can be about complex issues surrounding the written word (in black-and-white), including legal matters. These animals speak of polarity: black and white, good and bad, and they enjoin you to look at both sides of a question, to study them in depth, instead of taking the easy answer. They can also be about choices, and about being confused as to which choice to make.

As a **totem animal**, the zebra continues the theme of polarity and balance, bringing an ability to see both sides of any question and to fit in with any community, despite having more than its share of eccentricity.

CHAPTER FIVE

Dead as a Dodo

Thanks to archaeology and the skill of the modeller and the CGI artist, animals long vanished from the Earth can be seen again, and can inhabit our imaginations: cue the theme from *Jurassic Park* (1993). Dinosaurs have long fascinated us, but of course extinct animals now go up to the current day, with some declared extinct yet occasionally glimpsed in the wild, such as the megalodon shark, the dire wolf and the thylacine. Some creatures, like the coelacanth, have returned from the dead, hence are known as *Lazarus* species – for these, see under living animals in Chapter Four.

Many creatures have also gone extinct which are still represented by similar living animals: e.g. the Atlas bear, the Barbary lion, the North African horse. For meanings, see the living animals listed in Chapter Four.

This section includes some of the better-known extinct animals, including dinosaurs and beasts from the Cenozoic Era, although I have kept these to a minimum; most people cannot list all the classified dinosaurs or megafauna so far identified, and they can therefore hardly have meaning for them or be used in magic. The best-known dinosaurs – Tyrannosaurus rex, Diplodocus, Pteranodon and the velociraptors – are another matter, especially since their appearance in movies. In some cases, attempts have been made to recreate extinct animals using gene technology or selective breeding from related species, as for example the aurochs (a huge extinct wild cow which the Nazis attempted to recreate by selective breeding from living cattle) and the thylacine, on which genetic research is ongoing in the twenty-first century.

BIRDS

We are all familiar with the poor dodo, a member of the pigeon family that was so friendly and harmless that it was hunted to extinction by Europeans who came to Mauritius where it lived. Yet other extinct birds might have been a tougher proposition for these hungry invaders, who might not have dared attack the elephant bird or the moa. Generally speaking, birds in dreams are about messages and communication, but some of these avian giants speak of fear as well.

Archaeopteryx

This creature is a link between the dinosaurs and modern birds. It had feathers, like a bird, but also teeth, a long lizard-like tail and other features like a saurian. Around the size of a bantam, or smaller, it may have had a bald head and neck like a vulture, and probably could not fly strongly like a modern bird, but rather glided. Astonishingly, modern scientists have been able to establish that it was probably black in colour.

If Archaeopteryx appears in **dreams**, he is talking about messages from long ago, perhaps from the start of a relationship or from a previous relationship or situation, which you must now consider and face up to.

As a **totem**, it brings a keen desire to do better, to develop and seek new horizons.

Dodo

The strange appearance of this bird is very familiar to us from, among other sources, the illustrations of the dodo in *Alice's Adventures in Wonderland*: Lewis Carroll included the character as a comical reference to himself: he stammered, and was wont to pronounce his real surname "Do-do-dodgson". A member of the pigeon family, the bird seemed to have been very stout-bodied, with a robust hooked beak. It was a little larger than a turkey and could not fly.

Appearing in **dreams**, the dodo speaks of a person who is clumsy, accident-prone, rather stupid and their own worst enemy: their ill luck may stem from their inability to do a job properly. Or it may be a message to you that you need to smarten up yourself, shape up or ship out!

As a **totem**, it is quite ill-omened, signalling unsuccessful ventures and unwise dealings with money or people.

Elephant Birds and Moas

At three metres tall and up to 1,000kg in weight, *Aepyornis maximus* is considered the largest bird ever to have lived on the Earth. Slow moving because of its heavy bones and obviously incapable of flight, its nearest living relative is the kiwi. Once common on Madagascar, it became extinct sometime between 1700-1880, probably due to hunting or habitat clearing for agriculture, or because its huge eggs were prized as food – they could feed a whole family.

The moas were species of giant flightless birds related to the modern-day kiwis, emus and cassowaries and found in New Zealand. They were not only flightless, but wingless: they did not even have vestigial wings or forelimbs at all. They had disappeared by the mid-fifteenth century as a result of hunting and habitat clearing.

These giant, heavy birds share a common meaning when they appear in **dreams**, and it is a warning. Take care, there is danger from some unknown source, so do not go blithely on your way as though nothing were amiss. If you know, within your heart, that there is something wrong, you must address it now, or disaster will ensue.

As a **totem**, these birds bring a shy nature, with a love of home and of things staying the same, a dislike of change.

Great Auk

The careless cruelty of man marks the end of this distant relative of the penguin and razorbill: the last egg was crushed by a fisherman's boot in 1844 as he and his crewmates attacked and killed the last known pair of auks on Geirfuglasker, an island off Iceland. Auks were hunted for their meat, their eggs, their feathers (which were often just plucked cruelly from the living bird) and, latterly, because collectors wanted specimens of this disappearing creature for their collections.

While it shares many meanings with the penguin (see Chapter Four), the auk became a symbol of extinction caused by man, and an aura of great sadness and regret seems to accompany this bird in all mentions in books and online.

So, regret for past actions is its chief meaning in **dreams**, maybe also a guilty conscience for the way you have treated others, and bad decisions you have taken for wrong reasons that have caused harm.

As a **totem**, the auk is connected to strong feelings for the environment and for the devastation man has committed against his fellow animals on the Earth, and with taking action for the good of the planet.

DINOSAURS

While most people will be familiar with half a dozen species of dinosaur – usually the largest or the most terrifying predators – the dinosaurs ran to thousands of species and existed on Earth over a period of around 165 million years, during which species evolved, became extinct and were succeeded by other species. All non-avian dinosaurs became extinct 66 million years ago at the end of the Cretaceous as a result of the Cretaceous-Paleogene event: a natural catastrophe, possibly caused by an asteroid, which caused an abrupt change of climate.

Dinosaurs speak of the ancient past, and particularly of ancient terrors, perhaps those from your childhood, yet each type has additional meanings to contribute. Because most people cannot classify dinosaurs, I have simply divided them into types and based the dream meanings on these.

Armoured and Horned Dinosaurs

(e.g. Ankylosaurus, Dimetrodon, Protoceratops, Stegosaurus, Styracosaurus, Triceratops.)
The armoured dinosaurs are telling you that life is hard, and you may need to fight your corner, for people will pick on you, harmless though you may be. Be prepared, and take thought for how you will defend yourself.

As **totems**, these animals speak of the ability to defend oneself against attack, bullying, injustice – and to prevail. Remember: the Triceratops could see off (and even seriously injure) the Tyrannosaurus, as long as he was not taken by surprise.

Large Carnivorous Dinosaurs

(e.g. Albertosaurus, Allosaurus, Tarbosaurus, Tyrannosaurus Rex, Tyrannotitan.)
These beasties show up in nightmares from time to time, and no wonder! Dreaming of one is simply and obviously telling you that you are very afraid of something in your life, an anticipated threat that is coming and one that you will have to deal with somehow or other. It might not be 12 feet tall with a hundred teeth, but it is just as frightening to you personally. Try to be calm and judge the situation carefully before it actually arrives; prepare a defence or other action to get around the problem.

As **totems**, these gigantic reptiles are all about confidence and fierceness, owning a situation and never feeling uncertain or intimidated.

Velociraptors

If you saw the movie, *Jurassic Park* (and its later incarnations), you might agree that these smaller predators were more frightening than the T-Rex, because they were clever and could plan, cooperate and anticipate; whereas the T-Rex just went roaring around looking for people to eat. They were a lot less scary in reality: the velociraptors were not the six-foot tall creatures that careened around the kitchen cabinets in the film, but nearer the size of a turkey. However, this is one instance where the cultural resonance overrides fact, and a velociraptor appearing in your **dreams and visions** is very much about terror, and not just the natural dread you might feel at one of the larger flesh-eating dinosaurs. This is about fear of someone cleverer than you, someone who has it in for you and will stop at nothing to bring you down and harm you. I would stick my neck out here and say: are there fears of a serial killer in your town? As this would fit the meaning of this creature to a T.

As a **totem animal**, the velociraptor brings great cunning, greed, the ability to plan and outmanoeuvre others, and implacable aggression.

Long-Necked Giants and Plant-Eaters

(e.g. Alamosaurus, Brachyosaurus, Cetiosaurus, Diplodocus, Iguanadon.)
These slow-moving vegetarians all have similar meanings when they show up in **dreams**, and that is about moving on from the past, shedding old habits and turning to new paths. They can speak of forgiveness and reconciliation, but the more likely scenario is that they speak of the urgent

need for moving on, lest you, like them, become irrelevant. Are you scared of modern technology? Take a course. Do you have outdated opinions and ideas? Maybe you need to rethink them, for they are damaging you in your career and your relationships.

As **totem animals**, the giant plant-eaters bring strength and invulnerability, but the message they bring is the same: move on, join the rest of us in the twenty-first century!

Pterosaurs (Flying Dinosaurs)

(e.g. Pteranodon, Pterodactyl.)
A toothy Pteranodon invading your **dreams** can be disturbing – in fact: a nightmare – but the winged dino is telling you not to get carried away. It speaks of wrong decisions and misplaced enthusiasms, which can lead you astray if you do not stop and think carefully before proceeding.

As **totems**, these creatures bring a sense of freedom and adventure, the need for exploring and a zest for life.

Marine Reptiles

(e.g. Archelon, Plesiosaurus, Ichthyosaurus, Mosasaurs.)
There were in fact no marine dinosaurs, as the extinct marine reptiles around at the same time as the land dinosaurs are classified as non-saurian reptiles, but they were every bit as toothy, predatory and enormous as their land-based remote cousins. An Ichthyosaur (that was a huge fish-shaped reptile with long tooth-lined jaws) fossil of 85 feet in length was discovered a few years ago. An enormous sea snake called *Palaeophus colossaeus* was the largest sea snake ever known, at 12 metres. The seas were also home to less dangerous reptiles such as archelon – a giant sea turtle around four metres long.

The mystery of the depths confers on these massive animals a magic that land animals cannot share: like the Loch Ness Monster (believed by some to be a Plesiosaur), these beasts would not have been visible to land creatures until they surfaced; causing terror and amazement to any land animal that had strayed into the water.

Their appearance in **dreams and visions** speaks of hidden terrors, of frightening memories returning to haunt you, or of unpleasant things (perhaps guilt) thought long-buried but now back to fill your life with pain. They speak of vulnerability to these things, and in general, of pain felt in the subconscious and long buried, but now needing to be addressed.

As **totem or power animals**, they bring their own mystery and magic, the strength of people who inhabit their own world and make the rules, so that all comers are at a disadvantage.

FISH

An extinct fish will hardly resonate with anyone, unless it is remarkable in some way. The coelacanth, as we have seen, is a Lazarus species, now known to be still with us. That really only leaves the terrifying monsters that once swam the Earth's oceans, such as **Megalodon**, a giant shark once believed to be the ancestor of our modern great white shark. Megalodon was a species of mackerel shark that reached up to 20 metres in length and had huge teeth: hence its name. It became extinct during the late Pliocene period, for reasons not properly understood.

Dreaming of this nightmare creature, perhaps of struggling in the sea and being pursued by it, carries some of the same meanings as dreaming of modern sharks, but where they speak of the need for staying focussed on one's goals, the megalodon speaks of the basic need for survival, for taking all measures against something very threatening which has entered your life.

As a **totem**, it brings the same qualities as the shark (see Chapter Four).

INVERTEBRATES

Invertebrates often achieved great size in ancient times: giant extinct millipedes 2.5 metres long, 70cm scorpions, dragonflies with a 70cm wingspan. Generally speaking, these animals have the same meaning as their smaller modern counterparts, but some extinct invertebrates are recognised by most people. Trilobites, ammonites, fossil sea urchins and extinct crustaceans, such as sea scorpions, share a common meaning when they appear in **dreams and visions.** These ancient "creepy-crawlies" – some of which could have been dangerous to a human had we been around at the same time – speak of dangers and disruptions that are passing, or have passed altogether, and the message is a positive one, unless they have left damage behind.

As **totems,** they need to be studied individually for their meaning, with reference to any living animals that descended from them.

MAMMALS AND MARSUPIALS

Many, many species of animals have existed on the Earth, and it would be impossible to list them all, nor would the gentle reader necessarily recognise any of them. Again therefore, I have taken a selection of creatures whose names might be known, or which might have formed part of an exhibit at a museum or appeared in a film/TV series or a documentary.

Aurochs

This giant cow became extinct in the seventeenth century, but there have been attempts to recreate it by selective breeding of extant cattle, firstly in the 1920s by a scientist called Heinz Heck. Heck cattle are still found in Germany and were used in the late twentieth century in another breeding programme which produced "Taurus cattle", though neither of these species can really be called genuine aurochs, as it is not possible to genuinely recreate an animal without the genetic material available from laboratory or museum specimens, mummies or frozen carcases.

The aurochs was a formidable animal which stood two metres at the shoulder, had metre-long horns and was extremely aggressive. I can do no better when it comes to its meaning in **dreams** than to speak of the Norse rune Uruz (U), which speaks of tribulation and ordeal: a terrifying experience that has to be gone through in order to achieve something necessary. This could be a driving examination at one end of the scale, or exploratory surgery for suspected cancer at the other.

As a **totem**, the aurochs is all about aggression and power, but not necessarily successful power. It speaks of bullies and senseless quarrels.

Dire Wolf

This large canid was a little larger than the modern grey wolf, and went extinct around 10,000 years ago – though sightings are reported today, and there are even videos posted on YouTube. Thanks to the George RR Martin fantasy novel series, *A Song of Ice and Fire*, dire wolves have entered the public consciousness, which may go some way towards explaining these sightings.

For meanings in **dreams** and as a **totem animal**, see **Wolf** in Chapter Four.

Horse Ancestors

The horse is such an important animal to modern man, that even its ancestors strike a chord with us. Looking at a majestic Clydesdale or Shire horse, it is difficult to imagine that these noble beasts descended from a rabbit-sized creature called Eohippus (dawn horse) or *hyracotherium*. Many horse species have gone extinct over the millennia, from the early ancestors like Eohippus and Mesohippus (which both had toes instead of hooves) to more modern casualties like the tarpan and Przewalski's horse and even domesticated horse breeds, such as the Old English black and the Yorkshire carriage horse, which were superseded as better suited breeds were created. It is worth bearing in mind that all modern heavy horses, the Shire, the Percheron, the Clydesdale and the Suffolk punch, are endangered: man does not value what he cannot use for profit.

For all types of horses seen in dreams, see the meanings for extant horses in Chapter Four, but with extinct ones consider that the situation indicated in the **dream or vision** is passing away. This may be an opportunity or a danger: look at the feel of the dream to decide.

For **totem** meanings, see the modern **Horse** in Chapter Four.

Hyaenodon

These large and terrifying predators went extinct around 25 million years ago, leaving no modern animals descended from them: their name means "hyena tooth" and does not imply they were related to hyenas.

With all prehistoric carnivores, including Hyaenodon, the dire wolf and the sabre-tooth cats, their appearance in a **dream or vision** speaks of fear and being under attack.

As **totem animals**, they bring power and many of the qualities of the unrelated modern hyena.

Mammoth and Mastodon

These ancient elephants conjure a picture of massive bulk and streaming long hair, yet only the later woolly mammoth (which had migrated north from its original stamping ground in Africa and Asia) is known to have had hair: specimens have been found preserved in the ice in Arctic regions in such good condition that it was possible to eat their meat! There has also been research into the possibility of cloning mammoths, using elephant DNA. The name "mammoth" has become a common adjective meaning of unusual size.

Mastodons were around a little earlier than mammoths, were smaller in size and not that closely related. They were found in North America and became extinct along with other megafauna in the late Pleistocene.

As you might expect, **dreaming** of a mammoth or mastodon (most people would not know the difference between them) speaks of size, yet not physical size. They signify feelings of being overwhelmed by a situation which is too big to handle ("this thing is bigger than both of us"), of pressure and stress and being unable to cope. If you dream of a herd of these creatures charging towards you, it could speak of an actual breakdown due to the stress you are under.

As a **totem animal**, however, the mammoth and the mastodon bring strength, calm and confidence: all the qualities you need to deal with the aforementioned stresses!

Megatherium

Seven feet tall at the shoulder and weighing two tons, Megatherium was one of the largest creatures ever to walk the planet, yet its size could not save it from extinction (partly as a result of being hunted by early man). Humans arrived on the American continents around 14.5 million years ago and targeted these giant ground sloths for their meat, also possibly because they were gentle and passive. Megatherium (*great beast*) lived exclusively on grass and on leaves, which it ate from large branches that it pulled down with its huge incurved claws – it could stand on its hind legs (which would have made it enormously tall indeed) to reach these.

This most impressive of the megabeasts may well turn up in dreams and visions: anyone who has read the E Nesbit books will be familiar with it.

In **dreams and visions**, Megatherium speaks of unexpected vulnerability, of someone who seems invincible, yet they fall in circumstances which could not have been foreseen.

As a **totem animal**, this creature gives the same qualities as its distant descendant, the sloth, of calm, peace, even of laziness, lack of ambition and utter contentment with one's life as it is, and the Megatherium may also add a touch of complacency to that.

Quagga

Extinct since 1883, this wild equine was closely related to zebras. For its meanings, see **Zebra** in Chapter Four, but bear in mind that the quagga will be referring to situations in the past.

Sabre-Tooth Cats

The best known of the sabre-tooth cats was Smilodon, the sabre-tooth tiger (actually not closely related to modern cats, although its largest species was tiger-sized), which would have been a very dangerous enemy of very early man. Its huge tusks (scientists are not sure exactly how they were used) possibly helped it bring down large prey like bison, camelids and tapirs. Its shape was more robust and muscular than most modern felids, and it had a lynx-like bobtail.

Like many large and fearsome creatures, the sabre-tooth's appearance in **dreams** is about fear and persecution, about powerful enemies trying to harm or even destroy you – or perhaps about your own groundless fears along these lines.

As a **totem animal**, it speaks of savagery, confidence and a relentless pursuit of your goals.

Thylacine (Tasmanian Tiger, Tasmanian Wolf)

The thylacine, a marsupial predator related to the Tasmanian devil, was declared extinct in 1936 when a specimen at Beaumaris Zoo in Hobart, Tasmania, died. Like the dodo and the great auk, its story is one of the short-sighted cruelty and self-interest of Europeans when they colonised far distant countries. Instead of cherishing and studying the unusual species they discovered, in many cases they set about eliminating them for fear they should attack farm stock or because they tasted good.

The thylacine, despite its common name of Tasmanian tiger or wolf, was only the size of a Labrador dog, and got its name from the stripes which decorated its rear end. Otherwise, it looked very like a dog, with a long snout and fox-like ears. The tail was stiff and often carried horizontally, and the jaws could open very wide: up to 90 degrees.

The animal had become extinct on mainland Australia very early on, possibly because of competition with the dingo, but it had survived on Tasmania. However, because of the supposed danger to sheep and other farm animals, bounty schemes were operated from quite early in the nineteenth century, encouraging people to shoot thylacines – there are quite a few photographs featuring smirking gunmen with their "trophies". It was shot on sight until every specimen was dead.

Or has it died out? People have reported seeing thylacines at a distance into the current century, and there are even very poor-quality photographs of animals which bear a resemblance to it (or they could be large dogs). The tiger has made its way into video games and movies, notably the 2011 film, *The Hunter*, in which a man is hired to hunt down the last one for a greedy corporation.

The meaning of the thylacine seen in **dreams** is given in some sources as timidity and insecurity, perhaps due to the rarely seen Looney Tunes animated character, Wendal T Wolf, supposedly a surviving thylacine who suffers from lonesomeness and fear because he is the last of his kind. Personally, I feel the animal has more to do with preciousness, with something wonderful that has been lost, but might still be regained under some circumstances (and remember research is ongoing into the possibility of recreating them from genetic material from lab specimens and stuffed animals).

As a **totem**, the thylacine speaks of toughness, of walking one's own path no matter what, and making no concessions or compromises.

REPTILES

Many reptiles have gone extinct, both in the distant past and in the last century, but most have left similar cousins behind. A few species are worth including here because they are unusual in some way.

Crocodiles

A flurry of sightings of what seemed to be a crocodile in the Avon River caused a stir in 2014…and it has to be said that climate change is making this less unlikely. The "Bristol Beast" aside, it is difficult to imagine crocodiles abroad in Britain in the present day, yet huge crocodiles clearly did roam this area millions of years ago, for giant fossil crocs (or crocodilian ancestors, to be more accurate) have been excavated at several sites, including Dorset's Jurassic Coast and the clay pits around East Anglia. These were marine crocodilians – large in size, with long snouts like a gharial.

Occurring in **dreams and visions**, these ancient creatures have quite a different meaning from a modern crocodile. They speak of the past and of fears that have been left behind, of happiness that has been achieved, despite the unhappiness of perhaps early childhood or young adulthood, and of coming to a place of contentment and feeling "comfortable in one's skin."

As **totem animals**, they bring courage, confidence and calm.

Megalania

This nightmare creature resembled a Komodo dragon, but was almost as long as a London bus and weighed in at two metric tons. One of the so-called Pleistocene megafauna, it is the largest lizard ever to have lived. Add to that a mouthful of razor-sharp teeth, and the probability that Megalania shared its modern relatives' ability to excrete toxins in their mouths to give them a venomous bite, and you have a fearsome monster indeed. It may have survived in the Australian Aboriginal legends of the whowie, a reptilian monster described as being seven metres long. Even scarier, it is believed by some to be still around in the desert vastnesses of the Australian interior, with sightings of giant lizards 20 and 30ft long (and sometimes tracks) reported well into this century.

Showing up in **dreams**, Megalania's message is simple: you thought you were home safe, but the danger is still here. Look to your past for the reasons you are afraid, and perhaps you will find the answer to ending your fear.

As a **totem animal**, it brings strength and confidence, but also the tendency to use less than ethical methods to get one's way.

Titanoboa

Snakes frighten many people, whether or not they are venomous. In fact, the constricting snakes can have a much greater effect on people with a snake phobia, simply because of their huge size. The very largest snakes alive on Earth are species like the anaconda, the boa constrictor and the reticulated python – none of which have venom.

Titanoboa made some of our living snakes look like earthworms: it would have measured up to 50ft (15 metres) in length and weighed over a metric ton, and could swallow quite large animals whole, although scientists now believe it had a similar lifestyle to the anaconda, living in water and eating fish.

This creature evokes mythological monsters like Jörmungandr, Mehen, Apep and Ouroboros, the snakes that bit their own tails and in the case of the former lay around the circumference of the world. This posture refers to cyclical nature and, in Jörmungandr's case to the end of the world, all meanings which should be taken into account when considering the Titanoboa when it appears in a **dream**. It can refer to time, especially long periods of time and particularly in the past, to history, to memory, but always tinged with fear and regret.

As a **totem**, it brings the qualities of the modern living **Snake** (see Chapter Four), but with particular emphasis on wisdom and knowledge.

CHAPTER SIX

Unearthly Animals

Mythical and cryptid animals go with magic and story as butter goes with bread: they are all forged from our beliefs and dreams. When considering their appearance in dreams and visions, it is good to keep this in mind; that they are not real (in this Universe, at least) and therefore the message can have a quite different meaning from that of a real animal. It will tend to be about your inner life, your spiritual path and your relationship with divinity, rather than about the day-to-day occurrences of your home life, your family, your love life and your career. Mysteries awaken our minds to possibilities beyond the mundane, outside the office or workplace, away from the telly, tablet or PC, out in the dark woods where everything you think you know is suddenly not so certain... Dreaming of one of these creatures is a sign that your mind is becoming more open, your imagination more accepting – and that can only be good.

Because mythical animals in stories and belief around the world run into many thousands, I have concentrated mainly on the creatures familiar to Europeans from their own folklore and from classical tradition. Note that this book is about animals, not humanoids, but I have included some part-animal, part-human creatures such as centaurs and mermaids.

Alien Big Cats

So much evidence exists for these mysterious cats that it may be stretching a point to include them in this chapter. Many areas of the UK have an "ABC", including the Beast of Bodmin, the Beast of Exmoor, the Surrey Puma, the Essex Lion and the Cotswolds Big Cat. Photographic and video evidence is of necessity sketchy, as these beasts presumably do not sit around waiting to be snapped, nor would any sensible person go up close to them – or they to him. However, many accounts of sightings are on record, and include actual attacks on people who have happened on the animal, including a young boy who was left with facial injuries after he encountered what he described as a black panther in a field in Monmouthshire; and a big cat which attacked a man through an open window in Porthleven, Cornwall.

The power of the black cat is magnified in this creature – ABCs are overwhelmingly black – they speak of the eldritch when they appear in **dreams and visions**, of witches and magic and things out on the moor that most humans never see or would not believe their eyes if they did.

In dreams and as a **totem**, they are also about power, both raw physical power and the power that some magical practitioners have. They are about the privilege of power and knowledge, signifying that this privilege carries responsibilities of studying and working for others.

Basilisk

Most people will have heard the expression "a basilisk stare" applied to a person with an intimidating expression who is very cross about something. This monster, always depicted as reptilian, often as a giant snake, is better known today after appearing in the *Harry Potter* books and movies, where it attacks the young wizard in the Chamber of Secrets. The snakelike appearance notwithstanding, there is some chicken DNA in this creature, especially when it is known as a cockatrice, and some depictions show it as having a beak, feathers and wattles like a rooster. Although it is depicted as a terrifying creature, quite capable of devouring a human being in one bite, the basilisk's super-power is being able to turn a person into stone by catching their eye, like the Gorgon Medusa in classical mythology.

In **dreams**, many mythological creatures speak of danger, yet that of the basilisk/cockatrice is of a particular kind. It says you will be stopped in your tracks by a calamity if you are not very careful. Do not play with things too powerful for you or meddle with things you do not properly understand. Keep to things within your knowledge and powers, or you will be sorry.

As a **totem**, this animal brings power – most mythological animals do – but in this case, it is power over others, power to silence your enemies, to leave them powerless and speechless before you.

Behemoth

This biblical term has come to mean any creature or even object of huge size, as has the name Leviathan, from the same source. But while **Leviathan** (see below) has some dire meanings, Behemoth speaks of peace and plenty, and seems to have been a grazing animal of some kind.

Dreaming of huge monsters speaks of desperate needs, perhaps sexual or even for the necessities of life, but in this case also of the means for satisfying them: it shares with large fish the idea of the gaining of riches and plenty, and for this reason is also a fortunate **totem**.

Bigfoot

Giant elusive ape-men are spotted all over the Northern American continent: they are black or brown or red or grey and sometimes have glowing eyes and a foul smell, but the thing they all share is size, including a 40cm or so footprint. Some reports speak of monsters over eight feet tall, but always more than man-size. Some people have suggested the Bigfoot may be a surviving number of Gigantopithecus, a 12ft Pleistocene gorilla that was the closest thing to King Kong that ever lived on the planet.

Proving Bigfoot exists is another matter. The controversial Patterson-Gimlin film, a few seconds of a shambling, hairy humanoid shot in woodland in Northern California, is still the best evidence for Bigfoot available 55 years after it was first shared with the world – yet it could be a man in a gorilla suit. Other countries also have their own versions of these creatures: the yeti in Asia, the European wild man and the Australian yowie, while Bigfoot is also known as Sasquatch in the US and has several cousins, including the Honey Island swamp monster and the skunk ape.

Don't look at the real great apes for meaning if you **dream** of any of these creatures; they are about self-esteem and self-criticism, particularly in the sense that you may feel ashamed of how you have behaved or would like to change your own personality to bring it more in line with your ideals about yourself.

As **totems**, these animals bring strength and power, but not much popularity.

Black Dog

Tales of supernatural black dogs were once common across the UK, but their place has been largely usurped by the alien black cats – after all, no one ever took a photograph of Black Shuck! These dogs crop up in fairy tales (for example, Hans Christian Andersen's *The Tinderbox*) and old local traditions, and were the inspiration for Arthur Conan Doyle's story, *The Hound of the Baskervilles*. Unlike the black cats, the dogs are not real live animals but phantoms, and are closely associated with Christian ideas of hell, and they may also be harbingers of death and misfortune. They are commonly described as having huge blazing eyes and even of smelling of brimstone (sulphur) – a substance associated with the Devil and hellfire – and of leaving scorch marks behind when they vanish. Some may claim their origins in a crime or in the selling of a man's soul to the Devil, but a few are considered benign.

Dreaming of a black dog speaks of psychic danger: it may be telling you someone has worked evil magic against you, or that you yourself are the culprit and will be sorry, having meddled in supernatural matters beyond your power to control.

As a **totem** the black dog brings protection, but often at a price.

Centaur

This creature from classical myth is formed from a man's upper body, from the waist up, joined onto a horse's body from the neck down. The Greeks believed there were several races of centaurs, one race having horns on their heads, but individuals also appear in classical stories, including the most famous one of all, Chiron, who was tutor to the infant Achilles. As well as classical literature and art, centaurs are found in Dante's *Inferno,* and in more modern books such as the *Narnia* books of CS Lewis and the *Harry Potter* books and films.

When they appear in **dreams and visions**, centaurs speak of welding two worlds together, whether these are two conflicting aspects of your own personality, or two parts of your life that need reconciling, or two pieces of your spiritual path that do not seem to work together. It urges you to use your head and strive towards wisdom and away from your more basic instincts.

As a **totem**, this creature gives wisdom and flexibility.

Chimera

Chimera, sometimes spelled chimaera, is now a general term for an imaginary animal composed of two or more parts of other animals: the griffin is a chimera, as is the Ancient Egyptian Goddess Ammit, who has a crocodile's head attached to a body that is part lion or leopard, part hippopotamus. However, the name originally belonged to a specific monster in classical mythology, which had a lion's body, a goat's head on its back and a tail which was a snake, complete with a snake's head. She also breathed fire. This creature was of divine origin and was eventually killed by Bellerophon (rider of Pegasus) on the orders of Iobates, King of Lycia.

This creature can be a tricky one to interpret when it shows up in **dreams**, as much depends on the nature of the chimera and the animal parts of which it is composed. While in classical myth she was a terrifying being, it would not be impossible to encounter a dream chimera composed of a kitten and a bunny rabbit, so take note of the nature of the animal. Its meaning will generally be very similar to that of the centaur or, if it evokes fear, it could be a warning of peril from something made up of parts, including a many-pronged problem at work or in your relationship.

As a **totem**, its qualities will depend on its parts and for these, see the relevant animals in Chapter Four.

Chupacabra

This modern monster dates from the 1990s, when a series of livestock killings in Puerto Rico were attributed to a vampire-like creature, subsequently named *el chupacabra* (the goat-sucker) because the animals' bodies were all exsanguinated. The first most of us heard of it was an episode in the TV show, *The X-Files*, called *El Mundo Gira*. The myth grew and spread, with reports of animal attacks and sightings of strange creatures soon spreading all over the Americas. The chupacabra is variously described as a large lizard-like creature which jumps along on two legs like a kangaroo, as a strange hairless animal like a dog, or sometimes as a humanoid variation on either of these. In all cases, it goes hand-in-hand (or paw-in-paw) with reports of mass killings of farm animals, which are said to bear distinctive round puncture marks.

The chupacabra is speaking of loss when it shows up in **dreams**, of something you used to have, but have no longer, whether this is youth, beauty or an ability of some kind. It is time to accept that you have moved on, and perhaps to develop new talents to replace what you have lost. It may also speak of spiritual loss, such as a loss of faith.

As a **totem**, it gives a sense of need and a keenness to hang on to what you have, and to deplore and resist anything which could take away your gifts.

Cockatrice: see **Basilisk.**

Dogman

Not a werewolf, although it certainly looks like something from a Hollywood horror flick, the dogmen are still glimpsed in the north-eastern parts of North America, and have apparently recently migrated to Australia as well. The Michigan Dogman and its Bray Road, Wisconsin, cousin are both described as tall and humanoid, usually walking on two legs only and having a wolf- or dog-like head with blazing eyes, blue in the Michigan Dogman and red or orange in the Bray Road creature.

Although my personal belief is that this creature has little in common with the werewolf, its appearance and the mythology that has grown up around it will cause its appearance in dreams to have roughly the same meaning for most people.

See **Werewolf**.

Dragon

Now we come to perhaps the most famous mythical beast of all, one that is found in all mythologies (if not as dragons, then as huge serpents sometimes described as worms or wyrms) and is still significant to us today, if only via Hollywood. While the term *dragon* may include huge snakes, generally speaking a dragon is a four-legged reptilian which can fly and breathes fire. Like a luxury car, it comes in a range of appealing colours including green, black, red and white.

In the West, dragons are monsters pure and simple, from the evil Fafnir who gnaws at the roots of the World Tree to topple the Universe in Norse belief to the bright green creature slain by St George. They are associated with the hoarding of treasure and with devouring maidens (and anyone else who gets in their way). A theme that runs through some stories is the idea that a greedy or unjust person can metamorphose into a dragon. They are also mortal, and can be killed by anyone with courage and a sharp sword or a bow and keen eye. Like Smaug, Tolkien's cynical and self-important dragon of the Lonely Mountain in his book, *The Hobbit*, many can speak and seem to have almost human personalities. They have had a huge impact on heraldry (and thus on pub signs) and latterly on corporate logos.

In the East, dragons are quite different, with the dragon in Asian culture being seen as a spiritual and divine entity, though it may look very similar to Western dragons. In Asian culture, dragons embody the elements and certain gods, and have been worshipped as divinities. The Dragon God is still present in Chinese ritual, and may be celebrated with a procession including a dragon figure formed of a row of men under a decorative dragon-shaped cover. And, increasingly, this view of dragons is moving into the West, with modern pagans speaking of "dragon lines" in the Earth, and dragon energies.

The dragon in **dreams and visions** is urging you to move towards your higher-self and to cast aside baser qualities, especially greed and rage, so that you may manifest your finer qualities and progress into a more spiritual being. Being attacked by a dragon in a dream is still about this fear: that your worst qualities will take you over altogether, or result in your downfall. The colour of the dragon may also have meaning, with a gold dragon being about the love of wealth, and a black or red dragon being about evil temper.

As a **totem or power animal**, the dragon brings leadership qualities with magnanimity and a great sense of justice.

Echidna

While an echidna is a real living animal (see Chapter Four), it is also the name of a monster in classical mythology who was half-woman and half-serpent, often shown as a woman-headed snake or even with many heads. Monster she was, with a venomous bite and a desire to eat human flesh. Her human head was said to be very beautiful with long hair. Her mate was the monster Typhon, and together they produced more monsters, including Cerberus, the three-headed dog that guarded the door to Hades, and Hydra, another snake monster with many heads.

Dreaming of snake monsters (whether they are Echidna or any other snake) is often about sex, and the dream is suggesting you examine your own behaviour in this respect. Do you prey on others or exploit them for your own satisfaction? Do you damage your own relationships, or those of your sexual partners, by your behaviour?

As a **totem animal**, Echidna brings a desire to improve oneself and to move away from destructive conduct.

Faun

The name faun sounds lovely, like a baby deer, and when you think of Mr Tumnus in *The Lion, The Witch and The Wardrobe*, you might think they are the cutest creatures in classical mythology. Although these Roman half-goat, half-humans are closely related to Greek satyrs (lustful naked creatures wont to pounce on any vulnerable female), fauns are much more innocent, benign creatures. However, they also serve their master, the God Faunus (or Pan) by instilling panic and fear in travellers in lonely places.

Fauns cropping up in **dreams** speak of the love of nature and the longing to be in and to experience the magic of rural places, perhaps forest walks or hill climbing, even a desire to get away from other people.

As **totem**, they bring a oneness with nature and an ability to use nature wisely: these are the people you will see enjoying wild swimming or hunting for edible fungi – and knowing where to look.

Gorgon

The Gorgons were three creatures who could turn a person to stone by looking into their eyes. Two were hideously ugly, with nests of snakes instead of hair, but the third, Medusa, was a maiden under a curse and despite her stony stare and snaky hairstyle, she was often depicted as very beautiful. The term *Gorgon* has become a term of abuse meaning a person so ugly that others cannot bear to look at them, or possessing such a threatening stare that people dare not approach.

Dreaming of a Gorgon is telling you that you will triumph over an adversary – unless the creature is attacking you, in which case the message is less favourable and may speak of an encounter you will regret.

As a **totem**, this creature gives you all the power you could wish for, a great sense of your own impact on others and your personal invulnerability, but not much in the way of popularity.

Griffin (sometimes Gryphon)

This jigsaw of lion and eagle parts is one of the more impressive and majestic heraldic beasts. He has the head (but with long pointed ears), forelegs and wings of an eagle tacked onto the rear parts of a lion, and is usually depicted as bright gold in colour – perhaps because the creature is associated with the mining, working and hoarding of this precious metal. In very early classical sources they sometimes lack the wings. They are found in many mythologies and were used by the Christian Church as a symbol of the nature of Christ. In heraldry, there is also a "sea-griffin", which is shown as having a fish's tail in place of the usual lion's parts. Like many magnificent heraldic creatures, the griffin has been used extensively in corporate imagery; for example, the Vauxhall car logo. The best-known example in literature is probably the nostalgic gryphon in *Alice's Adventures in Wonderland*, who introduces Alice to the Mock Turtle.

Dreaming of a griffin is said to signify news or gossip but, personally, I feel such a magnificent golden animal speaks of more important matters, of truth, justice, courage and idealism.

As a **totem animal**, it brings these and other higher qualities, with the desire to be the best person you can be.

Harpy

The harpies get a very bad press. From classical and Roman mythology, they are shown as birds of prey with the faces of women – sometimes hideous, sometimes beautiful – but their main quality is their tendency to seize and carry away food or sometimes people, often as agents of the gods' wrath directed at wrongdoers. Violent, cruel and implacable, they are also prone to defiling food – if they do not steal it – by dropping faeces on it.

The name "harpy" has become a term of abuse for a woman of strong personality, taking a meaning akin to shrew or termagant, and it is this meaning which is most likely if you **dream** of harpies, for it is with this meaning you will most likely think of them. Do you have a difficult mother-in-law or a female boss who is making life hard for you? She may be represented by the harpy in your dream, so watch the content of the dream for an additional message about her.

As **totems**, these creatures bring resilience and a desire for justice, which may make them unpopular.

Hellhound: see **Black Dog.**

Hippocampus

This rather beautiful creature is a mer-horse: a sea-horse – a chimera with the foreparts of a horse and a fish's tail. It is sometimes shown with wings. It is especially associated with the Greek Sea God, Poseidon (to whom horses were sacred) and His Roman counterpart, Neptune. These Gods were often depicted driving Their chariots, drawn by hippocampi, through the waves. Hippocampus is also the Latin classification for the real seahorse, a tiny horse-shaped fish.

Dreaming of hippocampi is about freedom and adventure, of exploring mysteries previously closed to you, of having the courage to go where your heart and your spirit are leading you.

As a **totem**, it brings a wild spirit – fond of adventure and ready for any experience, danger or fun.

Hippogriff

This equine chimera is of relatively recent vintage. Although it could well have been designed by the classical myth-makers, it actually dates back only to the sixteenth century, to an epic poem by Ludovico Ariosto called *Orlando Furioso* – a tale of a paladin driven mad by thwarted love. The hippogriff is basically a griffin with eagle foreparts, but with a horse's hind parts instead of a lion's. It is probably better-known to most people today from the *Harry Potter* books: the young wizard rides a hippogriff called Buckbeak.

There are few traditional meanings for this creature, but the thing that came to my mind as I meditated on it was the Ancient Greek theatrical concept of the *Deus ex Machina* (known to us today by the Latin translation, as it was adopted by the Romans as well): the *god out of the machine*. This was an expedient device employed to rescue the hero of the play from a sticky situation when the playwright was out of ideas, and onstage made use of a lift which brought a rescuer, usually divine, flying onto the stage to save the day.

The hippogriff has a gentler but more adventurous vibe than the griffin and, as a **totem**, brings many of the same ideas as the hippocampus.

Hydra

Sometimes referred to as the Lernaean Hydra, this is a water monster with a twist: it was almost impossible to kill, because although it had many heads which *could* be cut off, they regrew from its neck immediately! In some versions they grew back double.

The Hydra was one of the monstrous children of Echidna and Typhon, and took the form of a huge snake with poisonous breath. The accounts of its head-count vary between nine and thousands. One of the labours of Hercules was to slay the Hydra but, as we have seen, he found it pretty hard to kill until he hit on the solution of having his charioteer, Iolaus, standing-by with a red-hot brand to sear the stumps as soon as the heads were cut off: this prevented them from regrowing and he was able to sever all of them, thus killing the monster.

When seen in **dreams and visions**, the Hydra is clearly about multi-pronged attacks, dangers from many sources at once, multiple problems all arriving together, or the scenario where sorting out one problem reveals several more. You must find a solution, but the good news is that one solution may work on many or all of them.

As a **totem**, the Hydra brings the ability to work on many fronts at once and to recover quickly and be ready for anything in a very short time.

Jersey Devil

The forested areas of New Jersey, USA, known as the Pine Barrens, are home to many supernatural creatures, but the Jersey Devil (sometimes the Leeds Devil) must be the most famous. A weird-looking thing with a horse's head and legs, goat's horns, a forked tail and bat's wings, sightings of it are still reported and there has even been a somewhat dubious photograph, taken in 2015.

The Jersey Devil's origins go back to a family called Leeds, who were historically living in the area in the first half of the eighteenth century. When Deborah Leeds found she was pregnant with her thirteenth child, the poor woman cursed the unborn child (and no wonder!), saying it would be born a devil. Sure enough, when the baby was born it transformed into a monster and flew screeching around the room, finally vanishing up the chimney.

Although a fearsome being which has supposedly brought terror to the area over the years, the Jersey Devil is not on record as having ever harmed a human being, although responsibility for the deaths of many farm animals are laid at its door. There have been reports it attacked a trolley car and a social club, but no people were harmed. It is said to be immortal, and shots fired at it have no effect.

The creature symbolises ancient family secrets when it shows up in **dreams and visions**, things you heard whispered as a child when your mother thought you weren't listening, skeletons in the ancestral closet of which you may be barely aware, and perhaps ancient abuse as well.

I think this creature would hardly be likely to be anyone's **totem animal**, but it might bring hidden knowledge.

Jörmungandr: see Leviathan.

Kelpie: see Lake Monsters.

Lake Monsters

Most large bodies of inland water have a monster of some kind associated with them, including the most famous, the Loch Ness Monster, and her cousins Morag (Loch Morar, Scotland), Teggie (Lake Bala, Wales), Champ (Lake Champlain, USA and Canada), Ogopogo (Okanagan Lake, Canada), Issie (Lake Ikeda, Japan), Mokele Mbembe (Congo River Basin) and Wally (Lake Wallowa, USA). Descriptions by people who have seen these creatures are strikingly similar: huge bulk, slimy scale-less skin, long serpent-like neck and flippers. The USA seems to have more than its fair share, perhaps because it has so many huge lakes, but the creatures are not always confined to lakes: the New Zealand monster Taniwha pops up in lakes, rivers and even caves all over the country, and Nessie has been sighted away from water on a couple of occasions, including in the notable report by the Spicers in 1933 of her crossing the road beside the loch in front of the couple's car. Mokele Mbembe appears to be a diplodocus from the descriptions given by native people, and is described as killing hippopotamuses if they get in its way. Otherwise, lake monsters do not appear to be very aggressive.

Water monsters are generally about secrets and hidden knowledge and the efforts and even danger that must be undergone to acquire these.

Many **dream** interpretations cite lake monsters as portraying personal power, and this may also be in the mix, but usually there would be an element of fear in the dream which does not seem to sit well with this idea.

As a **totem**, the animal may bring power but as a dream figure, it is not as comfortable or reassuring.

Leviathan

Another biblical mega-beast, Leviathan is described as a massive sea serpent or dragon, although the name later came to mean any enormous creature or object, including whales. Although it shares some aspects with the land monster, Behemoth, Leviathan is an aggressive creature that breathes fire and swallows people. She is analogous to the Midgard Serpent Jörmungandr in Norse myth, a monster which lies under the ocean and whose destiny it is to kill the God Thor at the end of time. Both Leviathan and Jörmungandr are said to bite their own tails and encircle the world, and both are destroyed by the forces of good. A third serpent of this kind is Ouroboros, a Gnostic symbol of renewed cycles and eternity.

The tail-biting serpent is a symbol of eternity, and yet both these creatures have numbered days. Leviathan is killed by God and her flesh preserved to feed the righteous after Judgement Day; whilst Jörmungandr is slain by Thor, although he fatally bites the God in the process.

In **dreams and visions**, these creatures are symbols of regeneration, but their terrifying aspects make this no easy prospect. Pain, fear and misfortune go with the process, which may even speak of physical death (and regeneration in the next world).

As a **totem**, they bring huge powers, wisdom, knowledge and invulnerability.

Manticore

The manticore definitely falls into the category of "thank goodness it isn't real" creations: a man's head on a lion's body and a venomous tail combine with an appetite for human flesh to make it one of the nastier mythological and heraldic animals. It appears to have become confused with the tiger at some period in heraldic descriptions. It is perhaps better-known to people today through the game, *Dungeons and Dragons*.

The manticore seen in **dreams** is said to be a warning of danger, but it is particularly about pretence: about someone trying to be what they are not, or putting on a kind face to entrap the unwary, while behind the face lies the reality of a predatory person.

As a **totem**, it brings the power of persuasion and the ability to always think one's own opinions are correct.

Mermaid

This chimera formed of a fish's body and the upper parts of a woman needs no introduction, thanks to Hans Christian Andersen, Disney and a number of folk- and fairy tales. She is found in the mythology of many cultures. Generally, the mermaid is seen as extremely beautiful, with long golden hair (which must be difficult to keep tidy underwater!) which she is often seen combing while she sings a *siren* song. Mermen also exist in stories, but they do not seem to have captured the human imagination in the same way. In 2011, the mermaid myth was given a new boost with a US TV drama presented as a documentary called, *Mermaids: The Body Found*, in which "scientists" were said to have found proof of the existence of merpeople. Sightings are still reported today.

In **dreams and visions**, mermaids are about longing – often longing for what we cannot have, although they are also connected to regeneration and transformation. Water creatures generally are often about emotion, and mermaids evoke feelings of love, perhaps for someone who cannot or will not reciprocate.

As **totems**, they bring great psychic ability and a comfort with one's emotions.

Minotaur

Pasiphaë, wife of King Minos of Crete, was a real animal lover. In fact, she got such a crush on a beautiful snow-white bull sent to her husband by Poseidon Himself that she ended up pregnant with the bull's offspring, and gave birth to a terrible monster with a man's body and the head of a bull – not a pretty white bull like its dad, but a bloody and terrible creature that fed on human flesh. Minos had a huge labyrinth created for the creature so it could be hidden away, but it still needed to eat, and grass was *not* its thing. The city of Athens owed Minos a favour, as it had been responsible for the death of his totally human son, so he demanded tribute of seven young men and seven girls to be sent to keep the monster fed. This unhappy state of affairs continued until the hero Theseus sorted it out by killing the Minotaur, but it still pops up now and again in horror films and games.

What does it mean? This chimera speaks of the worst parts of human nature, of greed, lust, rage, selfishness – all the dark parts of the human soul, the parts that make us monsters ourselves. We hide them away in the dark labyrinths of our subconscious, but they are still there and have to be dealt with.

As a **totem**, the Minotaur brings strength and the ability to overpower and intimidate.

Mokele Mbembe: see Lake Monsters.

Mongolian Death Worm

This creature certainly slithered straight out of a nightmare, but there are many people around the world who believe in its existence. Unlike many other monsters, it is quite small, no more than 60cms in length, though fat like a sausage. Its terror lies in its poison: it can supposedly spray venom and is so poisonous that just touching it is instantly fatal. Other accounts say its ability to kill has to do with an electric discharge. The people around the Gobi

Desert where it is alleged to live call it *olgoi-korkhoi*, "large intestine worm", which may refer to its looking like a section of bowel or like a tapeworm. It is generally said to be red in colour and to create waves in the sand as it moves underneath.

A **dream** of this creature would certainly be a nightmare. Worms generally are linked to death in dreams, but not usually as the cause. This is a danger sign: there is something you know can harm you, and you should not approach it or continue with it. This might be drugs or even smoking, or a dangerous course of action.

As a **totem**, it brings invulnerability and knowledge.

Mothman

Most myths are manmade, but the Mothman was created from newspaper reports and a subsequent novel and movie after just one sighting, which may have been of a heron or crane, in 1966. The legend grew and the Mothman was seen regularly around Point Pleasant, West Virginia, until after the collapse of the Silver Bridge in December 1967, killing 46 people who were on it at the time. He was said to be the size of a very tall man, but with large wings and glowing red eyes. The original sighting was of a white creature, but by the time John Keel wrote his novel, *The Mothman Prophecies*, it had become black and had a complete mythology of its own, including a name, Indrid Cold, and the ability to predict disasters. Since 2002, Point Pleasant has held an annual Mothman festival to celebrate the incident.

Seeing Mothman in **dreams and visions** speaks of mysterious warnings, for that is the meaning of the creature in the novel and its seeming relevance in light of the Silver Bridge disaster, 13 months to the day after its first sighting. This is a warning which is non-specific, and leaves you wondering what is going to happen, and frustrated because you can do nothing to avert the misfortune.

As a **totem**, Mothman is about looking out for others the best you can.

Ningen (sometimes Ninggen)

This whale-creature from twenty-first century Japanese folklore has the distinction of having been apparently captured on Google Earth. In 2002 - predating the Google Earth appearance of Nessie by seven years - the image of a vast white object that appears to have limbs and even digits was photographed in the Antarctic Ocean; it is estimated to be between 20 and 30 metres in length. Internet users dubbed it "Ningen". Descriptions vary from a man-faced smiling whale to a bipedal creature that can emerge onto ice floes.

In **dreams**, this modern monster is very benign, speaking of friends yet to be met and pleasures yet to enjoy.

As a **totem**, it brings happiness and freedom from cares.

Owlman

A distant cousin of Mothman, this Cornish cryptid was first seen in the 1920s by two young boys who described being chased by a huge, ferocious bird. The Owlman continued its practice of appearing to pairs of children when it flew over Mawnan church in 1976, frightening two young girls so much that their family opted to cut short their holiday there and then. Three months later, two teenaged girls reported seeing the creature on the ground in the churchyard, stating that it was as tall as a man, with huge claws and glowing eyes.

Though the 1976 accounts were collated by Tony "Doc" Shiels, a known hoaxer, the Owlman has left a legacy in the public mind, and has been reported as late as 1995. Barn owls living in the church have been put forward as an explanation, but it is difficult to reconcile a barn owl – commonly no bigger than a bantam – with the six-foot creature described by the children. Unlike Mothman, this cryptid seems to have no other motive than scaring those who see it.

Owls are about wisdom, but the Owlman seems to be about fear and frightening people – it chased the 1926 boys until they took refuge behind a metal grating.

Appearing in a **dream**, it may just be about fear, but also perhaps the justified fear of staying away from a danger.

As a **totem**, it is about courage tempered with prudence.

Phoenix

A glorious being which rises from its own ashes...what could be more inspiring? The phoenix is commonly portrayed as a burning red-gold bird, crested, beautiful and immortal. It appears in many cultures and has of course made an appearance in the *Harry Potter* franchise. The bird is said to know when its current life is coming to a close, when it builds a funeral pyre and climbs into the flames. After it has been completely consumed, a young bird emerges, reborn from the ashes. E Nesbit's idiosyncratic bird in *The Phoenix and the Carpet* lays an egg which has to be placed in the fire in order to hatch, and then goes off to die, being reborn in its own egg. The phoenix comes from classical mythology, but may have been inspired by the Ancient Egyptian *bennu* bird, which seemed to have been some kind of heron and was associated with Sun worship and regeneration.

In **dreams and visions**, the message of this creature is so obvious that I hardly need to state it: fear not, for though you may be at your lowest ebb now, a better time is coming and you and your fortunes will be reborn.

This ability to rise again after catastrophe and reinvent oneself is also the gift of the phoenix as **totem animal**.

Queensland Tiger

Accounts of this animal go back to the nineteenth century, with Aboriginal stories before that of a smallish striped predator called the *yarri*. The descriptions of it tally pretty closely with the Tasmanian tiger, so it may have been a population of these or perhaps another animal which shared a common ancestor.

For meanings, see **Thylacine**.

Sasquatch: see **Bigfoot.**

Satyr

What is the difference between a Roman faun and a Greek satyr? Largely sex: while the faun is a more innocent, arboreal spirit, the satyrs were well known for their *satyrism*, their amorous proclivities directed towards anything female, human or nymph. They were usually portrayed as having enormous erections and being in drink, as they were the followers of the wine-and-revelry God Dionysus. While fauns are half-goat in appearance, satyrs seem to have been based on horses; they have the ears, mane and tails of horses, and often the rear legs. They are not shown as attractive creatures, having typically balding heads, thick lips and squashed noses. Silenus, the elderly, drunken companion of Dionysus, usually shown crowned with vine leaves and riding on a donkey, is a satyr.

In **dreams**, satyrs symbolise the sexual drive, and they may well appear in *that* sort of dream. Is your sex life dull and unsatisfying, or is it your wider existence which leaves you feeling you are missing out on good times? Maybe you secretly wish to cut loose, shed your respectable image for a while and party to the max.

As a **totem**, the satyr brings you the ability to live as you please, provided you are prepared to lose the benefits brought by a more sedate life.

Sea Serpent

Close cousins of the lake monsters, these creatures have been seen all over the world from very ancient times to relatively recent times, and there are ancient illustrations of them wrapping their bodies around ships and destroying them.

For meanings see **Leviathan**.

Sphinx

Sphinx may refer to an individual creature from Greek myth or the chimeras produced by the Ancient Egyptians to decorate their tombs and temples, which were clearly the origins of the Greek beast. The most famous example is the Great Sphinx of Giza, a huge temple lying on the Giza Plateau. It is the oldest known Ancient Egyptian monument, predating the pyramids of the pharaohs Khufu and Khafre nearby, although its face has been altered to resemble that of the latter. In both cases, the sphinx has the body of a lion and the face of a human, although animal-headed sphinxes are known in Egypt, including the ram-headed examples at Karnak. The human-headed examples usually have the face of a pharaoh.

The Greek sphinx (which had the face and breasts of a woman) famously asked a riddle, and if the person could not answer it, she ate them. The riddle was: *what walks upon four feet in the morning, two feet in the afternoon and three feet in the evening?* The answer being "man", as he crawls when he is a baby, then walks as an adult, then uses a stick when he is old.

In **dreams**, the sphinx represents ancient mysteries and the important questions in life – what matters most to you and what are your greatest goals in life? Its appearance in a dream also speaks of a mysterious, inscrutable person, one who does not share their thoughts or emotions – qualities that also accompany the sphinx as **totem**.

Tiamat

This mighty serpent-being from Babylonian lore shares with the Norse giant Ymir the quality of primordial creation: she spawns thousands of creatures, gods and monsters, and her body is used as materials to create the Universe after she is killed by the God-hero Marduk. Portrayed as half-woman, half-dragon or snake, she is both a Goddess of the primordial sea and of chaos, a mother of all creation, often described as "the shining one". Though her mythology is very different to that of Leviathan, most people may not recognise the distinction; however, where Leviathan is a fire-breathing, flesh-eating monster, Tiamat is a universal mother, a creatrix and nurturer.

Dreaming of her speaks of a need for one's very ancient roots and ancestors – perhaps because the dreamer is an ex-pat in an alien country and longs for home – or of being filled with nostalgic longing for the things one knew as a child.

As a **totem**, she is about nurturing, about the fiercely protective nature of motherhood.

Unicorn

These beautiful and fantastic creatures have been downgraded during the twentieth and twenty-first centuries from the majestic and heraldic to plastic toys in dayglo colours for little girls! The unicorn is very familiar to everyone: a horse's body with a single spiral horn growing from the centre of its forehead. In heraldry, it also has cloven hooves like a goat or antelope, often a beard like a goat, and its tail seems rather more leonine than equine. It is always white (unless it is a toy!).

The unicorn is an ancient concept indeed, appearing on objects from the Bronze Age and found in mythologies all over the world. From the mediaeval period in the West it was seen as a symbol of purity, and the concept of it being tamed only by a virgin was added to its canon of lore: the beast was supposed to come and lay its head in the girl's lap if she were truly pure. Very important in heraldry, it is a symbol of Scotland and appears as a supporter on the coat of arms of the United Kingdom, thanks to King James I and VI. The unicorn was seen as the traditional enemy of the lion, as celebrated in the old nursery rhyme, *The Lion and the Unicorn.* The LGBT community adopted the unicorn as a symbol early this century, thus also associating it with alternative sexualities and the rights of minorities.

A unicorn's horn supposedly had magical and therapeutic properties, so if the virgin bait failed to attract one, quack doctors turned to other animals' horns, notably the spiral horn of the narwhal.

In **dreams**, the unicorn is a welter of contradictions. It speaks of immense power, but also gentleness, compassion and submission. It seems a sexless beast and strongly connected with old fashioned ideas of sexual purity and virginity, yet it is now firmly tied to communities with alternative sexualities. It is white, yet associated with rainbows. But at heart we feel it is a white horse, with all that implies: that it speaks to us of ideals, grace, honour and courage, and striving to be the best person we can.

These are also the ideas it brings as a **totem**, but there is something more about the animal which is hard to define, perhaps the word is uniqueness, perhaps just *magic.*

Werewolf

Shapeshifting into animals is a theme that runs through all cultures, from the were-tigers of India to the English witch who takes on the form of a hare to escape her enemies. The most famous of all is the werewolf, springing from ancient beginnings to enjoy a full career in Hollywood. It is easy to imagine his origins, in bygone ages when wolves might prowl round a small village, making the night uncanny with their howls, threatening livestock and causing children to be kept at home. The stories may also have been given a kick-start by ancient serial or sex killers preying on the young of the community.

The werewolf has a well-developed folklore which has been added to down the centuries, especially since he became a movie star, but the ideas associated with him are not necessarily the same in all cultures. However, in the West he has a generally agreed set of rules, including turning into the wolf at the full moon (or through the five nights around it), being vulnerable to silver weapons and being able to generate other werewolves by biting a victim but leaving them alive. In some cultures, the belief has been that a werewolf is born, not made, with signs of the curse upon its body, and that it can also rise from the dead, vampire-like, unless certain precautions are taken with the corpse.

Ancient belief was that the afflicted person turned into a wolf, indistinguishable from a natural animal but again, Hollywood has bent the rules, and most people would now imagine a creature with some human characteristics, including walking on two legs.

Unsurprisingly, the werewolf in **dreams and visions** speaks of transformation, but not in a positive sense. The myth has always spoken of the metamorphosis as negative, that of the human nature giving in to its baser, animal instincts, of a person who might be good and kind becoming a monster and slave to his vilest thoughts and desires. Whether the message is directed at the dreamer or points to someone in their life, the warning is clear: do not give in to evil thoughts, not lust nor anger nor revenge, lest you become a monster and your own downfall.

As a **totem,** the werewolf brings mixed blessings: strength and easy adjustment to all situations, but also the tendency to rage and to wish others ill.

Winged Horse

What animal, real or imaginary, could represent the idea of freedom and adventure better than the winged horse, a creature found through many mythologies from Pegasus, the mount of Bellerophon, who slew Medusa to the mythical talking animals encountered in CS Lewis' *Narnia* books? The winged horse in art is an astonishingly beautiful creature, usually white, sometimes with golden wings. In reality, it is of course impossible, as no mammal has six limbs, nor could it fly without pectoral muscles so huge they would drag on the ground.

The winged horse in **dreams and visions** speaks of freedom and travel of a special kind, such as escape or adventure, but also shares with the hippogriff the idea of a miraculous rescue, that *Deus ex Machina* moment. It can also speak of encounters with the divine, of psychic visions involving higher beings, as well as hope and joy.

As a **totem**, it brings hope and joy as well, with a complete lack of fear and anxiety.

Winged Lion

The icon of the city of Venice and its patron saint, St Mark, the winged lion is another creature that is found across many cultures representing kingship and divinity; as though people found the need to take an already majestic and beautiful animal and improve it still further to personify the ruler or deity they wished to adore. It is distinct from a griffin in that it retains its lion's head and foreparts instead of having eagle foreparts. It is generally coloured golden like a lion, and with golden wings. It is found as commercial logos, and the arms of NATO feature a winged lion holding a sword and shield with the inscription PAX (peace) on its shield.

Where the terrestrial lion is seen as a symbol of kingship and power, the winged version goes still further, speaking of divine protection and a guardian, with ultimate power, courage and glory. It could not be a more positive and blessed sign ... unless, in the **dream** it is attacking or threatening you, then it clearly represents something or someone else, someone of great power, perhaps the very state itself.

It goes without saying that this **totem animal** is about as fortunate and powerful for you as you could get.

Wyvern

This beast is a close relative of the dragon, but differs in that it has only two legs, does not breathe fire and has a venomous point or barb on the end of its tail. It is important in heraldry, where it is often pictured seated on its coiled tail, almost like a cat, and in commercial logos and the logos of organisations such as football clubs. The arms of the Dukes of Marlborough, for example, feature two wyverns as supporters; and a red wyvern was the symbol of the kingdom of Wessex.

In **dreams and visions,** the wyvern has a very similar meaning to the dragon, but may be warning you about someone with a toxic personality, or that you yourself need to keep a rein on your own feelings of envy and dislike.

For **totem,** see **Dragon.**

Yeti: see **Bigfoot.**

Yowie: see **Bigfoot.**

Milton Keynes UK
Ingram Content Group UK Ltd.
UKHW022220071223
433949UK00012B/273

9 781915 580054